The Fight Against Unemployment

The Fight Against Unemployment

Macroeconomic Papers
from the
Centre for European Studies

edited by

Richard Layard and Lars Calmfors

The MIT Press

Cambridge, Massachusetts   London, England

First MIT Press edition, 1987

This book was typeset in Oxford by Cotswold Press Ltd. and printed and bound in the United States of America.

Library of Congress Cataloging-in-Publication Data

The Fight Against Unemployment.

Bibliography: p.
1. Unemployment—Europe.   2. Europe—Full employment policies. I. Layard, P.R.G. (P. Richard G.) II. Calmfors, Lars, 1948- III. Centre for European Policy Studies (Brussels, Belgium)
HD5764.A6F54 1987   339.5'094   87-5356

ISBN 0-262-12122-0

Preface

This book is the second in the series of collections of macroeconomic papers from the Centre for European Policy Studies (CEPS) published by The MIT Press. The series began in 1986 with the title *Restoring Europe's Prosperity*. This new volume is based on two elements in the Centre's annual programme: the work of the CEPS Macroeconomic Policy Group and the output of the CEPS Macroeconomic Policy Workshop.

The Macroeconomic Policy Group was formed in 1982 under the chairmanship of Professor Rudiger Dornbusch. It meets at least three times a year in Brussels to prepare reports on the European economy for the Commission of the European Communities and a wider circle of policy-makers. Although funding for the programme comes from Directorate-General II of the Commission, which is responsible for Economic and Financial Affairs, the group's location in CEPS is intended to symbolize and safeguard its independence.

Membership of the group changes each year in order to ensure a proper balance between continuity and fresh ideas. In the twelve-month cycle represented by the essays reprinted in this volume, Professor Franco Modigliani joined the group in place of Professor Olivier Blanchard, though the latter remained a member until March 1986, which enabled us to draw on his advice in the preparation of the group's annual report. Professor Richard Layard chaired the group during preparation of the report, and then handed over to Professor Jacques Drèze, who will act as chairman during the new cycle.

The CEPS Macroeconomic Workshop met for the first time in September 1986. The idea behind the initiative was to bring together a small number of economists from the academic world, government, and international organizations to discuss at a high professional level a major issue in the European economic policy debate. The theme for the 1986 workshop, "Rigidities in the European Labour Market", virtually selected itself; it also fitted very well with the output of the Macroeconomic Policy Group.

The chairman of the workshop was Dr. Lars Calmfors of the Institute for International Economic Studies, University of Stockholm. Dr. Calmfors, who had worked with CEPS before, proved to be an ideal chairman: shrewd in his choice of collaborators, efficient in the organization of the workshop itself, and firm in his editorial role.

Funding for the CEPS Macroeconomic Policy Group is provided annually by the Commission of the EC through Directorate-

General II. Funding for the 1986 CEPS Macroeconomic Workshop was provided by the Ford Foundation, BMW AG (through the Stifter verband für die Deutsche Wissenschaft), and the Danish National Bank. We are grateful to all these institutions for their help. It should be stressed, however, that the views expressed by the authors of the various papers in this volume are attributable only to them in a personal capacity and not to CEPS, the funding organizations, or any other institutions.

Centre for European Policy Studies,   *Peter Ludlow*
Brussels, 1987

Contents

List of Tables

List of Figures

Reducing Unemployment in Europe: The Role of Capital Formation

Labour Market Flexibility and Jobs: A Survey of Evidence from OECD Countries with Special Reference to Europe

Hysteresis, Persistence, and the NAIRU: An Empirical Analysis for the Federal Republic of Germany

Work-Sharing: Why? How? How Not...

Notes on Authors

Lars Calmfors is Associate Professor of Economics at the Institute for International Economic Studies, University of Stockholm.

Jacques H. Drèze is Professor of Economics at the Universit Catholique de Louvain and President of the European Economic Association.

Michael Emerson is Director of Macroeconomic Analyses and Policies in the Directorate-General for Economic and Financial Affairs of the Commission of the European Communities.

Wolfgang Franz is Professor of Economics and Director of the Institute for Social Research at the University of Stuttgart.

Herbert Giersch is Professor of Economics at Kiel University and President of the Kiel Institute of World Economics.

Richard Layard is Professor of Economics and Head of the Centre for Labour Economics at the London School of Economics and Chairman of the Executive Committee of the Employment Institute.

David Metcalf is a Professor in the Industrial Relations Department and Centre for Labour Economics at the London School of Economics.

Franco Modigliani is Professor Emeritus of Economics at the Massachusetts Institute of Technology and winner of the 1985 Nobel Prize for Economics.

Mario Monti is Professor of Economics at Bocconi University, Milan, where he is also Director of the Institute of Economics and Director of the Centre for Monetary and Financial Economics.

Christopher A. Pissarides is Professor of Economics and Research Director of the Centre for Labour Economics at the London School of Economics.

Paul Van Rompuy is Professor of Economics at the Katholieke Universiteit Leuven.

Eckhardt Wohlers is a Research Fellow at the Institute of Economic Research (Institut für Wirtschaftsforschung, HWWA)-Hamburg.

Charles Wyplosz is Professor of Economics and Associate Dean for Research and Development at the European Institute of Business Administration (INSEAD).

European Unemployment
— An Introduction

Lars Calmfors

The theme of this volume is the persistence of high unemployment in Europe. An instructive way of sketching the background may be to go back to the conventional wisdom on inflation and unemployment prevailing in the late 1970s and early 1980s.[1] According to it, there exists an equilibrium (natural) rate of unemployment at which inflation will remain stable: the non-accelerating inflation rate of unemployment or the NAIRU. When unemployment is below this rate, inflation accelerates; when it is above the NAIRU, inflation decelerates.

Because of the inertia in wage setting, due to sluggish adjustments of expectations and overlapping contracts, changes in the rate of inflation will entail deviations of unemployment from the NAIRU. More specifically, a reduction of the rate of inflation from the high levels recorded in the 1970s required an increase of unemployment above the NAIRU. But according to the theory, the deviation should only be temporary: once the downward adjustment of inflation is completed, unemployment should fall again. The distressing European experience of the 1980s is that this has not happened. It looks as if the NAIRU has increased *pari passu* with actual unemployment. Four major explanations for this have been set forth.

(i) *Supply shocks in combination with rigid real wages.* The idea is simply that the increases in raw material prices and tax wedges in the 1970s required a downward adjustment in the real take-home pay of workers in order to maintain a real labour cost to employers consistent with earlier employment levels. But because of trade union resistance to real wage cuts, the real wage adjustment has been insufficient.[2]

(ii) *Hysteresis or persistence.* According to this hypothesis the NAIRU is affected by actual unemployment, with the consequence that a prolonged period of unemployment will raise the NAIRU. There are several possible channels for this.

A *first* explanation is the insider-outsider hypothesis.[3] According to this employed workers (insiders) carry more weight in the wage-setting process than the unemployed (outsiders). As a result any unemployment increase due to a temporary demand or supply shock tends to perpetuate itself, because a reduced number of employed workers can raise their wages without risking their jobs.

A *second* explanation, as argued by the CEPS Macroeconomic Policy Group in 1985,[4] is that the human capital of those who remain unemployed in the long term will gradually depreciate, with the consequence that they become harder to employ. Even if this does not actually occur, the hiring propensity of employers

3

may fall if past employment experience of job applicants is used as a screening device.

A *third* explanation offered is that since high unemployment is likely to covary with low investment or even a falling capital stock, a "capital shortage" may develop that prevents high employment from being attained in the short run even if real wages fall drastically.[5]

(iii) *Insufficient allocative efficiency in the labour market.* This may be due either to an insufficient ability of labour to respond to relative wage or quantity signals *or* to a failure of relative wages to adjust to market conditions. The result will be a coincidence of excess demand in some segments of the labour market and an excess supply in others, creating a "mismatch" between job applicants and available jobs.[6] As a consequence the unemployment rate consistent with stable inflation will rise.

A more sophisticated version of this argument stresses the importance of the internal wage structure for promoting incentives for workers to perform efficiently. It points to the risk that a compression of wage differentials will reduce productivity growth with obvious unemployment consequences.[7] Furthermore, since screening of job applicants is costly, firms usually prefer to adopt a wage structure with a steep earnings-age profile, under which workers are paid a wage below their expected marginal productivity in the beginning of their employment and above towards the end, in order to deter low-productivity applicants. To the extent that unions have succeeded in compressing wage differentials, firms have probably become more reluctant to hire.[8]

(iv) *Labour market regulations.* Finally, various types of labour market regulations may decrease labour market flexibility. High unemployment benefits may reduce the supply of labour.[9] Minimum wage legislation may price low-productivity workers out of the market.[10] Employment protection laws are likely to increase the expected fixed costs of workers, and will thus both induce a substitution of hours for workers and cause negative scale effects on employment. Although the latter type of legislation will reduce the variability of employment in the case of shocks, overall employment is likely to fall and to become more unevenly distributed.[11]

The papers in this volume all deal in varying degrees with the issues raised above and their policy implications.

The paper by **Franco Modigliani** and his colleagues is the 1986 annual report of the **CEPS Macroeconomic Policy Group**. It focuses on the issue of the capital constraint as a possible factor limiting growth in Europe. The group points out that, to achieve a major reduction in unemployment in Europe, the annual growth rate of output will need to rise substantially (to around 5% for some years). Such rates of growth have occurred before when labour has been in abundant supply, but at present the capital constraint may serve as a brake. In the past capacity has generally grown in step with the demand for output, but capacity utilization in Europe is now estimated by the group to be only slightly below previous peaks.

The group estimates that a growth of capacity on the scale needed would require that the share of investment in GDP could need to rise by as much as 5 percentage points. This could be financed partly by increased domestic saving out of extra income, and partly by capital imports. To make way for sufficient domestic saving, the group recommends that the fiscal stimulus to higher output should come from time-limited investment subsidies and marginal employment subsidies (rather than from incentives to a consumption-led boom). A coordination of the fiscal stimulus across countries and a coordinated cut in interest rates are also advocated. The efficiency of the European capital market could be greatly improved by liberalization of capital flows and by the wider use of index-linked debt.

David Metcalf gives a broad survey of our empirical knowledge on labour market rigidities in Europe and their effects on unemployment. In the first part, on *aggregate real wage flexibility*, he presents various estimates of the NAIRU and its determinants, as well as measures of real wage flexibility in different countries. He then discusses the links between corporatism, consensus, and macroeconomic performance, and comes to the conclusion that "a model of social organization in which groups rather than individuals wield power and transact affairs" is conducive to macroeconomic success.

The second part of Metcalf's paper deals with *relative wage flexibility* and questions the widespread belief that the industrial wage structure is more rigid in Europe than in Japan and the US. In the third part, on *intra-firm flexibility*, Metcalf raises doubts about the quantitative importance of the rigidities imposed by job security legislation. This part also looks at the question of whether high internal mobility (within the firm) of the Japanese type can act as a substitute for high external mobility of the US type and thus explain the high degree of adaptability of these two polar cases.

Wolfgang Franz's contribution empirically tests a variant of the *hysteresis* (persistence) hypothesis for the Federal Republic of Germany (FRG). He focuses on the screening hypothesis discussed above, according to which employers are reluctant to hire the long-term unemployed. He produces empirical support for the view

5

that the increased share of long-term employment may be an explanatory factor for the outward shift of the Beveridge curve (relating vacancies and unemployment) in the FRG. He also manages to explain an increased NAIRU in this way. Since the rate of inflation in his model depends, *inter alia*, on vacancies, an outward shift of the Beveridge curve must result in higher inflationary pressures at a given rate of unemployment.

Finally, by linking the share of long-term unemployment to past unemployment rates, Franz calculates a *steady-state NAIRU* that in general will differ from the contemporaneous NAIRU prevailing at any point in time. His conclusion is that the present contemporaneous NAIRU in the Federal Republic is far above this steady-state level.

Jacques Drèze discusses whether the present low total employment in hours can be distributed more efficiently through a reduction of individual working-time. The main argument for a redistribution of work between employed and unemployed is cast in terms of implicit contract theory. Because newcomers to the labour market are excluded from the benefits of income — and some employment insurance offered by firms to their employees — there exists a market failure that can be corrected through *work-sharing*. An employment increase through real wage restraint is ruled out by Drèze on the grounds that it would presuppose an excessive and inoptimal burden of income adjustment on the part of workers. Because a hiring decision entails fixed "investment" costs for firms and they, according to implicit contract theory, are likely to practice labour-hoarding (paying workers a wage above their marginal productivity in recessions) Drèze assumes a low short-run wage elasticity of labour demand.

He discusses three forms of work-sharing: (i) trading jobs by replacing older workers with younger ones through early retirement schemes, (ii) sharing jobs through part-time work, and (iii) trading hours for jobs through a reduction of working-time. The first type of work-sharing is seen as the most promising. Since young workers are likely to place a higher value on a regular job than older workers, an early retirement scheme is likely to have a positive welfare effect and interfere less with the organization of work. Such disturbance costs will be far higher if hours are traded for jobs.

Analytically, the most controversial issues are raised in the papers by Metcalf, Franz, and Drèze, as evidenced by the comments on them. A tentative list of some of the more important questions would look as follows.

(i) How general are the phenomena discussed in the papers? As **Michael Emerson** asks in his discussion, are the contributions of various factors to the growth of unemployment in Britain, which Metcalf discusses, typical for Europe as a whole? Can the results on asymmetries in relative wage responses in Sweden, France, and Britain, quoted by Metcalf, be generalized to other European countries as well? Can an outward shift of the Beveridge curve be explained in terms of an increased proportion of long-term unemployed in other countries as well as in the FRG? For how many other countries does a hysteresis explanation of the increase in NAIRU work?

On the last question other empirical studies point in various directions.[12] There is a serious risk — implicit in the whole Eurosclerosis debate — that too far reaching conclusions on European conditions are drawn from specific country examples. To minimize this risk there is a need for more systematic, cross-country, empirical analysis.

(ii) How robust is Franz's conclusion that unemployment persistence is explained by the screening hypothesis? His analysis is partial in the sense that he does not test for the alternative explanations of persistence. Indeed, as pointed out by both **Charles Wyplosz** and **Paul Van Rompuy** in their comments, the evidence produced may very well be consistent with the insider-outsider hypothesis. Van Rompuy also makes the crucial point that the screening hypothesis alone is not enough to explain persistence: it must be combined with the insider-outsider idea to give a complete story. The reason he gives is that a deterioration in human skills or increased uncertainty on the part of employers could otherwise be compensated by a lowering of outsider wage demands.

(iii) Which policy conclusions are to be drawn from the existence of unemployment persistence effects? It is common to see them as a motivation for aggregate demand expansion, as Franz seems to do. But this conclusion does not necessarily follow. The existence of such persistence effects only means that any change in employment is self-enforcing. It does not tell us anything about the appropriate methods of increasing employment. Nor does it alter the standard conclusion that a monetary expansion will only succeed in bringing down unemployment to the extent that money-wage rigidities can be exploited. Moreover, the policy measures adopted must not contribute to expectations of future government policies that provoke wage reactions which offset the initial employment effects.[13]

Another caveat concerns the fact that the NAIRU is usually defined without any reference to the external-balance constraint. Even though the NAIRU, as conventionally defined, can be reduced under certain assumptions by aggregate demand expansion or via reductions of the tax wedge, it does not follow that this can be done without serious negative effects on the external balance. Unless this external-balance constraint is incorporated into the definition of the NAIRU — e.g. by ensuring that the levels of aggregate demand and relative price *vis à vis* foreign competitors is consistent with a zero trade balance[14] — it may not represent a full equilibrium that can be sustained over time.

(iv) A fourth point concerns the corporatism-consensus-macro-economic performance nexus. As pointed out by **Eckhardt Wohlers** in his comments on Metcalf, the causal direction is unclear. Moreover, the concepts of corporatism and consensus are far less operational than most other concepts used in economics. To the extent that willingness of labour market organizations to concert real wage restraint is used as an indicator of corporatism or consensus, as is done in some of the studies quoted by Metcalf, the definitions are more or less circular. Of course, one must observe correlations between these "modes" of social organization and a macroeconomically favourable wage-setting; but this only reflects the proposition that cooperative solutions are likely to yield higher utility to all parties involved, including the government.

In my view, research in this area should focus more on the links between organizational structure (which can be classified more unambiguously) and wage-setting behaviour, although the problems of causal direction will still remain. More interest should also be devoted to the links between bargaining structure and relative wage flexibility: it is a common observation that attempts at incomes policies and centralized wage-setting seem to go hand in hand with a compression of the wage structure.[15]

(v) Finally, as concerns work-sharing, one must distinguish between the possible benefits of a more equitable distribution of work and whether a reduction of working-time will actually succeed in bringing about such a redistribution. It is quite possible — and in my view even probable — that a general reduction of working-time would entail such increases of wage and capital costs that employment would actually fall.[16] **Christopher Pissarides** in his comments on Drèze also points to the danger of adjusting to what may be a temporary phenomenon of unemployment through institutional changes that cannot be easily reversed in the case of a boom, and therefore risk contributing to inflationary pressures and slower growth.

As can be seen, there is no shortage of topics for future controversy.

Notes and sources

1. See, for example, F. Modigliani, "The Monetarist Controversy or, Should We Forsake Stabilization Policies?", *American Economic Review*, March 1977; or R. Layard, D. Grubb, and J. Symons, "Wages, Unemployment and Income Policies", in M. Emerson (ed.), *Europe's Stagflation*, Oxford University Press and Centre for European Policy Studies, 1984.

2. This line of thought is associated primarily with M. Bruno and J. Sachs, *The Economics of Worldwide Stagflation*, Basil Blackwell, Oxford, 1985. Formal wage-setting models giving such results have also been developed; for example, see I. McDonald and R. Solow, "Wage Bargaining and Employment", *American Economic Review*, 71, 1981; and J. Sachs, "High Unemployment in Europe — Diagnosis and Policy Implications" in C-H Siven (ed.), *Unemployment in Europe*, Timbro, Stockholm, 1987.

3. It was originally developed by A. Lindbeck and D.J. Snower, who summarize their approach in "Wage Setting, Unemployment and Insider-Outsider Relations", Papers and Proceedings, *American Economic Review*, 76, 1986. See also O.J. Blanchard and L.H. Summers, "Hysteresis and the European Unemployment Problem", in S. Fischer (ed.), *NBER Macroeconomic Annual 1986*, MIT Press, Cambridge (Mass.); and N. Gottfries and H. Horn, "Wage Formation and the Persistency of Unemployment", Institute for International Economic Studies, University of Stockholm, Seminar Paper No. 347, 1986.

4. O. Blanchard, R. Dornbusch, J.H. Drèze, H. Giersch, R. Layard, and M. Monti, "Employment and Growth in Europe: A Two-Handed Approach, " 1985 Report of the CEPS Macroeconomic Policy Group, in O. Blanchard *et. al.*, *Restoring Europe's Prosperity, Macroeconomic Papers from the Centre for European Policy Studies*, MIT Press, London and Cambridge (Mass.), 1986.

5. See, for example, E. Malinvaud, "Wages and Unemployment", *Economic Journal*, 92, 1982; or H.R. Sneesens and J. Drèze, "A Discussion of Belgian Unemployment Combining Traditional Concepts and Disequilibrium Economics", *Economica*, Vol. 53, No. 210(S), 1986.

6. See, for example, OECD, *Employment Outlook*, 1984 and 1985.

7. See, for example, R.J. Flanagan, "Efficiency and Equality in Swedish Labor Markets", in B. Bosworth and A. Rivlin (eds.), *The Swedish Economy*, The Brookings Institution, Washington, 1987.

8. See, for example, R.J. Flanagan, "Labor Market Barriers to Economic Growth", mimeo, Graduate School of Business, Stanford University, 1986.

9. This has been argued especially by P. Minford in "Labour Market Equilibrium in an Open Economy", *Oxford Economic Papers*, Vol. 35, 1983.

10. See especially OECD, *Employment Outlook* 1984.

11. For a thorough documentation of employment protection laws in various European countries, see M. Emerson, in "Regulation or deregulation of the labour market: the case of policy regimes for the recruitment and dismissal of employees in the industrialised countries," *Economic Papers*, Commission of the European Communities, Brussels, 1987.

12. D. Coe and F. Gagliardi, "Nominal Wage Determination in Ten OECD Countries", OECD Economics and Statistics Department, Working Paper No. 19, March 1985, do not find evidence of hysteresis in the European economies, whereas R. Layard and S.J. Nickell, "Unemployment in Britain", *Economica*, Vol. 53, 1986, find such evidence for the United Kingdom, as do O. Blanchard and L. Summers, op. cit., note 3, for the UK, FRG, and France.

13. This has been analysed by, for example, L. Calmfors and H. Horn, "Employment Policies and Centralized Wage Setting", *Economica*, Vol. 53, 1986, and "Classical Unemployment, Policies and the Accommodation Adjustment of Real Wages", *Scandinavian Journal of Economics*, Vol. 87, 1985; and E.J. Driffill, "Macroeconomic Stabilization Policy and Trade Union Behaviour as a Repeated Game", *Scandinavian Journal of Economics*, Vol. 87, 1985.

14. See, for example, the final version of R. Layard and S.J. Nickell, op. cit., note 12.

15. See, for example, R.J. Flanagan, D. Soskice, and L. Ulman, *Unionism, Economic Stabilization and Income Policy: European Experiences*, The Brookings Institution, Washington DC, 1983.

16. See my comment on Drèze in this volume, p.198.

Reducing Unemployment in Europe: The Role of Capital Formation

Franco Modigliani, Mario Monti, Jacques H. Drèze, Herbert Giersch, and Richard Layard

Synopsis

For the third year in succession European output is rising at 2-3% per annum. The problem is how to prolong and accelerate this upswing. For, despite the upswing, unemployment in the European Community remains stubbornly high — at 11% of the work-force. This involves a huge waste of economic resources and much human misery. To deal with it, our 1985 report advocated a "two-handed approach", with supply-side measures accompanied by demand expansion.[1] The same approach is still needed today.

But in the last year two major changes have occurred which, if handled well, can make the task a good deal easier. First, the price of oil has roughly halved. Just as the oil price rises of the 1970s increased inflation and reduced employment, so an oil price fall now can be expected to reduce inflation and increase employment. Employment will increase slightly, because a fall in oil prices raises real income in the Community (a net importer of oil) and this may increase aggregate demand more than reduced exports to OPEC countries decrease it.

The second change in the last year has been the fall in the value of the dollar. This provides a second bulwark against inflation, by reducing the ECU price of goods imported from dollar-linked currency areas. But it also reduces the competitiveness of European exports, and thus poses a threat to employment. A further threat to jobs comes from a possible fiscal contraction in the US. These events make the two-handed strategy of expansion in Europe even more urgent.

The risks of expansion-led inflation are now less than before due to both the oil prices and the new position of the dollar. Thus we have two new grounds for hope if the opportunities are taken. But expansion still has many problems. In our 1984[2] and 1985 reports we highlighted the problems arising from rigidity in the *labour* market. In Part I we review these briefly, together with the key features of the current European economic situation. But in our current report we focus on the potential problems in the *capital* market. First, there is the risk of a shortage of physical capital as the expansion proceeds. In Part II we discuss the size of this problem and conclude that, though it is not now binding, action has to be taken to ensure that it does not become so. In the light of this, we review in Part III what scale of expansion could be hoped for and the appropriate mix of macroeconomic strategies to be adopted. In particular we focus on the question of how improved capital formation would be financed — in terms of the broad flow of funds.

On top of this, there is the important question of the micro-economic efficiency of the institutions of the capital market.

In Part IV we look at how this needs to be improved both within each country and in terms of the international integration of the capital markets in the Community. Part V summarizes our conclusions.

But first we need to review some of the basic features of the current European situation.

I. Setting the scene

As Table 1 shows, the economy of the European Community (EC) has now recovered from the inflationary shocks of the 1970s and early 1980s, and returned towards a level of inflation similar to that of the 1960s. The rate of growth is still somewhat lower than that observed in the 1960s, but it is on the unemployment front that the present situation in Europe stands out. It is extremely serious in quantity, quality, and probable persistence.

• The rate of unemployment in Europe is about five times higher than it was in 1960-73; it is also much greater than the current rate in the US or Japan. (See Table 1.)

• Even if it were not larger in size, European unemployment would present more problems, economically and socially, due to its qualitative structure. Youth unemployment and long-term unemployment have increased substantially in the last few years and are much larger than in the US or Japan. (See Table 2.)

• If policies are not significantly changed, the unemployment problem in Europe is likely to remain severe. According to the EC's baseline projection, on present policies the rate of unemployment in 1990 would still be as high as 10.4%, almost twice the US level and more than six times the Japanese level. (See Table 1.)

For this reason, our report will again focus on the issue of unemployment in Europe. It will try to identify a strategy to increase both the rate of growth of output and the employment content of growth. The philosophy underlying our recommendations is in line with the "two-handed" approach advocated in 1985. We are still convinced — and developments of the last year confirm this view — that neither supply nor demand measures will by themselves create and sustain employment growth. Structural changes on the supply side are required if employment growth is to be sustained, but a boost is needed to accelerate the process. This boost must come from timely supply measures, sustained and validated by demand.

Our 1985 report noted that high material prices, labour costs, capital deepening, labour market rigidities, and deficient demand

13

Table 1. Inflation, growth, and unemployment[1]

	1961-73	1974-81	1982-85	1985	1986[2]	1987[2]	1986-90[3]
Inflation (p.a., GDP deflator)							
EC	5.0	11.3	7.3	6.0	5.6	3.3	4.2
US	3.5	8.0	4.7	3.2	3.0	4.3	5.4
Japan	5.8	6.7	2.4	1.6	0.8	0.1	3.0
Real GDP/GNP Growth (p.a.)							
EC	4.6	1.9	1.5	2.3	2.7	2.8	2.5
US	4.2	2.3	2.4	2.2	2.5	2.7	3.0
Japan	9.9	3.9	4.0	4.6	3.2	3.2	4.3
Unemployment rate[4]							
EC	2.2	5.3	10.4	11.1	10.8	10.5	10.4
US	4.9	7.0	8.5	7.2	6.9	6.6	6.3
Japan	1.3	2.0	2.6	2.6	2.9	2.9	1.7

Notes: 1. Growth rates are year on year, i.e. 1985 means 1985 on 1984, 1961-73 means 1973 on 1960.
2. Forecast presented in April/May 1986.
3. Baseline projection presented in October 1985 as in *European Economy*, No. 26, November 1985, pp.21 and 141.
4. Average of period, except for 1986-90 (end of period).
Source: Commission of the European Communities.

Table 2. Youth unemployment and long-term unemployment

	Youth unemployment (% rate)		Long-term unemployment (% of total)			
			6 mos. and over		12 mos. and over	
	1980	1985	1979	1984	1979	1984
EC(4)[1]	13.6	21.9	34	61	28	38
US		12.5		19		12
Japan		4.7		38		15

Notes: 1. France, FRG, Italy, and the UK.
Source: OECD, *Employment Outlook*, Paris, September 1985.

all share some responsibility for the current employment woes in Europe. It would be ineffective to tackle only some of these aspects of the problem. Thus, our policy recommendations stressed, as a necessary condition, the importance of removing barriers to entry and rigidities in the labour market and of allowing for more wage flexibility and more potential wage dispersion. At the same time we noted that measures aimed at those goals could only make a gradual contribution to employment growth. Only a set of supply incentives as discussed in our 1985 report would make possible the extra employment needed in Europe. On the other hand, we pointed out that supply measures would be insufficient without accommodating demand policies. If firms do not anticipate improved sales, they will not increase capacity to the extent that we deem necessary. Fiscal and monetary policies should therefore be combined with supply measures.

There seems to be broad agreement presently on the merit of this approach. Official documents stress the need for a strategy of this nature.[3] Policy simulations provide indications of its possible effectiveness. In particular, the recent simulation by the Commission of the EC for the period 1986-90 shows that an expansionary fiscal policy alone would result in a relatively poor

Figure 1. Industrial investment in the EC and other macroeconomic indicators

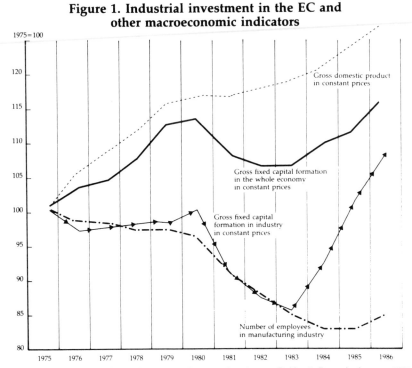

Source : Commission of the EC, *European Economy*, Supplement B, No. 1, Brussels, January 1986.

performance of the European economy, compared with a scenario of supply measures (wage moderation) and demand measures. Not only would the latter option bring lower inflation, lower labour costs, and small public deficits, but it would also lead to more significant improvements in employment and to less crowding out of investment.[4]   Our call for a two-handed strategy, therefore, seems to offer a genuine way out of the current difficulties.

But one key question is: "Will the expansion of capacity needed to restore employment be forthcoming?"[5] The investment record in Europe since 1980 has been poor, as Figure 1 shows. Total investment is barely higher than in 1980.   Industrial investment has recovered rather more, but the shortfall in the intervening period is so large that the existing stock of capital is still severely depleted. As noted by the Commission, "the volume of investment planned by firms for 1986 is at the level which it would have reached arithmetically if the investment trend observed in the period 1976-80 had continued. However, if the severe investment shortfall in the period 1981 to 1983 is to be made up, at least in part, it will not be sufficient for investment to continue on this earlier trend in the years ahead. It needs to continue for several years to grow as buoyantly as in the period 1984-86 if there is to be any appreciable reduction in unemployment".[6]

II.   Is capital a constraint on growth and employment?

II.1. Facts

We first ask whether and to what extent growth of output in Europe is made impossible, or at least severely hindered, by insufficient capital. We begin by looking at some facts relating to the availability of capital as measured by productive capacity in manufacturing industries,   where the concept is relatively well defined and measures are readily available. Figure 2 shows the recorded levels of capital utilization since 1974.   As can be seen, capacity utilization has been rising for three years. It is now only slightly below its level in 1979 and 1974 (though this is not generating the normal pressure on price expectations, due to the slackness of the labour and commodity markets).

We can now use the capacity utilization figures to produce a measure of capacity (in Figure 3). First we plot the actual level of industrial production (Y). Then we plot the level of capacity (C), measured as output divided by the rate of capacity utilization (CU): C = Y/CU. This is the middle line on the graph.

This approach to measuring capacity has several advantages over

Figure 2. Capacity utilization in industry (%)

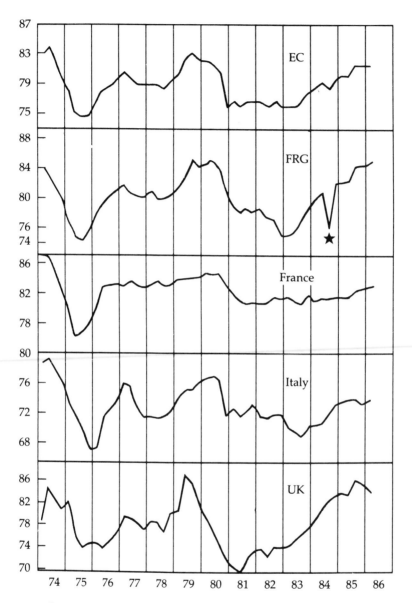

Note: ★ Mainly due to metal workers' strike in the Federal Republic of Germany (FRG).
Source: European Community business surveys.

Figure 3. Industrial output, capacity, and full-employment capacity

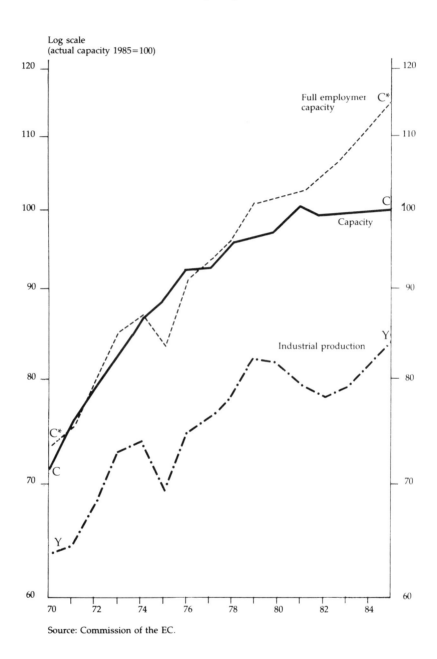

Source: Commission of the EC.

18

estimate the output which the existing capital stock can produce we also have to know the capital-intensity embodied in it. This in turn depends on the extent to which the investment which produced the capital was capital-widening or capital-deepening, which raises further problems of estimation. Second, our calculations get round the problem of obsolete capacity in that they rely on firms' own implicit judgements about what capacity is usable. They also circumvent problems of unmeasured scrapping of machinery. By dealing in terms of productive capacity, we partly circumvent these problems.

The distance between Y and C in Figure 3 measures the level of underutilization of existing capacity. As we have said, this gap is now quite low compared with most of the last ten years. So capacity is becoming relatively scarce compared to the existing level of output. But we also need to ask how it compares with the level of capacity that would be needed if output were sufficiently high to provide full employment. For this purpose we need to make an illustrative assumption about the level of full employment. We shall assume that it would be the average level for 1961 to 1980, namely 3%. (But the reader can easily see the result of different assumptions.) We also need to make an assumption about the rate at which output would have to change if unemployment were to be reduced. Here, for illustration, we shall assume that if unemployment is to be reduced by 1 percentage point, industrial output has to grow by an extra 2%.[7] This enables us to compute full-employment output as $Y[1 + 2(U - 0.03)]$, where U is the unemployment rate. The corresponding capacity required has been assumed to be greater than this by a multiple of $1/0.85$, on the assumption that capacity utilization rates of over 85% are difficult to attain. Thus full-employment capacity is C^*, where

$$C^* = \frac{Y}{0.85} [1 + 2(U - 0.03)]$$

The calculation is purely illustrative, to give some feel for what has been going on.

So what does Figure 3 suggest? Until 1978, the available capacity (C) was adequate, or more than adequate, to produce the estimated full employment output. However, it then began to fall short of the required level, and the gap increased steadily. By 1985 capacity, on these assumptions, was 15% below what is needed for full employment.[8]

II.2. Implications

Does this mean that there is no hope of returning nearer to full employment? No, for at least five reasons. First, as Figures 2 and

3 show, aggregate capacity utilization in industry is still 4% below the level of 85%, which we have posited as a critical level. So *some* expansion is possible with the existing capital used in the existing way.[9]

Second, the capital could be more fully utilized. At present much capital is only used for one shift. For example, in the UK 86% of worker-hours in manufacturing are worked between 8 a.m. and 6 p.m. The existing stock of capital will be consistent with a larger output if capital is used for a larger number of hours per day or per week. Measures should be taken in the field of labour organization — at the national level and at the level of individual firms — to permit and encourage this more intensive utilization of capital.[10] It would be particularly helpful if longer periods of capital utilization could be organized at firms operating in the "capacity-producing" sectors. This is not only because these sectors produce "capacity" for the others, but also because they are currently characterized by the highest degrees of capacity utilization, as conventionally measured. (See Section III.3.)

Third, the fall in oil prices relative to wages and output will make profitable again a certain amount of the capital which otherwise would be unprofitable to work. This will again expand effective industrial capacity. Similarly if our policies for wage flexibility, wage restraint, and removal of barriers to entry were followed, this would make it possible for many European industries to take more advantage of any growth in world demand. Such improved profitability would again expand effective capacity.

Fourth, the calculations which we have done relate to industry, where the capacity problem is the most severe. In services, which produce much more than half the output of the Community, the physical capacity constraint is much less clear (even when there is one-shift working). For example, the capacity of a shop is highly elastic, as we experience at Christmas, and offices likewise can be used to a greater or lesser intensity.

Finally, and most importantly, capacity can be increased. This makes it essential to understand what affects capacity and to what extent extra demand for output might generate sufficient capacity to supply it.

II.3. Determinants of capacity

There are two textbook types of explanation of changes in capacity: supply factors and demand factors.

According to the supply hypothesis, the prime determinant of changes in capacity is profitability, which depends in turn on real factor prices and on other matters, such as the regulations affecting the use of factors of production. On this line of thought, the recent standstill in capacity has been caused by the fact that labour costs have jumped up during the 1970s, with a faster rise in real labour cost (in terms of product wages) than in productivity. This occurred particularly from around 1974 to the early 1980s. Aside from higher wages, growing rigidities in the structure of employment relations, tenure arrangements, and so on have resulted in an increase in the effective hourly cost of labour.

Whether set in terms of a putty-clay model or a putty-putty competitive model, higher labour costs in the short run will tend to reduce the output worth producing. This will reduce our measure of capacity — depending in practice on how this is calculated by employers. In the long run, higher labour costs would tend to reduce the capacity worth maintaining as well as the output worth producing. This would certainly be the case if the real interest rate did not decline.

Following on this, one might expect to see a decline in domestic interest rates under the impact of the reduced investment, though the extent would depend on what happens to interest rates elsewhere and on capital mobility. If this fall occurs, there might be some tendency for the capital/output ratio to rise, thus partially offsetting the fall in investment. However, even with given saving and investment, one should find investment taking more capital-intensive forms, so that the capacity would become increasingly inadequate to employ all the labour.

According to the demand explanation, on the other hand, the capacity level is set with reference to expected output. (Even though in this model the real wage does not directly affect the level of output, it could affect it indirectly via an influence on the feasible level of aggregate demand. This holds, in particular, in an open economy when the real wage and aggregate demand determine the current account balance. Therefore, given external balance requirements, the real wage may control the level of target aggregate demand chosen by the authorities.)

The two explanations are not mutually exclusive. In particular, real unit costs and other supply factors influence market shares (of Europe in the world economy) and demand factors influence market size. In the short run, the output of a firm is determined by effective demand (given its costs and world prices), subject to the limit of physical capacity. In the longer run, net investment tends to bring physical capacity into line with effective demand, both at the level of the firm and in aggregate. Equilibrium degrees of

Figure 4. Industrial output (Y) and productive capacity (C)

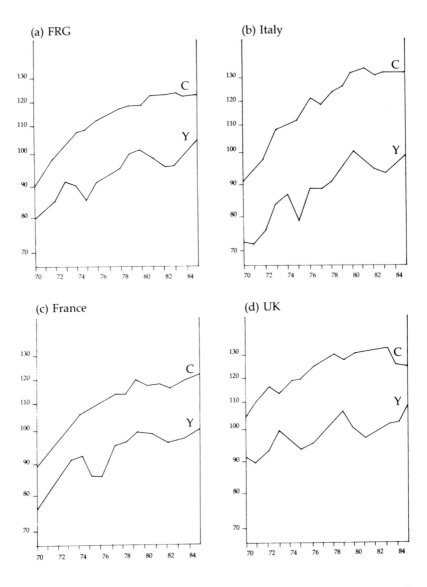

Source: Commission of the EC.

capacity utilization reflect both the relative costs of capital and labour, and the (relative) short-run variability of demand, productivity, and factor availability.

As Figures 3 and 4 show, in 1974 capacities were fully used and output was constrained by the availability of factors (both labour and capital). The decline in capacity utilization in 1975 reflected mainly the downturn in aggregate demand. From 1975 to 1978, capacity rose in line with the increase in output. From 1980 capacity utilization fell sharply and, in line with this, capacity ceased to grow.

From now on, it may be expected that effective demand growth would trigger investment for capacity expansion. But the situation differs widely both across sectors (with spare capacities least visible in the capital goods industries) and across countries (with spare capacities least visible in Denmark, the FRG, and the Netherlands).[11]

The questions then arise as to how rapid an expansion could be hoped for, what policy mix would be appropriate to encourage it, and how the additional investment would be financed.

III. Macroeconomic policy

III.1. The feasible scale of expansion

If European output continues to grow at say $2^1/_2\%$ a year, unemployment will not fall. Suppose that instead we aim to reduce it with reasonable speed to the level of the late 1970s. This means that unemployment will fall by 6 points (from 11 to 5%). How much output would have to grow in order to achieve this depends on the complex issue of the relation between the growth of output and the change in unemployment. The Commission's projection of the cooperative growth scenario implies a coefficient of 1.2. A reasonable estimate is somewhere between this figure and the figure of 2 that we used earlier. On any of these assumptions we suggest that if unemployment is reduced by 6 points with reasonable speed, conditions must be created for growth to build up to a level of 5% a year for a limited period.[12]

Such rates of growth have been by no means uncommon in the past, especially at times of high unemployment. In fact in some countries unemployment has fallen quite rapidly after reaching a high peak. For example, in the five years 1932-37 unemployment in Britain fell by $8^1/_2$ points (from 17 to $8^1/_2\%$) and unemployment in the US fell by 14 points (from 23 to 9%). Of course, both economic and institutional conditions during the 1930s were very different to those which exist today. It is also true that the 1970s were years of experience which cannot simply be rolled back in their entirety. Perceptions and reactions have changed. Nevertheless, the recovery of 1932-37 is not without interest.

III.2. Inflation and the need for wage restraint

But will not a faster rate of growth inevitably bring an increase in the inflation rate? This is, after all, probably the greatest fear at present. There is no doubt that inflationary pressure would be higher than otherwise. Thus, as we have argued in earlier reports, wage restraint should be a crucial element in the policy, with wages rising little faster than prices.

But the exact scale and nature of the inflationary problem remains a matter of considerable debate. Unfortunately, even though the relation between wage and price inflation and aggregate activity — the so-called Phillips curve — has been a subject of intensive inquiry in the last decade, there is disagreement on many issues, and in particular on the role played by the rate of change of unemployment (or employment).

Some, like Blanchard and Summers,[13] have argued that wage behaviour depends mainly on the change in employment. This, if true, would mean that, in the absence of induced wage restraint, *any* permanent decrease of unemployment would lead to a prolonged period of higher inflation. The mechanism that is said to explain this is the fact that existing workers (insiders) only care about keeping their own jobs, and thus the existing level of employment is always the critical level above which inflation increases (and vice versa).

Others, such as Layard and Nickell,[14] argue that there *is* in fact a long-run NAIRU (non-accelerating-inflation rate of unemployment). But if unemployment is driven above it, as in the last few years, there is a short-run NAIRU which is a good deal higher than the long-run NAIRU. This is because rises of unemployment lead to disproportionate increases in long-term unemployment, and the long-term unemployed are an ineffective source of labour supply. Given that unemployment is now above the long-run NAIRU, it can be reduced without increasing inflation provided it is reduced slowly. But faster reduction of unemployment can only be achieved without extra inflation if jobs are explicitly targetted at the long-term unemployed or if there is effective wage restraint. In support of their view, Layard and Nickell point to the rise of unemployment at given vacancies which has happened in many countries. This cannot be explained by the Blanchard/Summers analysis but can be partly explained by the

24

increase in long-term unemployment and other supply-side factors. In addition the Blanchard/Summers analysis cannot explain why in the long term the rise of the labour force affects the level of employment.

Others still, such as Sneessens and Drèze,[15] argue that the inflation/unemployment relationship cannot be isolated from the degree of capacity utilization. There are two sources of inflation — cost push and demand pull — and there are two determinants of employment — effective demand and production capacities (places of work). Rates of unemployment and of excess capacity compatible with given levels of inflation are determined simultaneously, against the background of income claims (wages and profits) and of classical unemployment (unemployment at full use of available capacities).

The three arguments have important elements in common. In all three there are elements of "hysteresis", meaning that the current non-inflationary level of unemployment is affected by past history. In the Sneessens/Drèze version the hysteresis is embodied in the capital stock. In the Blanchard/Summers version there is total hysteresis, and in the Layard/Nickell version there is partial hysteresis. Thus it seems wise to proceed on the assumption that what can be attempted in Europe is limited by our recent past.

There have of course been episodes in other times and places where this has not appeared to be the case. The US reflations of 1961-64 and 1982-86 proceeded without contemporaneous increases in inflation. (The second was helped by a massive terms-of-trade gain and growing unemployment in the rest of the world.) Even the huge US recovery from 1938 to 1941 saw inflation rising from 1.4% in 1938 to only 1.4% in 1940, and then to 7.5% in 1941. But we could not safely rely upon the same degree of luck in Europe now.

We would therefore suggest that, to ward off the inflation risk, the recovery plan needs to have the approval and explicit support of all economic actors — business and labour. This should include a pledge to contain wage increases within the limits of price increases as long as unemployment remains above some stated level, which means essentially during the duration of the recovery programme. This could be matched by a pledge on the part of business not to try to expand profit margins, which should not be a serious sacrifice considering that profits should be greatly swelled by the large rise in volume. Those pledges might, of course, be reinforced by a formal and binding type of incomes policy in countries where this was feasible or appropriate.

In a country like Italy, which still makes widespread use of escalator clauses, one might suggest a set-up ensuring roughly 100% inflation-coverage as the combined result of escalator clauses and new nominal contracts. In the United Kingdom a taxed-based incomes policy might be the natural route. The most obvious success of incomes policy in recent years has been in France (a policy applying strictly in the public sector and followed by agreement in the private sector). This has helped to reduce inflation from $12^{1}/_{2}\%$ in 1982 to 4% today without any large increase in unemployment.

So wage restraint is necessary, and so are the other supply-side measures discussed in our last report.[16] But, in terms of the inflation risk, it is hard to imagine a better moment to embark on a policy of expansion, with both oil prices and the dollar on our side.

III.3. Generating and financing the expansion of capacity

We can therefore revert to our initial focus and ask how an adequate expansion of capacity can be achieved and how it can be financed. In the last 15 years, the largest increase in capacity for the Community has been 6% per annum (about the same as for output), and the maximum for a single country has been about 10% (Italy 1976). Increases of this size have not raised any problem, but significantly the expansion required now needs to be sustained over a longer period than has been the case in the examples given.

If output were to grow $2^{1}/_{2}$ percentage points a year more than otherwise (at 5% rather than $2^{1}/_{2}$) and we assume an incremental capital/output ratio of 2, the share of investment in total output would have to rise by 5 percentage points GDP ($2 \times 2^{1}/_{2}$). This is probably an exaggeration, given the existing spare capacity and the role which services will play in the expansion. Even so, an expansion on the scale we envisage poses a substantial challenge. Two issues need to be confronted.

First, there is the challenge to the equipment-producing industry. The capacity utilization in this area was high by 1985; in that year equipment investment rose some 6%, substantially more than the rise in capacity of the equipment industry, whose capacity utilization rose, therefore, 3 to 4% in most subsectors, reaching rates of 82-86%. Furthermore, by year end the rates had risen to the 84 to 88% level.

It is not clear how fast capacity and output can grow in these industries, though it is encouraging that they are reported to plan an increase in investment by 15% in 1986 on top of a 15% rise in 1985.[17] In any case, some of the equipment would be imported from outside Europe.

The second question is where the finance will come from to pay for the extra share of investment in national income. It will mainly come from two sources. First, the European current account surplus will come down as Europe expands and the effects of the lower dollar come through. This year the Community's current account surplus is forecast at roughly 1% of GNP. As this turns round, the unhealthy deficits of the US and the third world debtor countries will come down and Europe will cease to be an exporter of capital. Second, the share of consumption in income will decline. This naturally tends to happen in an upturn, since a substantial fraction of any rapid rise in output does not get consumed. (In the longer term, a permanently higher rate of growth would also increase the savings rate by about 2% of income for every 1% of growth, in a steady state.)[18] However, to generate the higher savings we have to ensure that our expansion package includes the right mixture of monetary and fiscal policies.

III.4. Monetary and fiscal policies

The standard view, though not universally accepted, is that the world economy has been suffering from inappropriate mixtures of monetary and fiscal policies on both sides of the Atlantic. The US has pursued a high interest rate monetary policy, in order to restrain the possible inflationary effects of an expansionary budget. The net effect of the expansionary budget and relatively tight money has been favourable to US employment and has helped unemployment to fall by about 4 percentage points over the last four years. But it also led to a strong appreciation of the dollar, which together with the high US activity rate generated the present huge US trade deficit.

Though this deficit provided jobs in Europe, Europe was forced to accept the high world real interest rates. The alternative would have been a further depreciation of the European currencies, sharpening the twin dangers of inflation in Europe and protectionism in the US. The high real interest rates were, in the absence of wage restraint, bad for European employment. On top of this the European governments also adopted much tighter fiscal policies. In the Community between 1979 and today, the share of taxes (and social security contributions) in the national income rose by between 3 and 4 percentage points.[19] At the same time the share of government expenditure (net of transfers) barely changed,[20] and as a proportion of potential output (however measured) such government expenditure fell substantially. Thus the net impact of the budget was contractionary.[21]

The situation has now changed substantially. First, the oil price fall has reduced the level of world inflation, just as the earlier oil price rises lifted it. Second, the US has relaxed its monetary policy enough to permit a fall in the dollar. Thus the danger of an unacceptably low value for the European currencies (with the associated inflation risk) has been removed. This makes it much easier for European countries to consider a coordinated monetary expansion.

Would this be the right thing to do? It is quite possible that in the process of increasing employment, there will be such a scarcity of capital that high real interest rates will correspond to the correct pattern of factor prices. In the light of this, long-term real rates may remain high for some time. But this does not argue against greater monetary ease in the short run. In the new context, lower short-term real interest rates and (where appropriate) less credit rationing would be important parts of a package for European recovery. Lower interest rates in turn will involve somewhat higher monetary aggregates, justified by a fall in the velocity of circulation of money.

III.5. The structure of fiscal policy

There is also a need for fiscal expansion in Europe. How should this be structured? Given our previous discussion, we must ensure that the requisite savings emerge to finance the construction of new capacity. We cannot have a consumption-led boom. In addition fiscal expansion must not lead to a permanently growing ratio of debt to income. It should therefore be focused mainly on temporary incentives to employing more labour and creating more capital.

Labour is the surplus factor, but owing to complementarity between the factors one *must* pursue both objectives simultaneously.[22] It is only when output is fixed that more capital implies less employment. But we clearly want the expansion of capital to take as labour-intensive a form as possible. In other words, we want capital widening rather than capital deepening. This means that, where possible, it is the real cost of labour that we want to reduce rather than the real cost of capital.

So let us first consider steps to encourage expansion of the capital stock. This consists of the public and private capital stock, both of which may need to grow when national output rises. In some countries the public capital stock has become quite run down and the case for infrastructure investment is quite strong. This must be judged on normal criteria for the social rate of return. Where it passes this test, an expansion of the government deficit to finance such investment can involve no crowding out of investment in total, since by definition it can at worst divert a given volume of savings from financing private investment to financing equally-profitable public investment.

However the main expansion is needed in private investment. Incentives to investment in the form of tax provisions and subsidies have apparently proved to be not very effective in stimulating investment.[23] In addition, they have the serious drawback of encouraging substitution of labour with capital at the time when labour is abundant and capital presumably scarce. So we see little use in trying more of that medicine except for an investment tax credit of relatively short duration.[24] In this case the dominant effect of such a measure is the desirable one of shifting investment forward in time.

More generally, regarding the existing widespread public-sector transfers to the corporate sector, we believe that a critical review should be carried out — for each member country and in a comparative way — of the complex network of grants, subsidies, tax reliefs, credits, participations, etc. While some of these interventions may be warranted, it does seem urgent to us that the arguments for their continuation on the present scale, diffusion, and lack of transparency should be reconsidered more closely. The EC Commission has recently undertaken a systematic review of these interventions for France, the FRG, and the UK, with comparisons with the US, and has identified a number of critical issues concerning the budgetary cost of financial supports to industry, their effects in terms of efficiency, their consequences on the EC internal market, and their degree of transparency.[25]

In some countries attempts have been made to estimate the macroeconomic consequences of a massive reduction in these government interventions, including the aggregate and sectoral effects on employment that would derive from a reduction in personal taxes matching the reduction of expenditure on subsidies.[26] Simulations seem to indicate positive net effects on employment and the subject is worth pursuing.

What has to be stressed, in the context of our proposed strategy, is that financial support by governments seems to go to a large extent to the protection of unproductive capacity at old firms in sectors facing declining demand, to the detriment of the creation of new firms and of capital formation in sectors facing high demand. This runs contrary to the requirements of a policy aimed at removing the capital constraint on employment growth.

If a factor is to be subsidized (or detaxed), it should mainly be the abundant factor — labour. Several methods have been suggested to implement this approach. The method we advocate is that of "marginal employment subsidies", preferably in the form of rebating to the employer some portion of payroll taxes on net additions to payrolls (in terms of number of workers, not in terms of hours worked or of wage bill). This scheme has a number of desirable features.

- Provided the rebate is guaranteed to last some time, it will encourage labour-intensive techniques.

- It will lower domestic costs of production relative to the rest of the world, increasing exports — and aggregate demand — and the increase in exports will be valuable to attenuate the effect on the balance of trade of a rapid expansion of demand. It is true that if this measure is adopted simultaneously, as it should be to avoid intra-Community raiding, its effect on the demand from this source will come only from that portion of trade that is directed to the rest of the world. However, it is also true that the gains obtained abroad by each country will spill over to the other member countries through intra-Community trade.

- One could expect some effects even in a closed economy by lowering marginal costs, thus shifting the supply curve. In addition, of course, the newly-employed create their own demand, as long as the incremental savings are absorbed into investment, which, as we have said repeatedly, is pretty safe to assume once output gets growing and monetary policy is accommodating.

Finally we should comment on public consumption. This again should be judged on its merits. There does not seem to be a major role for big expansion of public employment in Europe except in the form of special programmes for the long-term unemployed, such as are advocated in our 1985 report. Many of these schemes could in any case be operated through the private sector.

A feasible policy for creating demand has to be such that at one and the same time it generates the capacity to supply the demand. Thus it must generate an increase in desired investment, as well as sufficient savings to finance this. But there is also the important question of the microeconomic efficiency of the process by which savings are allocated to investment, to which we now turn.

IV. Improving the financial system in Europe

IV.1. Capital formation and the efficiency of the financial system

Along with the macroeconomic policies suggested above, supply-side policies should be pursued in a complementary manner in all three crucial markets: the labour market, the output market, and the financial market.

Actions to achieve continued wage moderation, to contain non-wage labour costs, and to substantially increase the flexibility of the labour market should still be considered as the central piece of supply-side policies in Europe. If we do not dwell on them here, beyond what has been said in Section III.2 above, it is simply because we discussed this subject at length in our 1985 report[27] and because appropriate measures have been spelt out in detail by the EC Commission.[28]

Policies aimed at increasing the supply response in the output market are also important and should be carried out both at the level of individual countries and at the EC level. A large set of measures contemplated by the plan for the completion of the internal market for goods and services belong precisely to this category. Their implementation will serve the purpose not only of a deeper integration among member countries, but also of increasing the supply elasticity in each country's market for goods and services. In addition, the establishment of a truly unified market will itself provide a powerful impetus for capital formation.[29]

Structural policies to improve the financial system in Europe are not less essential. We wish to deal with them at some length for two reasons. First, capital formation in Europe in the next few years is not likely to find a substantial and permanent stimulus in an overly expansionary demand management for the reasons mentioned above. It will have to rely more, therefore, on improvements in the financial system that may facilitate the allocation of financial resources to promising initiatives.

Second, the link between the employment goal and structural financial policies needs to be stressed. Measures to increase the efficiency of financial markets and intermediaries — in individual countries and in the EC — are usually perceived by public opinion as having little or no relationship with the employment issue. However, as one key constraint to employment growth is now the capital constraint, and since it cannot be removed through macroeconomic policies alone, it should become clear that any step towards a more efficient financial system which will allow a larger capital formation for any given set of macroeconomic conditions is to be viewed as a positive contribution to employment policy.

Once this link is acknowledged, a strategy to improve financial allocation in Europe is likely to benefit from wider political support than has been the case so far. For this strategy to be effective, it has to consist of two coherent sets of policies, aiming respectively at improving domestic financial systems and at achieving a deeper integration among them.

IV.2. Improving domestic financial systems

Through the improvement of their domestic financial systems, European countries may increase the formation of productive capital associated with any given volume of aggregate private savings and current account position. Three main aspects of public policies come into play here, concerning respectively public sector investment, public sector financial transfers to firms, and public policies affecting the structure of the financial system. Issues related to the first two aspects have been discussed above, in the context of fiscal policy. We now consider policies affecting the structure of the financial system, i.e. the array of monetary, financial, and equity markets and the various types of institutions which operate in them.

Although measurements in this field are particularly difficult, it is commonly agreed that several European countries have financial systems which cannot be regarded as optimal from the point of view of supporting the formation of productive capital. In particular, there seems to be room for improvement in two respects: *greater operational efficiency*, leading to the provision of financial services to the economy at lower costs, and *greater allocative efficiency*, assuring that savings flow to those uses with the highest expected real rates of return — private or social — for any given risk level.

The specification of these objectives and the measures to achieve them will of course differ from country to country. A strong case can be made, however, that in general European financial systems can become more efficient in both respects outlined above if domestic public policies (by the regulatory bodies and the monetary authorities) (i) create more competitive conditions in and among the markets making up the financial system, and (ii) reduce the "hidden taxes" that are presently levied from the financial system.

These are essentially the two components of the process that is sometimes called "domestic liberalization" of financial markets. It should be stressed, however, that "deregulation" as such is neither a necessary nor a sufficient condition for this two-sided policy to be implemented. In several cases regulatory instruments will have to be oriented towards positively achieving more competition, rather than simply dismantled.

(i) Greater competition tends to increase the operational efficiency by inducing financial institutions to contain their production costs and to operate with lower profits. Both circumstances result in lower intermediation costs for the economy (see Appendix). Furthermore, keener competition leads also to a greater allocative efficiency by enabling financial resources to respond more easily to the attraction of the different rates of return obtainable from the various uses.

As to ways to increase competition, most of them should be identified in changes in those controls by which the authorities themselves to a large extent determine the degree of competition (barriers to entry, specification of the types of financial operations that each category of institutions is allowed to carry out, policies towards cartels, etc.). These changes should go in the direction of a certain relaxation of the "protection" granted to existing financial institutions, while at the same time relieving them from the various "portfolio constraints" imposed upon them in several countries (see below).

(ii) Hidden taxation results from different forms of coercion exerted by the authorities on the allocation of financial resources, most typically through portfolio constraints placed upon banks and other financial institutions (compulsory investments in certain types of securities, ceilings on specified kinds of loans, high reserve requirements bearing no interest or a strongly penalizing one, etc.), but frequently also upon non-financial firms (e.g., compulsory financing in foreign exchange for certain operations) and on households (e.g., restrictions on the purchase of foreign assets). "Taxation" is involved, both because coercion is applied — which is typical of fiscal instruments rather than of traditional monetary policy instruments — and because it produces effects similar to those of explicit taxation, though in a "hidden" way.

It can be shown that such systems of controls do impose hidden taxes on the economy (through lower returns to savers and higher costs for certain borrowers, usually in the private sector), the "revenue" of which accrues mostly to the public sector (through a larger supply of funds at lower rates to that sector).[30]

A reduction of such taxation can be achieved by means of appropriate structural changes in financial regulation and changes in the methods of monetary control, so as to make it less dependent on portfolio constraints and more dependent on market mechanisms. This reduction in hidden taxation not only has the advantage of bringing about a greater transparency (notably concerning the cost of the public sector), but also that of increasing both the operational efficiency of the financial system (smaller margins between lending and borrowing rates) and its allocative efficiency (especially when the effect of the portfolio constraints is to encourage the flow of financial resources to uses with low or nil productivity, e.g., financing of public sector current account deficit or dissaving).

Along with a reduction in explicit taxes (and subsidies) on financial markets — to the extent allowed by budgetary

33

considerations — a decrease in hidden taxation of the financial system would really amount to reducing the burden on the savings-investment process and at the same time increasing the efficiency with which financial markets perform the allocative function in that process. These two results are of crucial importance in the framework of a strategy for productive capital formation to sustain employment growth.

It will be noted that there is close complementarity between reducing hidden taxation and increasing competition in the financial system. Greater competition is necessary to ensure that the easing of inappropriate burdens on financial institutions, which would flow from a lower degree of hidden taxation, is passed on to users of financial services, i.e., is fully reflected in lower intermediation costs for the economy, rather than in higher profits for financial institutions themselves.

A revision of financial policies along the lines suggested here also aims at stimulating efficient capital formation through a greater allocative neutrality on the part of the authorities than has been observed in the past. This does not necessarily mean that governments should refrain altogether from influencing financial allocation. Within our strategy, however, they should do so more by making use of efficient financial markets than by impeding their efficiency through direct controls. Furthermore, to the extent that allocative purposes remain in governments' objectives, they should be oriented mainly in favour of new firms and of growing small and medium-sized firms, especially those characterized by relatively low capital intensity. Much remains to be done in order for those firms to gain easier access to capital markets.[31]

In the last few years, several European countries have started to move in the directions suggested above. Increased competition among financial institutions has been encouraged. Less use has been made of hidden taxes, especially in the form of direct controls over credit flows. The level and structure of interest rates have moved more freely. The more liberal environment has permitted the emergence of many new types of instruments and intermediaries, reflecting the needs of borrowers and lenders.

Although there are problems associated with these developments — in particular, supervisory problems in relation to financial stability — we consider it important that this trend be continued and be intensified to the advantage of capital formation in Europe. Certain countries, which in the last few months have temporarily reverted to previous practices based, in particular, on credit ceilings, should resume the new trend of domestic financial liberalization as soon as possible.

IV.3. Government debt and capital-market liberalization: the role of indexed bonds

Perhaps the main reason that keeps the authorities of some countries from further pursuing financial liberalization (both domestic and in the field of capital movements) is that in a regime without hidden taxation of the financial system the Treasury would have to pay more competitive interest rates on its issues. Besides the adverse budgetary consequences, this may contribute to keep up interest rates also for other borrowers in the bond market (although, for example, bank lending rates would be lowered by the elimination of hidden taxation, where this took the form of ceilings on bank loans).

We believe that this probelm could be solved at least in part by introducing index-linked bonds among the financing instruments of the Treasury. This is an innovation that we would recommend also in those countries that have already proceeded to a substantial liberalization of their financial system, if they wish to give some stimulus to the saving-investment process for any given demand policy stance.[32]

In several financial markets many agents still maintain fairly high expectations concerning the underlying rate of inflation, in spite of the recent remarkable declines in observed inflation rates. These expectations may take the form of a high expected rate of inflation (relative, for example, to government plans or to consensus forecasts) and/or a large variance associated with the inflationary expectation. In such conditions, a borrower issuing a long-term bond with principal linked to the general price level is likely to be able to raise funds at a lower real cost than would be implied by issuing conventional bonds of the same maturity, as it does not have to compensate the lender with an inflation-risk premium. At the same time, the borrower itself acquires the certainty concerning the real cost of financing over the whole life of the bond, rather than being exposed to unexpected changes in the real cost, as is the case with both conventional bonds and floating-rate nominal bonds. This may be of particular importance in connection with the financing of capital-widening investment — which should be increased under the strategy advocated in this report — because that kind of investment implies an extension of the forecasting horizon and therefore more uncertain inflationary expectations.

It is true that a company issuing bonds linked to the general price level would be exposed to a relative-price risk, as prices of its outputs may move differently from the general price level.[33] But it should be noted that this does not apply to the Treasury. Since its receipts — taxes — are indeed linked to the general price level (indexation of the tax system, even if applied, would simply

35

make this relationship proportional rather than progressive), the Treasury is possibly the only agent in the economy which, without incurring relative-price risks, can "sell" inflation coverage on financial instruments, obtaining as revenue a decrease in its own real cost of financing. It is paradoxical for a government not to exploit this sort of "natural monopoly" it potentially enjoys, and at the same time to impose artificial distorting elements of monopoly through various types of constraints in order to make Treasury financing easier.

There are possible objections to the indexation proposal, but they may be overcome. Issuing indexed bonds, it is sometimes feared, may appear a surrender to inflation; but clearly this preoccupation might have been more serious a few years ago than it is under the present conditions of low inflation. It is contradictory — states another argument — to index financial instruments while trying to reduce indexation in the labour market. But it should be noted that wage indexation has by now been substantially reduced in several countries, and that at any rate no simple symmetry can be established between wage indexation and asset indexation, for a number of reasons made clear by the literature.[34]

Setting the "appropriate" real rate on indexed bonds is difficult and may make an issue either unattractive or else too attractive at the expense of non-indexed issues of the Treasury itself or other borrowers. But this difficulty is reduced if indexed bonds — which should be fully negotiable instruments — are issued by tender. Finally, some monetary authorities are concerned that indexed bonds, as they reduce nominal interest payments relative to conventional or floating-rate bonds and shift the servicing burden over time, may give the fiscal authorities the impression that more room is available for other expenditures. But this can be avoided by establishing that the Treasury should make annual payments into a sinking fund, possibly with the central bank, for an amount corresponding to the nominal appreciation of the principal of the outstanding stock of indexed bonds.

The policy suggested here — financial liberalization supplemented and made easier by some indexation of government debt — would bring benefits not only to the Treasury, but probably also to other borrowers. To the extent that they issue bonds, firms would find Treasury pressures in the conventional and floating-rate bond markets somewhat eased. To the extent that they have recourse to bank loans, they would benefit from the more abundant supply and the lower rates that would be brought about by the elimination of ceilings and other constraints that still exist to facilitate Treasury financing. Furthermore, firms as well as savers would benefit from having a more competitive financial system. This would stimulate the savings-investment process without the need for a substantially more expansionary monetary policy at the aggregate level. It may be added that savers would benefit also because indexed instruments (savings deposits, insurance policies, etc.) would become more easily available if financial intermediaries were in a position to match them with indexed government bonds on their asset side.

Of course, indexed bonds would have to complement, and certainly not to substitute for, present forms of financial instruments issued by governments. There is in the markets a considerable demand for diversification and indexed bonds should satisfy a portion of this demand. Indeed, diversification might perhaps be considered even within indexed bonds themselves. Along with indexed bonds bearing a fixed real rate of interest, as those referred to so far, a government may find it appropriate to issue indexed bonds bearing a real rate of interest which varies (but in a predetermined way, not in a way which is unspecified *ex ante*, as is the case for real rates implicit in conventional or floating-rate bonds). A case could be made, in particular, for indexed bonds bearing a real rate of interest linked to the real growth rate of GDP. This would have stabilizing properties from a theoretical standpoint and, at a time when the principles of the "share economy" are being regarded with favour, would represent for a government a form of financing which is the closest possible to some concept of "equity capital".

In conclusion, introducing indexed bonds in the array of government debt instruments may make capital-market liberalization easier and may reinforce its effect of stimulating the savings-investment process for any given monetary policy stance. (See Appendix.)

IV.4. Financial integration

While domestic financial systems are in the process of being improved, they should also be integrated more deeply. Besides supplementing from the financial side the completion of the EC internal market, progress in integration will reinforce the trend towards more efficient financial systems in member countries, thus contributing to a more effective savings-investment process in support of growth and employment.

In fact, financial integration may be seen as the natural extrapolation of domestic financial liberalization. In common with the latter, it is based upon the two elements of increased competition (opening up domestic financial markets to international competition) and decreased recourse to hidden taxation (in particular of the form deriving from restrictions on capital flows).

In turn, financial integration is a component of a wider strategy aiming at creating in the EC an area of effective monetary and financial union. This wider strategy consists of the process leading to greater exchange rate stability among national currencies (monetary integration) and of the process leading to the liberalization of financial services and of capital movements (financial integration). While substantial progress has been made through the European Monetary System (EMS) on the front of monetary integration, advances have been much more limited towards financial integration, which is by no means less important in view of supporting the savings-investment process in Europe.

Yet, present circumstances seem to be rather favourable to an acceleration and deepening of financial integration, for two reasons. First, macroeconomic conditions denote a clear convergence among member countries, as indicated in particular by the narrowing of inflation differentials. This should reduce the risks, as perceived by national authorities, associated with phasing out the restrictions on capital flows and other obstacles to financial integration. At the same time there is an increasing concern that market rigidities bear considerable responsibility for the relatively poor performance of the EC in terms of growth and employment. This is gradually inducing national monetary authorities to reduce on their part some of the rigidities in the financial sphere as well. They may even come to realise that financial openness would put greater pressure on the budget process and on the labour market for the achievement of the adjustments that remain to be made.

Second, those countries which have a longer way to go in the direction of financial integration have recently initiated a liberalization process. This is the case for France and Italy, which have recently taken some measures of liberalization in the field of foreign exchange controls, as well as more incisive measures reducing the constraints on the allocation of funds through domestic intermediaries and markets. The two sides of this dual policy tend to reinforce each other because as less recourse is made to financial constraints domestically, the level and structure of domestic interest rates become more market-determined and more in line with those prevailing in international markets. This makes it less necessary to keep restrictions on capital flows for any given balance of payments or exchange rate target.

In this new environment, the recently announced EC plan to achieve gradually a full liberalization of capital movements is an important and feasible contribution not only towards financial integration, but also towards the more general strategy for growth and employment advocated in this report. The plan[35] involves two phases.

In the first phase, the objective would be to achieve the unconditional and effective liberalization throughout the Community of the capital operations most directly necessary for the appropriate functioning of the Common Market and for the linkage of national markets in financial securities. This implies the ending of the exceptional arrangements authorized in the past for some member countries and an extension of Community obligations to cover unconditional liberalization of long-term common credits, the acquisition of listed and unlisted securities, and the admission of securities to the capital markets. The second phase would aim at achieving the complete liberalization of all monetary and financial flows, including those unrelated to common transactions.

The trend towards liberalization of capital movements by countries such as France and Italy may also make other countries, the FRG in particular, more prepared to adopt a favourable stance concerning the development of the ECU and further institutional steps for the development of the EMS, thus increasing the potential for a Community-wide financial system with its own identity. On the other hand, it seems justified that there should be only limited support for these developments as long as both the ECU and the EMS are severely eroded in their scope by the high degree of financial fragmentation still existing in the EC, mainly due to restrictions on capital flows.

Further progress towards the improvement of domestic financial systems and towards their deeper integration may of course imply relevant transitional costs and problems for economic agents as well as for the national policy-makers. However, in view of the proximity of a capital constraint for the European economy, a general improvement of Europe's financial system is as important as appropriate macroeconomic policies if growth and employment are to be sustained.

V. Summary

Finally it may be useful to summarize our main points, somewhat baldly.

1. The falls in the price of oil and of the dollar provide a new climate of low inflation. It is now safer than before to expand the European economy. The fall in the dollar, by destroying jobs in Europe's export industries, also makes it more necessary than before to provide a specifically European stimulus to demand. This will be even more necessary if there is a US fiscal contraction.

2.   Europe's industry is now working only slightly below previous peak levels of capacity utilization. More shift work might make higher utilization possible, and employment in services is less limited by physical capacity. But major increases in employment will not be possible unless there are major expansions in capacity.

3.   To reduce unemployment to its level in the late 1970s (5% of the labour force), output will have to grow faster than the $2\frac{1}{2}\%$ a year growth currently projected. High growth rates have occurred in the past, especially starting from high unemployment, and they can occur again in the future. We must create the conditions for growth to build up gradually to 5% a year for at least a few years.

4.   But there would be a danger of inflation increasing. To prevent this, supply-side policies — leading to low barriers to entry and more flexibility of all markets, and including appropriate policies on wage restraint — are essential.

5.   The extra investment would be financed partly from a reduced trade surplus (i.e., reduced capital outflows) and partly by higher savings as consumption lagged behind the growth of income.

6.   To encourage investment, Europe should relax its tight fiscal policy and have a coordinated monetary expansion. The fiscal relaxation should be mainly temporary, in order to get the economy moving faster. There should be time-limited investment incentives and marginal employment subsidies. Public employment growth should be mainly limited to programmes for the long-term unemployed.

7.   The success of the proposed expansion depends in large measure on its occurring more or less simultaneously in all members of the Community. Any one country that tries to do it alone (except possibly the FRG) would soon face a current account deficit, to be financed by capital imports. If capital cannot be attracted, this would create a serious risk of depreciation and renewed inflationary pressure. But if the expansion is simultaneous, much of the negative effect on the current balance would be avoided through additional exports generated by the expanded imports of the other countries. Whether these considerations call for some explicit form of coordination is a political issue beyond the scope of this report.

8.   The allocation of savings to investment would be more efficient if there were less quantitative regulation of financial markets. Liberalization is needed in relation to capital flows within countries and between member states. Access to the capital market should be eased for small firms.

9. Governments should be more willing to issue index-linked bonds. This would reduce the inflation risk both to governments and to savers and thus help to reduce real interest rates.

10. With the measures outlined in this and our 1985 report it should be possible to make a major attack on the problem of European unemployment.

Appendix: Improvements in the financial system

Consider a very simple framework for the analysis of the financial market:

$$D = D(\underline{i_D}, \overline{\sigma i_D}, ...)$$

$$S = S(\underset{+}{i_S}, \overline{\sigma i_S}, ...)$$

$$i_D = i_S + m$$

$$D = S$$

where D is the demand for funds, S is the supply of funds, i_D is the expected value of the real interest rate for borrowers, i_S is the expected value of the real interest rate for savers, σi_D and σi_S are the standard deviations of the probability distributions of those respective real interest rates, and m is the margin charged by the financial system (intermediation cost).

If both the agents who demand and those who supply funds are risk-averse (in that the former will be prepared to bear a higher expected real cost on borrowings if the cost can be anticipated with greater certainty, and savers will be content with a smaller expected real return on assets if that return is exposed to less inflation-risk), the response of the demand and supply of funds to changes in the arguments will be those indicated by the signs.

As shown by Figure 5, any policy intervention resulting in a decrease in the spread will shift the D schedule upwards by the amount of such a decrease, because any given borrowing rate will now be associated with a higher level of the rate of return to savers i_S, shown on the vertical axis. There will be an increase in the volume of all funds supplied and demanded (from OE to OE´, likely to be associated with greater savings and investment), an increase in the equilibrium rate of return to savers (from i_S to i_S´), and at the same time a decline in the equilibrium interest rate on borrowings (because the increase in i_S, AF, is more than offset by the decline in the spread, AC).

In terms of the policies discussed in the main text, this is the case of an increase in competition, of a reduction in the (explicit or hidden) taxation of the financial system, and — at the EC level — of greater integration among domestic financial systems.

The effects of introducing indexed bonds can in turn be considered by looking at Figure 6. Indexation allows for a reduction in the inflation-risk and thus shifts both schedules to the right. The volume of funds supplied and demanded (and the scale of the savings-investment process), will increase (from OV to OV'). The changes in real interest rates cannot be determined unambiguously. However, the smaller the elasticity of D with respect to the interest rate and to its standard deviation (as is likely to be the case for the government sector), the more likely is a decrease in the real interest rate.

Figure 5. Policies reducing the cost of intermediation

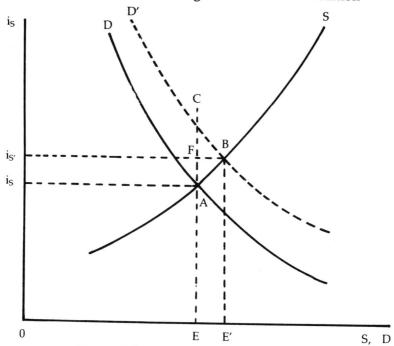

Figure 6. Introduction of indexed bonds

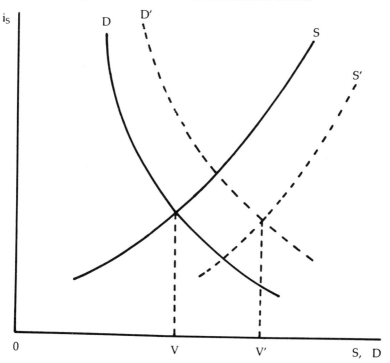

Notes and sources

1. O. Blanchard *et al.*, "Employment and Growth in Europe: A Two-Handed Approach", in O. Blanchard *et al.*, *Restoring Europe's Prosperity: Macroeconomic Papers from the Centre for European Policy Studies*, MIT Press, London and Cambridge (Mass.), 1986.

2. R. Layard *et al.*, "Europe: the Case for Unsustainable Growth", in O. Blanchard *et al.*, *Restoring Europe's Prosperity, Macroeconomic Papers from the Centre for European Policy Studies*, MIT Press, London and Cambridge (Mass.), 1986.

3. See, in particular, Commission of the EC, "Annual Economic Report 1985-86", in *European Economy*, No. 26, Brussels, November 1985, and OECD, *Economic Outlook*, Paris, December 1985.

4. Commission of the EC, *European Economy*, op. cit., pp. 140 ff.

5. See also O. Blanchard *et al.*, "Employment and Growth in Europe: A Two-Handed Approach", op. cit., Section III.2.

6. Commission of the EC, *European Economy*, Supplement B, No. 1, Brussels, January 1986, p. 2.

7. This involves assumptions about how total GDP would change with unemployment and how industrial production would change with total GDP. On the latter point, we assume a unit elasticity, assuming unit income elasticity of demand for industrial products in consumption plus a disproportionate growth in investment, offset by negligible growth in Community exports and in government purchases of industrial products. On the first point, we base our Okun coefficient partly on "How Fast Can Europe Grow?", *Quarterly Review*, Federal Reserve Bank of New York, Summer 1985. This suggests that for the recent period the Okun coefficient is 1.8 for the FRG and 1.6 for the UK. One may query whether even coefficients of this order are fully relevant when one is considering a once-for-all expansion of output and employment (rather than a cyclical change). In addition the labour-intensity of marginal output will also be very important. The calculations are therefore illustrative.

8. This is broadly in line with the findings of the Compact model that in 1982 the excess of labour supply over the maximum labour force that the capital stock could employ was 7.4%.

9. The EC has asked firms their reasons for not employing more people. Insufficient production capacity came tenth out of the reasons tabulated. (*European Economy*, Supplement B, April 1986, p. 8.)

10. On this problem see Jacques H. Drèze, "Work-Sharing: Why? How? How Not...", in this volume.

11. *European Economy*, Supplement B, February 1986, Tables 1 and 3. The UK data are not a reliable measure of capacity-utilization levels, though they are a valid measure of changes over time.

12. If the coefficient were 2, output growth of 5% a year would reduce unemployment by 1.25 points a year (the 2 $1/2$ "extra" growth, divided by 2).

13. O. Blanchard and L.H. Summers, "Hysteresis and the European Unemployment Problem", in S. Fischer (ed.), *NBER Macro-economic Annual 1986*, MIT Press, Cambridge (Mass.).

14. R. Layard and S.J. Nickell, "The Performance of the British Labour Market", London School of Economics, Centre for Labour Economics, Working Paper No. 846, 1986.

15. H.R. Sneessens and J.H. Drèze, "A Discussion of Belgian Unemployment, Combining Traditional Concepts and Dis-equilibrium Econometrics", *Economica*, Vol. 53, No. 210 (Supplement), 1986, pp. 589-119.

16. At the European level, general support for wage restraint has been expressed by both the official trade union and employers' organ-izations, TUAC and BIAC. See "Full Employment and Growth as a Social and Economic Goal — A Joint Statement by BIAC and TUAC", OECD, Paris, April 1986. According to the statement, "The employment situation remains very unsatisfactory in most OECD countries, and recurrent unemployment is specially intolerable. Changing the present unemployment situation and achieving full employment through more investment and higher economic growth should thus be the main objective of economic and social policy". (p.3).

17. *European Economy*, January 1986, Supplement B.

18. See F. Modigliani, "Life Cycle Hypothesis of Saving and Intercountry Difference in the Saving Ratio", in A. Abel (ed.), *The Collected Papers of Franco Modigliani: The Life Cycle Hypothesis of Saving*, Vol. 2, MIT Press, Cambridge (Mass.), 1980, pp. 382-412. A 1% increase in the trend growth of income is found to increase the saving ratio between $1^1/2$ and 2%. In a later paper, "Determinants of Private Saving with Special Reference to the Role of Social Security — Cross Country Tests" (with Arlie Sterling), it is found that the effect of pure productivity rise, which may be expected to be a large component of the advocated growth, is even larger: between 2 and 3%.

19. *European Economy*, November 1985, pp. 183 and 134.

20. *European Economy*, November 1985, pp. 166 and 134.

21. The fact that the share of the budget deficit in GNP is still the same as in 1979 is irrelevant. This is due mainly to higher payments to unemployed workers (which respond passively to unemployment and do not explain its level) and to higher interest payments (whose demand impact is small, especially to the extent that they reflect nominal rather than real interest).

22. In the short run there is no conflict between pursuing increased use of labour and of capital. This is clear even in a strictly neo-classical

framework. In this case employment is determined by capital and the real cost of labour:

$$\frac{N}{K} = f\left[\frac{W}{P}(1 + t)\right] \qquad (f' < 0)$$

where N is employment, K capital, W/P the real wage, and t labour taxes. In addition, capital growth is determined by the rate of return on capital, $\varrho(N/K)$, relative to the cost of capital (c):

$$\frac{\dot{K}}{K} = g\left[\frac{\varrho(N/K)}{c}\right] \qquad (g' > 0;\ \varrho' > 0)$$

So for any given path of W/P, the path of N will be higher the lower t and the lower c.

23. Commission of the EC, "Annual Economic Review, 1985/86", *European Economy*, No. 26, November 1985, Chapter 3.

24. See "Employment and Growth in Europe: A Two-Handed Approach", op. cit.

25. Commission of the EC, Document EC II-107/85.

26. In a study based on a simulation model, Gerken *et al.* suggest that an overall reduction of subsidies by 50% over a period of five years, combined with corresponding tax cuts, could increase the number of jobs in the FRG by 1 million. Gerken *et al.*, "Mehr Arbeit-splaetze Durch Subventionsabbau", Discussion Paper No. 113/114, Kiel University, 1985.

27. "Employment and Growth in Europe: A Two-Handed Approach", op. cit.

28. Commission of the EC, "Annual Economic Report 1985-86: A Cooperative Growth Strategy for More Employment", and "Annual Economic Review", *European Economy*, No. 26, November 1985.

29. F.D. Weiss, and H. Giersch, "Internal and External Liberalisation and the European Economies' Structural Development", May 1985.

30. This analysis has been carried out in detail, for example in the case of Italy. See "Report on the Italian Credit and Financial System", *Quarterly Review*, Banca Nazionale del Lavoro, Special Issue, June 1983.

31. Consider, for example, that since 1963 fewer than 600 companies have been listed on the second tier of exchanges in the EC, while during the ten years from 1974 to 1984 the nationwide electronic dealing network in the US has created an active market of 5,000 listed equities with an annual trading volume of $153 billion — bigger than the combined volume of business on the stock exchanges of the UK, FRG, France, Italy, and the Netherlands. While the EC countries produce as many new start-ups in a year as the US (about 600,000), no large-scale mechanism exists for trading

the equity of these companies. Partly as a consequence of this situation, European investors have provided US venture companies with a fifth of their capital in recent years. In 1985 alone, Europeans provided more than $600 million towards the $3.2 billion raised in venture capital in the US. (See *Euromoney*, February 1986.)

32. A discussion of this issue, including references to the British experience, is in M. Monti, "Indexation of Government Debt — and its Alternatives", in B.P. Herber (ed.), *Public Finance and Public Debt*, International Institute of Public Finance, Wayne State University Press, forthcoming.

33. It can be noted, however, that a company may not avoid risks associated with relative prices even when issuing nominal debt instruments.

34. See, for example, N. Liviatan, "On the Interaction between Wage and Asset Indexation", in R. Dornbusch and M.H. Simonsen (eds.), *Inflation, Debt and Indexation*, MIT Press, Cambridge (Mass.), 1983.

35. The plan, announced by President Delors on 12 May 1986, is outlined in the Communication from the Commission to the Council of 23 May 1986, "Programme for the Liberalization of Capital Movements in the Community".

Labour Market Flexibility and Jobs: A Survey of Evidence from OECD Countries with Special Reference to Europe

David Metcalf

The author is grateful to Lars Calmfors and to participants of the CEPS Macroeconomic Workshop for helpful comments on an earlier version of this paper.

I. Introduction

Some pundits and policy-makers attribute the relatively high European unemployment rates to sclerotic labour markets. For example, the British government's recent White Paper, *Employment, the Challenge for the Nation*,[1] stated "The biggest single cause of our high unemployment is the failure of our jobs market, the weak link of our economy." By contrast, the expert OECD investigation into labour market flexibility[2] was far more cautious: "It is worth emphasising yet again that labour market flexibility is but one and probably not the most important factor affecting progress in these respects [economic adjustment, unemployment]. In the first instance, macroeconomic policies promoting non-inflationary growth are needed. For them to be successful, a set of structural measures has to be added. Labour market flexibility has its place in this structural set." Given such a divergence of views about the importance and role of labour market rigidities, it is vital to examine how more flexible labour markets can boost employment.

The aim of this paper is to assess the extent to which rigid labour markets are responsible for current high levels of European unemployment. After surveying the evidence we conclude that such rigidities do have adverse effects, but that they account only for part of the rise in European unemployment in the last decade.

Three aspects of labour market flexibility are considered. The *aggregate labour market* is studied in Part II. Sections II.1 and II.2 concentrate on the link between jobs and nominal and real wage pressure, while the role of institutions in achieving flexibility in pay is discussed in Section II.3. In Part III *relative wage and relative employment flexibility* is analysed by breaking down the labour market into its component industrial and occupational sectors. Employment flexibility *inside the firm* is inspected in Part IV. Section IV.1 examines the way in which job security influences firms' employment; in Section IV.2 flexibility in job tenures and in the internal labour market — craft demarcations and productivity agreements, for example — are discussed. The summary and conclusions are presented in Part V. This progression from the aggregate labour market through industrial and occupational sectors to the firm's labour market would seem to be an illuminating way of setting out and studying the various types of labour market rigidity that have been discussed.

In recent years the performance of the European labour market has often been unfavourably contrasted with Japan and the United States. For example, an editorial in *The Financial Times*[3] stated that "Japan's low unemployment is primarily a reflection of very high internal mobility, America's a reflection of high external mobility. Europe suffers high unemployment because it lacks either sort of mobility." Therefore a main point throughout the analysis is to make comparisons between Europe and Japan and the United States. Many of the particular examples are drawn from the United Kingdom.

II. The aggregate labour market

The OECD has described the importance of aggregate labour market flexibility in a nutshell:[4]

> The issue of labour cost flexibility is both difficult and controversial. It is difficult because wage setting in member countries is intimately bound up with collective bargaining, and institutional settings and practices in this area vary widely across countries. It is also controversial because it raises major analytical and empirical questions on which no consensus exists.

In Section II.1 we examine economy-wide labour cost flexibility. Estimates of the non-accelerating inflation rate of unemployment for nine countries over time are presented and discussed and the causes of the large rise in British unemployment since the 1950s are analysed. Then in Section II.2 the association between real labour costs and employment is studied. The relationship between the institutions of collective bargaining and the performance of the aggregate labour market is examined in Section II.3. This discussion therefore permits us to take a view on many of the current controversies, including the role of union power in causing high unemployment and the case for and against corporatism.

II.1. Economy-wide labour cost flexibility

Non-accelerating inflation rate of unemployment

One indicator of flexibility in the aggregate labour market is the non-accelerating inflation rate of unemployment (NAIRU) which shows the level of unemployment necessary to keep inflation constant. The NAIRU can be compared across countries or over time (Table 1). Differences in the NAIRU among countries or over time within the country are frequently attributed to corresponding differences or changes in variables reflecting labour market flexibility, such as the unemployment benefit to wage ratio, the mismatch between vacancies and the unemployed in the occupational or geographic composition of the labour force, or the power of organized labour in striving for and achieving higher than warranted real wages.

Table 1. Estimates of the non-accelerating inflation rate of unemployment[1]

	Time	Actual unemployment rate (%)	Estimate of NAIRU (%)
Austria	1969-73	1.4	1.1
	1980-83	3.0	2.4
Canada	1967-69	4.2	5.6
	1980-83	8.5	7.2
France	1971-75	2.7	4.6
	1981-83	6.3	5.8
FRG[2]	1967-70	1.0	0.8
	1981-83	6.3	5.8
Italy	1966-70	5.5	6.2
	1981-83	9.1	5.8
Japan	1972-75	1.5	1.2
	1981-83	2.2	2.3
Netherlands	1969-73	1.4	1.1
	1980-83	3.0	2.4
UK	1967-70	2.2	4.9
	1981-83	10.6	7.7
US	1967-69	3.6	4.9
	1982-83	9.7	5.2

Notes: 1. The NAIRU is calculated from a three-equation system: an augmented Phillips curve, a cost mark-up price equation, and an adaptive expectations equation. Full details of the estimation method are given in the source.
2. Federal Republic of Germany.
Source: D. Coe and F. Gagliardi, "Nominal Wage Determination in Ten OECD Economies", Working Paper No. 19, Economics and Statistics Department, OECD, Paris, March 1985, Table 11.

Four points stand out from Table 1. First, currently the level of unemployment necessary to keep inflation constant is lower in the US and Japan than in most European countries. (Austria and the Netherlands are the exceptions.) This must reflect, in part, some dimensions of flexibility in the labour market, including the power of organized labour, in the different countries.

Second, there is a tendency for the NAIRU to rise over time. This implies that labour markets have become more rigid or that the work-force is striving for too high a real wage.

Third, movements in the estimated NAIRU are strongly associated with movements in actual unemployment. Perhaps growing unemployment destroys human capital and undermines the work ethic.[5] Alternatively labour markets may have become more rigid in the last two decades. Or it may simply reflect the method of estimation. (If so, this is a damning indictment of the statistical methods used.)

Fourth, in many countries current unemployment levels are way above the estimated NAIRUs. If the estimates of NAIRUs mean anything, this suggests that unemployment could be reduced in these countries without running into problems of accelerating inflation.

The rise in unemployment in the UK

The factors associated with the rise in the British unemployment rate, including the NAIRU, have been thoroughly documented[6] and are set out in Table 2. (Unfortunately no similar work seems to exist for other European countries.) Changes in the replacement ratio, payroll taxes, union power, and mismatch account for roughly half the increase in unemployment; changes in demand account for the other half.

The change in the benefit-to-wage ratio (replacement rate) contributes only 0.4 percentage points — a far more modest contribution to the rise in unemployment than saloon bar pundits would have us believe. Although benefits did rise relative to pay in the period 1968-78, since then the replacement ratio has fallen

Table 2. Breakdown of the change in UK male
unemployment rate: 1956-83

Variable	% point increase in unemployment
Benefit replacement ratio	0.4
Employers' labour taxes	1.9
Unions	2.3
Mismatch	0.8
Demand factors	6.4
Total	11.8
(Actual change)	(11.8)

Note: This table is estimated from a three-equation system: labour demand, price and wage equations 1954-83, non-linear 3SLS estimates. See Table 4 of the source.
Source: R. Layard and S. Nickell, "The Cause of British Unemployment", National Institute Economic Review, February 1985.

back as certain benefits have been axed and others have been made subject to income tax. Anyway, when there are few vacancies, if benefits deter one person from taking a job, someone else will snap it up, so benefits are unlikely to have much of an impact on aggregate unemployment. However, it is possible that changes in the administration of benefits have influenced unemployment. For example the divorce in the 1970s of the job-finding and benefit-paying functions of employment exchanges may have reduced pressure on unemployed people to seek work and reduced the resources devoted to helping longer-term unemployed individuals into work.

Since the early 1960s, non-wage labour costs — mainly employers' National Insurance contributions and pension contributions — have risen by more than 13 percentage points. This has made labour more expensive to employ and is estimated to have added nearly two percentage points to unemployment.

Union militancy may raise real wages above that warranted by productivity. Such militancy might reflect, for example, a shift in the relative valuation of real wages and employment. Union militancy is often measured by the union mark-up, i.e. the pay of union members relative to otherwise similar non-union members. [Though whether this is a truly independent measure of power or whether it is (negatively) associated with changes in employment is a moot point.] This union mark-up rose substantially over the period and, consequently, it is calculated that the direct impact of union power on unemployment since 1956 is 2.3 percentage points. This may, in fact, understate the total impact of such power on unemployment. For example, if wages do not adjust properly to changes in employment taxes, is this also because of unions? Further, non-union wages may be affected by union wages.

The long-run rate of unemployment will rise if the mismatch between unemployment and vacancies worsens. There is little evidence that this has happened by region or by occupation. However, the industrial structure of the economy has changed substantially in the last two decades, and particularly since 1979. In 1966 half the employed labour force was in the production industries (mining, manufacturing, construction, utilities), but by 1985 this production sector only accounted for one-third of employment. The large switch out of production industries worsened the industrial matching of vacancies and people and so may have raised unemployment. But the table indicates that worsening mismatch between jobs and vacancies only accounts for less than one percentage point of the rise in unemployment.

More than half the increase in unemployment over the period is associated with inadequate demand. This is measured by fiscal stance, world trade trends, and international competitiveness. In the period since 1979 these demand factors are particularly important in accounting for the rise in unemployment.

There is a complication here. When a structural factor (i.e. replacement rate, payroll tax, union power, or mismatch) moves adversely, it has both a direct and an indirect effect. The direct effect is that reported in Table 2. The indirect effect of the adverse change arises because it serves to reduce the level of demand consistent with unchanging inflation. Thus some of the unemployment associated with the demand factors reflects the government's attempt to keep inflation stable in the face of worsening structural factors.

According to Layard and Nickell, the NAIRU rose over the period from around 2% in the 1950s to around 11% in the 1980s. This way of thinking about unemployment brings out two important policy implications. First, as actual unemployment is well above the NAIRU, it can be cut — without fuelling inflation — via measures which increase aggregate demand. Second, the essence of "making the labour market more flexible" is to improve the underlying structural factors. This has a favourable direct effect on unemployment, but also a favourable indirect effect, because the economy can now be run at higher aggregate demand without compounding inflationary pressure.

II.2. Real labour costs

The association between employment and real labour cost refers both to movements in pay and jobs over the cycle and to how the labour market responds to shocks like big changes in import prices. It is sometimes held that the Japanese and US labour markets are more adaptable over the cycle or to shocks than labour markets in major European countries and that this accounts for their superior employment performance. These links between real wages and employment and the adjustment of western economies to shocks are described here.

The OECD[7] recently examined evidence for a number of countries and concluded that "The results point clearly to a negative long-run association between real wages and employment, with the mean wage elasticity being about unity." Thus the level of, and movements in, real wages are one factor (but only one) in determining employment. But we should remember that it is nominal pay that is decided by collective bargaining, while the real wage is determined also by firms' pricing decisions.[8] Therefore, as Solow noted, the useful questions for policy "are better phrased in terms of nominal wage behaviour even when the desired answers relate to real wages".[9] It is worth noting, in passing, that the sensitivity of employment to real wages was above average in Japan and below average in the United States.

If the terms of trade worsen or the trend growth of aggregate productivity slows down, real wages have to be adjusted downwards; otherwise employment will fall as capital gets substituted for labour and as unprofitable output gets cut back. Countries with rigid real wages will tend to suffer more unemployment in the face of an external shock than countries with flexible real wages.

In the mid-1970s the industrialized countries experienced an unfavourable movement in the terms of trade due to the rise in the price of oil. Evidence on the subsequent degree of adaptability of real wages across 10 OECD countries is given in Figure 1, which also shows the growth in unemployment between 1975 and 1982. It certainly appears that real wage rigidity has serious consequences. The rank correlation coefficient between real wage rigidity and the growth in unemployment is 0.76 (significant at 1%); countries where real wages are most rigid tend to experience the biggest rise in unemployment and vice versa. They also tend to have higher NAIRUs than countries with more flexible real wages. (See Table 1.)

Figure 1. Short-run real wage rigidity and unemployment

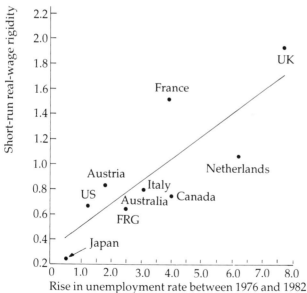

Note: A value of unity in the real wage rigidity measure indicates that a 1% increase in the unemployment rate is required to offset a real shock which would otherwise result in a 1% increase in inflation.

Source: D. Coe and F. Gagliardi, "Nominal Wage Determination in Ten OECD Economies", Working Paper No. 19, Economic and Statistics Department, OECD, Paris, March 1985, Figure 13 (corrected), p. 37.

The two countries at the top and bottom of the league table stand out starkly. Japan has flexible real wages and experienced a growth of unemployment of only 0.5% between 1975-82. By contrast, the UK had rigid real wages and suffered an increase in unemployment of nearly 8%. Furthermore, the estimated NAIRU for the UK is treble the Japanese rate.

The difference between the United States and much of Europe on this measure of real wage adaptability is much less pronounced than is sometimes asserted.[10] For example, the Federal Republic of Germany (FRG), Austria, and Italy all have similar adaptability, on this measure at least. Coe and Gagliardi[11] conclude that "The results cast some doubt on the conventional wisdom that real wages are relatively flexible in the United States ... [and] make it somewhat difficult to attribute the more robust employment performance in the United States primarily to more flexible real wages."

II.3 Consensus and economic performance

The association between consensus in the labour market and economic performance has been systematically investigated across and within a number of countries. The evidence suggests that superior macroeconomic performance goes hand-in-hand with consensus and corporatism (though such associations beg the causal mechanism).

Corporatism is identified by Bruno and Sachs[12] as a "model of social organization in which groups rather than individuals wield power and transact affairs." Their indicators of corporatism are: whether negotiations take place at national or local level; the power of national vis-à-vis local labour organizations; the extent of employer coordination; and the power of local union stewards. A country is defined as corporatist if wage bargaining is highly centralized; if wage agreements do not have to be ratified at local level; if employers are organized; and if local union officials have limited influence. The ranking of countries which emerges from these criteria seems sensible. The most corporatist countries are Austria, the FRG, the Netherlands, and the Scandinavian ones; the least corporatist are the US and Canada. Japan and the rest of Europe rank in the middle.

Bruno and Sachs themselves suggested that corporatism is an important influence in economic performance and this is confirmed by a thorough recent analysis[13] which shows that:

• more corporatist economies display a greater response of wage change to unemployment in both the short run and long run (i.e., a smaller increase in unemployment is required to get a given reduction in money wage inflation in corporatist economies);

• the impact of tax changes and import prices is lower in corporatist economies (i.e., it is easier to adjust to oil shocks, for example, because there is less real wage resistance in corporatist economies);

• both the increase in unemployment in the last two decades and the level of unemployment in the 1980s is lower in the more corporatist economies.

It might be thought that corporatism only matters when unions are powerful, or to put it another way, that powerful unions without the corporatist consensus is the worst of all worlds. The authors analysed this possibility and rejected it; it is corporatism per se that is associated with economic performance.

The association between corporatism and macroeconomic performance has also been investigated recently by Newell and Symons.[14] Their analysis is specially illuminating because they not only compare performance indicators across five countries but also split three countries — the FRG, the UK, and Japan — into corporatist and non-corporatist episodes. Their main findings are reported in Table 3. The unemployment consequences of a wage shock (such as an increase in militancy) or of an employment shock (such as a rise in real interest rates) are less in corporatist Sweden than in the non-corporatist US. In addition, and perhaps more interesting, these shocks result in far more unemployment within a country when it is pursuing a non-corporatist policy than when it has a corporatist strategy — twice as much in the FRG, three times as much in Japan, and six times as much in the UK. Further, row 3 indicates that in corporatist countries or in corporatist periods a far smaller increase in unemployment is required to obtain a given cut in real wages. The authors (who have sometimes been criticized in Britain for their hard-line neoclassical approach to labour market issues) conclude that "Corporatism is undoubtedly a good idea to control unemployment."[15]

The consensus-performance connection has also been investigated by an OECD Working Party.[16] They compared for 16 countries the Okun "misery index" with the extent of consensus. The misery index is defined as the sum of the inflation and unemployment rates. The degree of consensus was based on three characteristics: the degree of centralization of collective bargaining, trade union and employer willingness to concert action with the government, and the reliability of dispute settlement procedures. The evidence — for three separate time-periods — shows an inverse association between consensus and misery. In each time-period high consensus countries like Austria and the FRG show up as low misery countries, while low consensus countries like the UK and Italy have poorer performance.

The *performance–consensus–corporatism* nexus does not, however, identify the causal mechanism. It is possible that good

Table 3. Impact of the industrial relations system on macroeconomic performance

	Sweden	Corporatist FRG	Non-corp. FRG	Corporatist UK	Non-corp. UK	Corporatist Japan	Non-corp. Japan	US
Unemployment consequences of wage shock	0.26	0.51	1.27	0.48	3.10	0.17	0.49	2.81
Unemployment consequences of employment shock	0.68	0.96	2.36	0.51	3.33	0.30	0.86	1.30
Impact of unemployment on real wages	3.28	1.53	0.38	1.90	0.14	5.61	1.82	01.9

Notes: Row 1 shows the cumulative increase in percentage points of unemployment stemming from a 1% real wage shock caused by (e.g.) a change in militancy or import prices.

Row 2 shows the cumulative increase in percentage points of unemployment stemming from a 1% employment shock caused by (e.g.) a change in real interest rates.

Row 3 is the short-run (percentage point) decrease in real wages resulting from a 1% increase in unemployment (capital held constant, output variable).

The authors adopt the Bruno and Sachs definition of corporatism. Thus the FRG is defined as non-corporatist after 1977; Japan is defined as corporatist after 1977; and the UK is defined as non-corporatist after 1979.

Source: A. Newell and J. Symons, "Corporatism, *Laissez-faire* and the Rise in Unemployment", Working Paper No. 853, Centre for Labour Economics, London School of Economics, 1986.

economic performance generates consensus in the labour market. But to the extent that the causal mechanism runs, even in part, from consensus to performance, it would seem sensible to pursue consensus. The OECD team believed that consensus evolves more easily under a centralized system where there are, for example, shared perspectives between unions and government, centralized bargaining, and effective contract enforcement. Again, this is food for thought for the direction of labour market policy in Europe.

III. Relative wages and relative employment

Efficient allocation of labour has two requirements. First, relative wages should adjust to reduce imbalances among markets. Thus relative pay should rise in sectors where there is excess demand, and vice versa. Second, the quantity of labour should adjust — for example among industries, skills, or geographic areas — in response to relative pay movements (wage signals) and to vacancies or unemployment rates (quantity signals). Layard and Nickell[17] provide a formal treatment of this. The evidence below suggests that labour does get adjusted in response to wage and quantity signals, albeit not necessarily at the right speed or by the right amount. But movements in relative wages are torpid and contribute only modestly to the flexibility of the labour market.

In Section III.1 we examine the industrial wage structure to see, in particular, whether the process of adjustment in relative pay across industries augments or reduces aggregate employment. Movements in relative pay and employment by skill are examined in Section II.2. Layard and Nickell[18] perform a similar analysis, splitting the labour market by geographic area, education, age, sex, and public/private sectors.

III.1. The industrial wage structure

The key issue concerning flexibility in the industrial wage structure is whether the nexus of *productivity change–wage change–employment change* across industries has a favourable or unfavourable impact on jobs.

The importance of flexibility in relative wages in allocating labour across sectors and its possible affect on aggregate employment is not a new topic. More than a quarter of a century ago Reddaway[19] compared and contrasted the "institutional" approach with the "competitive" model of allocation in the labour market. In the institutional approach "the essential characteristic is that the *main* way in which employment will either be increased or reduced is through 'direct action' by the employers, and that only exceptionally will they have to include employers, and that only exceptionally will they have to include a change in the relative wage offered in order to secure the desired number of workers." By contrast the competitive approach puts wage flexibility to the fore and suggests that, in the short run, sectors expanding (contracting) employment will raise (lower) their relative wages.

An OECD Working Party examined this controversy and reported in 1965 that they "inclined to the view that the allocation of labour had been sensitive primarily to job vacancies and not to movements in relative wages."[20] This finding is replicated in a thorough study of industrial wage determination in Britain.[21] It found sector-specific excess demand influenced sector real wage movements in only two out of 13 sectors and concluded that "This result casts considerable doubt on the role of relative wages in allocating labour between sectors of the economy, since it suggests that relative wages are not very responsive to sectoral shifts in labour requirements."

These different views of the labour allocation process have recently been set out in a novel way by Bell and Freeman.[22] Their approach is particularly helpful in the present context because it concentrates on whether the wage-setting and labour-allocation process across sectors aids aggregate employment.

They distinguish two types of flexibility. Under *competitive flexibility*, industry wages are responsive to shifts in demand for and supply of workers in particular industries and employment will be greater than if wages are inflexible. Under *industry-productivity wage flexibility*, the flexibility is due to industry-specific conditions independent of shifts in demand or supply of labour and need not have beneficial employment effects. Consider a labour market where wages respond flexibly to industry-specific changes in value productivity per worker which do not reflect shifts in demand. The downward pay flexibility in response to declines in productivity per worker can certainly "save" jobs, but the upward flexibility of wages in response to increases in value productivity will, in the same sense, "cost" jobs; those industries experiencing a rapid growth of productivity will hire too few workers. In this system, if wages fall less with relative productivity declines than wages rise with relative productivity increases, the system of flexible wages will, net, result in less employment than would otherwise have been observed. Therefore in principle there are two situations where wage flexibility among industries has positive employment consequences. First, when wages reflect competitive forces. Second, when wages are more flexible downwards than upwards to industry-specific productivity developments. We consider the two situations in turn.

The most up-to-date and comprehensive evidence on the issue of flexibility in the industrial wage structure is in two reports from the OECD.[23] These documents survey important previous studies and present new information for OECD countries. There is no strong evidence that competitive forces dominate any observed flexibility in relative wages. For example, over the period 1973-79 the correlation between the change in wages and the change in employment for a large sample of manufacturing industries (3-digit or 4-digit SIC) is:

Canada	-0.18	*(significant at 95%)*
Japan	0.12	*(significant at 99%)*
UK	0.03	
US	0.01	

The competitive approach also states explicitly that because the labour supply curve facing a sector is more elastic in the long run than in the short run, the positive correlation across industries between pay changes and employment changes should be stronger the shorter the time-period. There is no evidence of this; indeed, half the correlations presented are negative.[24] The first OECD report concludes, reasonably, that the results "suggest the possibility that the importance of relative wages is outweighed or supplemented by many other factors as an allocation mechanism".[25]

The second OECD study[26] uses regression analysis with a highly disaggregated sample of 3-digit and 4-digit industries in Canada, France, Japan, Sweden, the UK, and the US to explain (cross-section) industry pay changes by changes in sector-specific value added, changes in shipments, and changes in the skill composition. Movements in value added are positively associated with pay movements in each of the six countries (but the association is not statistically significant in France or the UK). Evaluated on the basis of sample means, the elasticity of sectoral wage changes to sectoral productivity changes is as follows:

Canada	0.116	*(manufacturing, 1970-80)*
Japan	0.208	*(manufacturing, 1970-79)*
Sweden	0.026	*(all industries, 1964-83)*
US	0.261	*(all industries, 1958-80)*

Thus employees do appear to get a share of industry-specific productivity changes. While this result holds across countries with very different systems of collective bargaining, the association is stronger in the US and Japan, where bargaining is decentralized, than it is in Sweden, where bargaining is more centralized.

We must now ask whether this association between pay changes and productivity changes across industries augments employment? The evidence in Table 4 tentatively suggests that this association does help employment in Canada, Sweden, and the US, but that it has adverse affects on employment in Japan, and has no effect in France and the UK. The reasoning is as follows.[27]

On the one hand, if relative pay falls in response to a fall in relative productivity, employment will be higher in these sectors than it would have been with no response in relative pay, i.e. some jobs are "saved". On the other hand, where relative pay rises in response to a rise in relative productivity, employment will be lower in these sectors than it would have been with no response in relative pay, i.e. some jobs are "lost". If the sectors where relative productivity is increasing and decreasing are of

Table 4. Association between relative nominal pay changes and relative value added changes holding other variables constant

	$\Delta(\text{VAI-}\overline{\text{VA}})$ coefficient (t)	
	Industries with below average changes in value added (1)	Industries with above average changes in value added (2)
Canada (manufacturing, 1970-80)	0.145 (2.8)	0.063 (1.1)
Sweden (all, 1964-83)	0.112 (4.6)	0.011 (2.3)
US (production, 1970-80)	0.272 (6.1)	0.143 (5.2)
Japan (manufacturing, 1970-79)	0.097 (1.5)	0.273 (10.8)
France (manufacturing, 1970-82)	- 1.65 (1.5)	0.104 (1.8)
UK (all, 1970-79)	0.050 (0.7)	0.034 (1.2)

Note: The dependent variable is the actual difference between each industry's wage change and the average wage change across all industries. The other controlled variables are the change in shipments, the change in the proportion of female and production workers, and the initial wage. Source: OECD, "Labour Market Flexibility", Manpower and Social Affairs Committee, MAS(85)25, mimeo, Paris, December 1985, Table II.8.

equal size and have equal elasticities of labour demand, and if the relative productivity movements are identical (but of different signs), then employment will be higher than it would have been provided there is a favourable asymmetry in the wage response. If relative pay falls more in sectors where relative productivity is falling than relative pay rises in sectors where relative productivity is rising (i.e. if column 1 is greater than column 2 in Table 4), employment will be higher than it would have been without this asymmetry.

These results do not suggest that the industrial wage structure is somehow more rigid — to the detriment of jobs — in Europe than it is in Japan or the US. In Japan there is a hint of competitive flexibility in that industry wages appear responsive to shifts in the supply and demand for workers in particular industries. But the further association between pay changes and productivity changes appears to have an adverse effect on employment. The US results are the reverse of those for Japan. There is no real evidence of competitive flexibility, but some evidence (from the OECD) that movements in pay in response to movements in productivity have, on balance, increased US employment.[28]

Thus the conclusion of the analysis here is that there is no strong evidence of competitive flexibility in relative wages. This does not mean, however, that we should not seek to achieve flexibility in relative wages to augment aggregate employment. But it is an open question whether such flexibility is more likely to be achieved under a corporatist system or under a system where collective bargaining is decentralized.

III.2 Occupation and skill[29]

In most western countries manual workers suffer more unemployment than non-manual workers. For example, in Britain in 1983 male unemployment rates were:

Non-manual	5%
Skilled manual	12%
Semi- and unskilled manual	23%

There is evidence that relative wages affect the relative demand for labour with different skills.[30] This suggests that a too compressed wage structure is one reason for relatively high unemployment rates among unskilled and semi-skilled people. The Dahrendorf Group certainly believes this to be the case: "There is however a problem with regard to skill differentials, especially in European countries. When methods of wage fixing reduce [the differentials] too much, a process of de-skilling is encouraged which is equally detrimental in terms of economic adjustment and technological change."[31] It should be recognized that it is not only union preferences for equality, expressed through collective bargaining, which might compress the occupational wage structure. Employers may have a view of a fair wage or an efficient wage in terms of morale and motivation in the internal labour market. Minimum wage legislation (via a national minimum wage or Wages Councils, for example) might also play a part.

In Britain recently both the relative pay and the relative employment of unskilled workers has fallen substantially: "differentials have widened for men to a level unprecedented since records began in 1886, so that relative unskilled wages (say at the bottom decile) have fallen since 1979 by roughly 10% relative to the mean".[32]   The fall in both relative wages and relative employment must reflect a fall in the relative demand for unskilled people because of technical change and the banishing of some restrictive practices. Unskilled people are now facing a difficult time in the British labour market.

There are two complementary solutions to this problem. Both involve state intervention and demonstrate that such intervention is often vital if the labour market is to be made more adaptable. First, there is a case for some form of subsidy to less skilled employment.[33] This reduces the NAIRU by bringing the demand for unskilled workers closer to their supply. Second, the less skilled can be trained to become skilled. This too reduces the NAIRU by matching supply more closely to demand.

There seems, in Britain at least, to be a strong case for bigger state subsidies to adult training, because the social rate of return is almost certainly greater than the private return in training unskilled workers. First, if the unskilled worker is unemployed, society is giving up nothing while the worker is being trained and will get higher output once the training is completed. Second, the increased supply of trained people may reduce the degree of wage pressure in the skilled labour markets and possibly in the aggregate economy.   Third, imperfect capital markets currently hinder the unskilled worker from borrowing against his or her higher future earnings.   Fourth, the state may have better information about future occupational requirements than any one individual or firm. Finally, the negative externality caused by poaching calls for at least a levy-grant system to finance training.

IV. Firm-level flexibility

Firm-level flexibility can be discussed with reference to both jobs and pay.[34] Here I concentrate on the jobs dimension, which has two main strands.   First, job security rules determined by legislation or collective bargaining influence the number and type of people employed. Second, labour mobility and the operation of the internal labour market provide for numerical and functional flexibility, i.e. flexibility in the numbers employed and the tasks they perform. These strands will be discussed in turn. Factors like job security rules, craft demarcations, and work patterns help to determine the level of employment associated with any particular stance of macroeconomic policy.

IV.1. Job security [35]

Employment security legislation spread rapidly in the 1960s and 1970s. It is often held that these measures inhibit job generation by distorting the market — that there is a tension between the efficient functioning of the labour market and the desire by those employed for job security.

Hamermesh[36] used economic theory to analyse the probable direction of the effect on employment of some of the policies. He examined policies which
(i) raised fixed employment of costs (e.g. guaranteed week agreements),
(ii) change the cost of adjusting employment (e.g. notice period, redundancy payments, unfair dismissal procedure, subsidies to retain workers),
(iii) change the process of adjustment (e.g. redundancy in reverse order of seniority, provision of information on impending redundancies).

Gennard[37] examined the actual (as distinct from theoretical) job security experience of seven countries: France, the FRG, Italy, Japan, Spain, the UK, and the US.

Both authors emphasize that we know very little about the *quantitative* effect of employment protection provisions on the aggregate level of the labour input (employment multiplied by hours). The theory-based approach of Hamermesh leads him to predict the likely *direction* of their effect. He concludes that most of the job regulations raise labour costs and thus reduce the *aggregate* labour input. But Gennard — who examines the actual practice across countries — is much more cautious.

Gennard is generally reluctant to take a position on whether the regulations have a positive or negative effect on the aggregate demand for labour. First, he points out that the three most efficient economies have very different degrees of regulation. He states that the FRG is highly regulated while the US government and courts have a "hands-off" policy. Japan splices lifetime tenure for some with an unregulated "buffer" sector that bears the burden of adjustments. Second, he indicates that only "partial answers" exist on all the important cost and benefit questions about the impact of these job regulations. Third, Gennard implicitly questions whether the regulations do raise costs and indicates that, on balance, they might lower costs. On the one hand the regulations may curb "employer flexibility to the extent that particular avenues and means for adjustment are foreclosed or degrees of adaption reduced". But on the other hand "regulation may be required to open up paths and space for flexibility which would not be available in its absence". Perhaps job security is a prerequisite for flexibility in the internal labour market.

Emerson,[38] who examined job regulations in many countries, comes to a similarly agnostic conclusion: "employment security provisions generate a number of effects on labour costs, employment and productivity, some favourable and some unfavourable".

Given the aggregate labour input, the theory-based discussion provides information on the *structure and cyclical* behaviour of that input. First, in the short run the regulations raise the ratio of hours to employment. But this effect will probably diminish over time if hours of work are decided on the basis of individual worker choice rather than by the firm. Second, the regulations lessen the upwards and downwards employment fluctuations over the cycle for those workers covered.

Hamermesh indicates that, in theory, the employment regulations provide a choice. Well developed regulations provide more employment stability for fewer workers on average. Fewer regulations result in greater employment fluctuations for more workers on average. Gennard goes nowhere near so far. Although he points out that more extensive regulations over time in some OECD countries have gone hand-in-hand with a growing secondary sector, he does not conclude that the one has caused the other.

Given this lack of agreement between the economic theorist and the industrial relations expert, it seems sensible to take a pragmatic approach. In 1985 the International Organisation of Employers reported how each country's employers' organization assessed the severity of the rules restraining the termination of employment contracts:[39]

Importance of obstacles to the termination of employment contracts

Fundamental	Serious	Minor	Insignificant
France	Austria	Denmark	UK
FRG	Belgium	Finland	
Italy	Ireland		
Netherlands	Norway		
Portugal	Sweden		
Spain			

68

It is plausible that job security provisions have a bad effect on *total* employment in countries like Italy and Spain, but it is unlikely they have much of an impact in the United Kingdom.

IV.2. Job mobility

It is important to distinguish between external and internal job mobility.[40] External mobility involves a change of employer or enterprise; internal mobility takes place within one enterprise or with one employer.

The OECD Group of Experts' Report on Labour Market Flexibility[41] suggested that internal mobility and external mobility are substitutes: "high internal and low external mobility in Japan contrasts with high external and low internal mobility in the United States; yet the labour market effect of both combinations may be similar." Although no evidence was given to justify this statement, it was immediately picked up. For example a *Financial Times* editorial[42] states that the two types of mobility are "close substitutes" and that "Europe suffers high unemployment because it lacks either sort of mobility." Some information on the extent of external and internal mobility is presented in this section.

The length of current ongoing jobs in the main OECD countries is given in Table 5. In every country except Italy more than one-sixth of employees have held their jobs for less than two years. But in every country except Australia, more than a quarter of employees have held their jobs for more than ten years. The completed tenure of jobs currently in progress will be approximately double the uncompleted tenure reported in Table 5. So, on average, jobs currently held can be expected to last a very long time before they terminate. Using the doubling theorem, the average job tenure ranges from 13 years in Australia to 23 years in Japan.

Cross country differences in job tenures are probably explained by factors like firm size, the age composition of the work-force, the process of human capital formation, the system of collective bargaining, and social attitudes. But there appears to be no consistent significant connection, across countries, between the length of job tenure and either the degree of wage variability or the level of unemployment. This negative finding is rather important because it implies that there is no necessary link across countries between wage flexibility and job tenure and, in turn, between job tenure and unemployment.[43]

The employment performance of many European countries is often contrasted unfavourably with that in Japan and the US. It is interesting to note that these two countries are at opposite ends of

Table 5. Distribution of ongoing jobs by current tenures[1]

Country	Year of data	< 2 years (%)	≥10 years (%)	Average job tenure in yrs
Australia	1981	39	19	6.3
Belgium	1978	18	36	8.0
Canada	1983	33	27	7.5
Denmark	1978	27	27	-
Finland	1983	28	32	-
France	1978	18	35	8.8
FRG[2]	1978	19	38	8.5
Italy[2]	1978	13	37	7.1
Japan	1982	21	48	11.7
Luxembourg[2]	1978	19	35	9.9
Netherlands[2]	1979	28	31	8.2
UK	1979	24	31	8.6
US	1983	39	27	7.2

Note: 1. The information here refers to average (uncompleted) duration of jobs currently in progress. There are three distinct concepts of average employment duration: (i) the average (uncompleted) duration of jobs currently in progress; (ii) the expected duration of employment for someone beginning a new job; (iii) the expected completed duration of a job which is currently in progress. The information in the table refers to concept (i). Under certain circumstances (iii) is equal to twice (i). Concept (ii) produces shorter durations than (i).
2. For these countries the information on average job tenure in years refers to 1972.
Sources: OECD, *Employment Outlook*, Paris, 1984, Table 31; OECD, "Labour Market Flexibility", Manpower and Social Affairs Committee, MAS(85)25, mimeo, Paris, December 1985, Table I.1; and OECD, "Job Turnover and Tenure in Selected OECD Countries", mimeo, 1985, Table 1.

the job tenure league table. Compared with Japan, the US has about double the number of people in current jobs lasting less than two years and only slightly more than half the number of people in jobs lasting ten years or more. Job tenures in most European countries generally lay in between the levels for Japan and the United States. Previously I concluded from this that "to the extent that job mobility and economic performance are associated it is, by implication, uncertain whether Europe needs more of it (like the United States) or less of it (like Japan)."[44]

Alternatively any mobility problems in Europe might concern the use of labour inside the firm. But there is evidence of considerable

70

adaptability in the use of labour in the internal labour market in some countries, like Britain and France.

First, the nature of the employment contract is changing.[45] Many firms are reducing the number of their full-time core employees and accommodating fluctuations in demand or peripheral tasks (like catering) by increasing the number of part-timers, temporary workers, and sub-contractors.

Second, changes in the development and use of skilled labour are taking place.[46] In some sectors, skilled workers are becoming partially competent in a number of crafts and some barriers to mobility between semi-skilled, skilled, and technician jobs are being eroded.

Third, work patterns are changing. A number of firms have struck collective agreements which move away from the traditional basic work week and instead encourage shift work, night work, weekend work, and part-time work.[47]

While Europe does not have the external mobility of the US or the internal mobility of Japan, its labour market is by no means as obdurate as is sometimes painted. The role of (insufficient) internal and external mobility in explaining high unemployment remains an open question.

V. Summary and conclusions

Both restrictive macroeconomic policy and labour market rigidities have contributed to the relatively high level of European unemployment in the 1980s. Furthermore, countries where real wages are relatively rigid suffered a larger increase in unemployment in the late 1970s and early 1980s than countries where pay is more flexible. But in most European countries the actual level of unemployment is currently above the level necessary to keep inflation constant.

There is strong evidence — both across countries and over time — that corporatism, consensus, and superior macroeconomic performance go hand in hand. Countries pursuing a corporatist strategy suffer smaller increases in unemployment in response to things like an upsurge in militancy or a rise in real interest rates. Moreover, they need a smaller increase in unemployment to obtain a given reduction in real wages. *Thus labour market flexibility must not be confused with decentralization.* It is quite plausible that countries with a highly centralized system of industrial relations exhibit the most adaptable labour markets.

Employment and the labour supply do respond (albeit possibly too little, too late) to movements in unemployment, vacancies, and relative wages, but relative wages move sluggishly and so play only a minor role in any adjustment process.

Movements in the industrial wage structure augment employment under two sets of circumstances. First, if they reflect competitive forces. There is little evidence that this has been happening in recent years in the US, UK, Sweden, France, and Canada, but it might be the case in Japan. Second, if relative pay changes are related to movements in value productivity but are more flexible downwards than upwards. This appears to have been the case in the US and Sweden.

Unskilled people suffer higher unemployment rates than the skilled. This may occur because the occupational wage structure is too compressed, but it should be noted that (in Britain at least) the relative pay of unskilled people has fallen substantially since 1980. The pay structure by skill (and also by age) has shown substantial flexibility in the face of a change in relative employment. So the higher unemployment rates of the unskilled cannot all be attributed to labour market rigidities. There is a strong case for state intervention via employment subsidies and via state finance for training to make the unskilled labour market more adaptable. *Labour market flexibility will not be achieved by withdrawing the state from its proper functions.*

Employment security legislation, which spread in the 1960s and 1970s, has been reined back in many European countries in the 1980s. Unfortunately there is no strong evidence one way or the other concerning the impact of this legislation on aggregate employment. Likewise, while Europe has less external mobility than the US and less internal mobility than Japan, it is simply not possible to state dogmatically that insufficient mobility is or is not a cause of high European unemployment levels.

Notes and sources

1. Department of Employment, *Employment, the Challenge for the Nation*, Cmnd 9474, HMSO, London, March 1985.

2. R. Dahrendorf, *et al.*, *Labour Market Flexibility*, OECD, Paris, June 1986, para. 45.

3. *The Financial Times*, 30 May 1986.

4. OECD, *Employment Outlook*, Paris, 1984, paras. 19 and 20.

5. As discussed by Wolfgang Franz, "Hysteresis Effects, Persistence, and the NAIRU: An Empirical Analysis for the Federal Republic of Germany", 1986, included in this volume.

6. R. Layard and S. Nickell, "The Causes of British Unemployment", *National Institute Economic Review*, London, February 1985.

7. OECD, "Labour Market Flexibility", Manpower and Social Affairs Committee, MAS(85)25, mimeo, Paris, December 1985, p. 38.

8. D. Metcalf and S. Nickell, "Jobs and Pay", *Midland Bank Review*, London, spring 1985.

9. R. Solow, "Unemployment: Getting the Questions Right", *Economica*, Vol. 53, 1985, p. 4, quoted by the OECD, "Labour Market Flexibility", op. cit., note 7.

10. For example by J. Sachs, "Wages, Profits and Macroeconomic Adjustment: A Comparative Study", *Brookings Papers on Economic Activity*, No. 2, Washington DC, 1979, pp. 260-333; and W. Branson and J. Rotenberg, "International Adjustment with Wage Rigidity", *European Economic Review*, May 1980, pp. 309-332.

11. D. Coe and F. Gagliardi, "Nominal Wage Determination in Ten OECD Economies", Working Paper 19, Economics and Statistics Department, OECD, Paris, March 1985, paras. 60 and 70.

12. M. Bruno and J. Sachs, *The Economics of Worldwide Stagflation*, Basil Blackwell, Oxford, 1985.

13. C. Bean, R. Layard, and S. Nickell, "The Rise in Unemployment: A Multi-Country Study", *Economica*, Vol. 53, No. 210 (S), 1986, pp. S1-22.

14. A. Newell and J. Symons, "Corporatism, *Laissez-faire* and the Rise in Unemployment", Working Paper No. 853, Centre for Labour Economics, London School of Economics, 1986.

15. I recognize that international comparisons involving such time series are fraught with difficulties. For example, the definition of corporatist and non-corporatist episodes is a matter of fine judgement. Further there may be lags in the impact of corporatism on labour market variables. A corporatist episode may bottle-up underlying labour market pressure which then rebounds just at the

very time a less corporatist system comes in. Unless such lags are allowed for the econometric estimates may be misleading. For instance, it may be the case that corporatism supressed wage inflation in the UK between 1975 and 1978 but it then collapsed in 1979. Collective bargaining then became more decentralized and wage inflation and unemployment both rose. It is quite possible that even if the corporatist system had been sustained the wage inflation and unemployment would still have worsened. Nevertheless, the results in Table 3 are so powerful and consistent that I endorse the Newell and Symons conclusion.

16. D. Soskice, "Collective Bargaining and Economic Policies", Manpower and Social Affairs Committee, MAS(83) 23, OECD, Paris, 1983.

17. R. Layard and S. Nickell, "The Performance of the British Labour Market", Discussion Paper No. 249, Centre for Labour Economics, London School of Economics, 1986.

18. Ibid.

19. B. Reddaway, "Wage Flexibility and the Distribution of Labour", *Lloyds Bank Review*, London, October 1959.

20. Quoted in OECD, *Employment Outlook*, Paris, 1985, p. 106.

21. C. Pissarides and I. McMaster, "Sector Specific and Economy Wide Influences on Industrial Wages in Britain", Working Paper No. 571, Centre for Labour Economics, London School of Economics, 1984.

22. L. Bell and R. Freeman, "Does a Flexible Industry Wage Structure Increase Employment? The US Experience", mimeo, Harvard University, November 1984.

23. OECD, *Employment Outlook*, Paris, 1985, Chapter 4; OECD, "Labour Market Flexibility", op. cit., note 7, Chapter 2.

24. OECD, *Employment Outlook*, Paris, 1985, p. 127.

25. Ibid., pp. 128, 129.

26. OECD, "Labour Market Flexibility", op. cit., note 7, Chapter 2.

27. Ibid., and L. Bell and R. Freeman, November 1984, op. cit., note 22.

28. It is possible that the Japanese result occurs because the bonus component of total pay compensation is not included in the Japanese data. (The source does not indicate whether bonuses are included or excluded.) K. Koshiro ("Labour Market Flexibility in Japan — With Special Reference to Wage Flexibility", Discussion Paper 86-2, Centre for International Trade Studies, Yokohama National University, 1986) reports that the elasticity of bonus payments with respect to profits in Japan is more than four times larger than the basic wage elasticity with respect to profits. If bonus payments are excluded from the Japanese analysis, and if profits and productivity movements are themselves related, it is possible

that the flexibility in the Japanese industrial wage structure may hinder employment less than indicated. It should be noted that the reverse results for the US found by the OECD are completely at odds with findings in two other major studies. Thus Bell and Freeman, op. cit., note 22, conclude their own analysis by stating that "the flexibility of industry wages to industry value productivity has been harmful to employment." And C. Lawrence and R. Lawrence ("Manufacturing Wage Dispersion: An End Game Interpretation", *Brookings Papers on Economic Activity*, No. 1, The Brookings Institution, Washington DC, 1985) invert the normal causal mechanism and argue that high relative wages *result from* declining competitiveness.

29. For an extended treatment, see Layard and Nickell, op. cit., note 17.

30. For example, for the US see D. Hamermesh and J. Grant, "Econometric Studies of Labour — Labour Substitution and their Implications for Policy", *Journal of Human Resources*, Vol. 13, 1979, pp. 518-542, and for the UK see J. Nissim, "The Price Responsiveness of the Demand for Labour by Skill: British Mechanical Engineering 1963-78", *Economic Journal*, Vol. 94, 1984, pp. 812-825.

31. R. Dahrendorf *et al.*, op. cit., note 2, para. 19. However, it is interesting to note that this compression in pay has probably been greatest in Sweden, which has a low absolute level of unemployment. The coefficient of variation of wages in Sweden (1972 = 100) fell from 180 in 1965 to 70 twenty years later.

32. R. Layard and S. Nickell, op. cit., note 17, p. 41.

33. G. Johnson and R. Layard, "The Natural Rate of Unemployment: Explanations and Policy", in O. Ashenfelter and R. Layard (eds.), *Handbook of Labor Economics*, North-Holland, Amsterdam, 1986.

34. Pay flexibility involves things like concession bargaining, two-tier wage structures, and profit-related bonuses. There is considerable interest in Britain in making pay more flexible in order to raise aggregate employment and reduce the variability of employment. (See Chancellor of the Exchequer, *Profit Related Pay: A Consultative Document*, HMSO, Cmnd 9385, London, 1986.) Unfortunately there is little evidence on this topic for Britain and it is not pursued here.

35. In this section I focus on the impact of job security policies introduced through legislation. But employment security and rigid work allocations can also come about via collective agreements. M. Piore ("The US Can Be Inflexible Too", *The Financial Times*, 12 May 1985) suggests that when this is taken into account, US firms are far less flexible than is commonly believed: "they can only [change employment] in accord with a complex set of rules and procedures designed to protect employee rights and insure equity in the distribution of jobs. Adherence to this imposes certain costs for lay-off and discharge and inhibiting expansion in precisely the same way as European rules." I should add that I am sceptical of much of the work on the impact of job security regulations because we simply

have no information of their incidence. If they are viewed as a tax on the firm, it does not follow that the firm bears the burden of the tax; it may be passed forward to the consumer or backwards to its employees.

36. D. Hamermesh, "Job Security Policy and Labour Demand: Theory and Evidence", paper prepared for the OECD, July 1985.

37. J. Gennard, "Job Security: Redundancy Arrangements and Practices in Selected OECD Countries", paper prepared for the OECD, September 1985.

38. M. Emerson, "Regulation or deregulation of the labour market: policy regimes for the recruitment and dismissal of employees in industrial countries", mimeo, Harvard University, June 1986, p. 30.

39. Quoted in Emerson, ibid.

40. R. Dahrendorf, et al., op. cit., note 2.

41. Ibid.

42. The Financial Times, 30 May 1986.

43. Using the information in Tables 1 and 2, and Figure 1 yields the following rank correlation coefficients for the eight countries with data on all three variables:

    Job tenure length and real wage flexibility   0.00
    Job tenure length and unemployment   - 0.58

    Although the second correlation has the correct sign, it is not significant at the 5% level. For further evidence on this, see D. Metcalf, "On the Measurement of Unemployment", National Institute Economic Review, August 1984.

44. D. Metcalf, "Labour Market Flexibility", report prepared for the OECD, mimeo, Centre for Labour Economics, London School of Economics, 1985, p. 7.

45. J. Atkinson, "Flexibility: Planning for an Uncertain Future", Manpower Policy and Practice, Vol. 1, summer 1985.

46. D. Marsden and J. Silvestre, "The Economic Crisis and Labour Market Regulation in France and Great Britain. Is There Convergence to a New Pattern of Regulation?", LSE mimeo, paper presented to International Working Party on Labour Market Segmentation, July 1986.

47. D. Thomas, "A Yearly Rate for the Job", The Financial Times, 12 May 1986.

Comments

by Michael Emerson

David Metcalf gives us a gentle review of the growing and much needed literature on the economics of labour market rigidity or flexibility and its relevance to the European employment problem.

I say "gentle", because he does not give a clear-cut answer to the basic question of whether European labour markets *are* too rigid. Metcalf's analysis is quite cautious. In several controversial domains — for example, the impact of job security legislation on employment — Metcalf remains firmly agnostic. He keeps his intuitions under wraps, except perhaps in indicating a sympathy for a corporatist and consensual approach to handling macro-economic policy and labour market questions.

I do not criticize Metcalf for being so cautious. On the other hand, politicians and economic policy advisers are obliged to take positions on some questions on which he declines to conclude, lacking sufficient evidence.

In the following paragraphs, I propose to review Metcalf's handling of the topics to which he gives prominence. I shall indicate where his analysis in places is a little too Anglocentric to represent the European situation as a whole, and also offer some conclusions where Metcalf has feared to tread.

Labour cost flexibility at the macroeconomic level

Metcalf presents the estimation of the non-accelerating inflation rate of unemployment (NAIRU) by Coe and Gagliardi.[1] An interesting feature of these data is that for France, Italy, and the Federal Republic of Germany (FRG) the same figure of 5.8% is found, with the United Kingdom higher at 7.7%. This makes an average of about 6.25% for the four countries, which is within the 6-7% range that the Commission of the European Communities (EC) has recognized as an indicative objective for 1990 in its Cooperative Growth Strategy, adopted in the Annual Economic Report for 1985-1986.[2] However, the Commission in its calculations (using the COMPACT econometric model) found that an accentuated policy of wage moderation for a medium-term period would be necessary to achieve this result, implying that these NAIRU estimates may be on the optimistic side.

Metcalf next presents the estimates prepared by Layard and Nickell[3] of the supply- and demand-side factors behind the

77

United Kingdom's increased unemployment. These estimates are a laudable, pioneering effort to give supply-side labour economics an objectively calculated place in diagnosis of the unemployment problem. The factors identified are

(i)   the evolution of unemployment benefits in relation to prior earnings,
(ii)   the growth of employers' social security charges,
(iii) the evolution of trade union power, and
(iv)   skill and regional mismatches between labour supply and demand.

I would like to see more research work of this kind for other European countries. With this in mind, I draw attention to some points that should be considered.

The finding that the increase in the unemployment benefit had a small influence on rising unemployment in the United Kingdom calls for a major cautionary remark should the same study be done for such countries as the FRG, Italy, Belgium, and the Netherlands. In several of these, the unemployment benefit ratio did increase somewhat in the course of the late 1960s or early 1970s. However, that indicator was only a small part of the story.

The major changes took place in the criteria for awarding early retirement and disability pensions.[4] These programmes have come to be massively used as permanent unemployment benefits, mainly for elderly workers within five to ten years of normal retirement age. The numbers of people drawn off the labour market through these programmes has come to equal — and in some cases exceed — the total number of officially registered unemployed.

In this way, an important institutional change has progressively taken place, substantially relieving labour market participants from the pressure of the weakening labour demand. The rising cost of these programmes, as reflected in social security taxes, has also contributed to this weakening labour demand in a movement of circular causation. Moreover, in this situation analysis of the evolution of officially registered unemployment becomes an artificial and limited exercise, compared to a broader analysis of employment and labour force participation trends.

Employers' social security taxes are found by Layard and Nickell to have made a significant contribution (nearly two percentage points) to the rise in UK unemployment. Methodologically there would be no problem in testing this for other European countries. As I have already hinted, the results would probably be more dramatic: FRG employers' contributions have risen twice as high as the British level, and those of Belgium, France, and Italy to around four times as high.

The union power variable is surely very difficult to give correct expression in econometric analyses, but no less important for that. Layard and Nickell found it to be of comparable importance to the social security taxes in the British case. However, the technique of observing the mark-up between union and non-union pay rates, as used by Layard and Nickell, is likely to be quite inappropriate in countries where the law or custom extends union negotiated rates to non-unionized employees or enterprises. Such is the case in Belgium, France, Italy, and the FRG.

Turning to the comparisons made between Europe and the United States on the relationship between real wage adaptability and unemployment, I have a problem with the way in which Metcalf uses material from Coe and Gagliardi. Metcalf presents data on the relationship between short-term real wage rigidity and unemployment to infer that the contrast between the European and US experience is not so clear (notably in the sense of a greater European rigidity being associated wtih a stagnant employment record). However, the second term in the graph reproduced by Metcalf p.57 should surely be employment rather than unemployment. Analytically, Metcalf concentrates the argument on employment, and correctly so. Why present unemployment graphically? It runs into all the problems of limited significance of the unemployment statistics to which I have already referred. After making this correction, the conventional conclusion in European-US comparisons could be restored, and Metcalf's agnosticism may therefore be too cautious.

Corporatism and consensus

I welcome Metcalf's presentation of material on corporatism. I am sure that this socio-political variable needs to be present in comparative analyses of macroeconomic performance, difficult as it is to integrate into econometric work. The work by Newell and Symons[5] distinguishing between corporatist and non-corporatist episodes in the FRG, Japan, and the UK is a useful enrichment of the earlier work of Bruno and Sachs.[6] However, the distinction between the two types of episodes may be easy to make for the United Kingdom, but less so perhaps for the Federal Republic and Japan.

Table 3 also prompts questions about time-lags. For example, is the choice of periods immune to criticisms that in some cases a corporatist incomes policy episode was unsustainable after some years, giving way to a non-cooperative wage explosion? (An example is the Healey-Wilson incomes policies, which broke down in 1978, shortly before the beginning of the Thatcher Government.)

Metcalf does not review recent years' experience in which the non-corporatist United States has stolen a march on the more corporatist Europe in terms of the evolution of the "misery index". Some correction for cyclical unsustainability of the US' recent showing is required in order to discount this in part. Also ignored are the serious arguments advanced by Calmfors[7] to the effect that centralized wage bargaining may work better in association with non-accommodating monetary policy.

Relative wages and employment

On the complex subject of relative wages and employment, I will just pick up two points.

Metcalf draws attention to the widening of pay differentials (as a measure of economy-wide income distribution) in the United Kingdom. In his conclusions, he generalizes this implicitly to Europe as a whole, and goes on to conclude that pay flexibility has existed without helping to resolve the unemployment of low-skilled persons. Although I do not have data for continental Europe, I doubt whether there has been a widespread tendency of the sort recorded in the United Kingdom, partly because minimum wage legislation or conventions are much more constraining than in the UK. It is a point worth further research. In general, in continental EC countries the minimum wages stand around 70-75% of the average wage, whereas in the United States and Japan they are about 33%.[8] I would be highly suspicious of any argument that suggested that the wide income hierarchy in the United States had not helped assure a relatively high volume of employment of low-skilled people (youths, the black population, poorly educated immigrants).

Metcalf next gets into the related argument of whether inter-industry pay flexibility helps employment, or helps keep unemployment down. The standard argument is that such flexibility helps clear the labour market in a competitive manner, rather than to bottle it up with lots of disequilibria (i.e., job-rationing effects where low productivity jobs are not offered because the pay rates of the corresponding level cannot be offered for reasons of minimum wage or collective bargaining constraints).

The counter-argument now introduced, most audaciously by Bell and Freeman[9] in two recent studies of the United States and the FRG, is that pay flexibility has an offsetting impact on relative productivity performance. The argument is, in its extreme form, that these productivity offsets can completely nullify the beneficial employment impact of the pay flexibility.

No one would reasonably doubt an endogenous relationship both ways between pay and productivity, especially in the medium to

80

long run. High pay pushes investment in equipment that increases labour productivity. High productivity growth is at least partly distributed in pay to the workers concerned. But I fear we are entering into a fanciful world of academic or politically motivated paradigms to suggest that these offsets between pay and productivity flexibility will as a general rule be so complete and prompt as to make pay flexibility irrelevant or counterproductive in relation to the objectives of employment policy.

External and internal job mobility

Metcalf reports from a recent OECD paper[10] the hypothesis that the United States exhibits high external job mobility (hiring and firing), Japan exhibits high internal job mobility (within one firm), whereas Europe suffers from a lack of one or the other, the two types being close substitutes. Metcalf notes these arguments but remains sceptical; he asks why Europe had relatively low unemployment rates in the 1950s and 1960s if it had deficient amounts of external and internal mobility.

There are two possible replies to this question. First, employment security legislation was considerably tightened in the subsequent period. Second, Europe's labour market institutions may have been reasonably well suited to the fair-weather macroeconomic conditions of the 1960s, but were particularly ill suited to coping with the kind of supply shocks and structural changes of the last 15 years.

Job security regulations

The last point I would like to discuss is Metcalf's account of the debate on employment protection regulations, or "hiring and firing rules". His conclusion is as follows: "Employment security legislation, which spread in the 1960s and 1970s, has been reined back in many European countries in the 1980s. Unfortunately, there is no strong evidence one way or the other concerning the impact of this legislation on aggregate employment."

I think this is excessively agnostic and provides implicit support for some unfortunate regulatory practices that have grown up in many European countries. On this subject I have supplied some detail elsewhere.[11]

In comparing the non-regulated regime of the United States with the highly regulated but dualistic regime of Japan, and the highly regulated but less dualistic regimes of many European countries, one can make the following observations.

The non-regulated United States is, in this specific domain of labour practices, much less of a free market ideal than many of its

81

political proponents at times suggest. On the one hand, the legal system for handling individual dismissals is in trouble, with an exploding growth in the number and cost of litigations over unfair dismissal. The absence of a general regulatory framework is leading towards a destabilized employment relationship, or at least a very costly system of court-room jurisprudence. On the other hand, an increasing number of analysts of personnel policies of large corporations are concluding that the traditional employment-at-will doctrine (i.e., free hiring and firing) is not well adapted to the needs of modern, technologically advanced enterprises. The Japanese model of employment security is observed with interest and in effect followed by some very successful firms, such as IBM and Hewlett Packard.

For Europe, the first conclusion I draw is that it is not necessary or desirable to consider the policy option of total deregulation. However, within Europe — and in making comparisons with Japan — it is possible to observe a wide variety of regulatory policies. They range from those which give a fair and efficient deal for employer and employee alike, to excessively onerous sets of regulations that can and do depress the employment propensity of the economy. By "excessively" onerous, I mean the following kinds of example.

Regarding individuals, is it reasonably possible, or practically impossible, to dismiss a shirking worker? — a question of particular importance to small enterprises and family businesses contemplating expansion. In some European countries (the United Kingdom is a good example) an apparently fair legal system operates with tribunals for settling disputed cases, assuring a balance of interest between employer and employee. In some other countries, dismissal is considered practically impossible because of heavy procedures or court practices.

Similarly there is a wide range of policies regarding collective redundancies. The effective costs of redundancies (through delays, amounts of compensation) and the extent of managerial prerogative (who can decide? — the company, the trade union, the government?) vary from being reasonable to being extremely onerous for the employer.

Thirdly, there is the question of conditions of engagement of temporary, part-time, and fixed-term-contract workers. Here Japan assures an important margin of flexibility alongside its predominant regime of permanent employment contracts. Some European countries are reasonably open on these atypical forms of work contract, but some surround such work with extraordinarily tight restrictions.

On balance, I would suggest that at least half the European countries still have reason to reflect whether they are not overly heavy-handed in the regulation of employment protection, without recommending to any that they consider total deregulation. Evidence of the range of severity is shown in recent surveys in Europe of employers' perceptions of the importance of such rules as obstacles to hiring more workers.[12] Countries which apparently needed to look most closely at their policies included Italy, France, Belgium, Spain, and the FRG; in some of these countries, changes are being made. Countries where employers apparently have few grounds to complain are the United Kingdom, Denmark, and Finland. Allaying the fear that these survey results are biased by political interests, there is a fairly good correlation between the severity of regulations as perceived by employers, and objective measures of labour market flexibility (average length of job tenure, number of unemployed who become so because of dismissal).

Notes and sources

1. D. Coe and F. Gagliardi, "Nominal Wage Determination in Ten OECD Economies", Working Paper 19, Economics and Statistics Department, OECD, Paris, March 1985.

2. Commission of the European Communities, "Annual Economic Report 1985-86", *European Economy* No. 26, Brussels, November 1985.

3. R. Layard and S. Nickell, "The Causes of British Unemployment", *National Institute Economic Review*, London, February 1985.

4. M. Emerson, "What model for Europe?", MIT Press, 1987, forthcoming.

5. A. Newell and J. Symons, "Corporatism, *Laissez-faire* and the Rise in Unemployment", Working Paper No. 853, Centre for Labour Economics, London School of Economics, 1986.

6. M. Bruno and J. Sachs, *The Economics of Worldwide Stagflation*, Basil Blackwell, Oxford, 1985.

7. L. Calmfors, "Trade Unions, wage formation and macroeconomic stability — an introduction", *Scandinavian Journal of Economics*, Vol. 87, 1985.

8. M. Emerson, op. cit., note 4.

9. L. Bell and R. Freeman, "Does a Flexible Industry Wage Structure Increase Employment? The US Experience", mimeo, Harvard University, November 1984. L. Bell, "Labour Market Behaviour in the US and Germany", mimeo, Harvard University, October 1985.

10. R. Dahrendorf, *et al.*, *Labour Market Flexibility*, OECD, Paris, June 1986, para. 45.

11. See M. Emerson, "Regulation or deregulation of the labour market: the case of policy regimes for the recruitment and dismissal of employees in the industrialized countries", *Economic Papers*, Commission of the European Communities, Brussels, 1987.

12. See G. Nerb, "Employment problems: Views of businessmen and the workforce", *European Economy*, No. 27, Commission of the European Communities, Brussels, March 1986.

Comments

by Eckhardt Wohlers

Insufficient labour market flexibility is often said to be an important cause of high European unemployment. In his paper Metcalf surveys several aspects of labour market flexibility in Europe and their consequences for employment. The following remarks refer to some of his conclusions.

Flexibility of real labour costs

Metcalf states that the difference in aggregate real wage flexibility between the United States and Europe is much less pronounced than is often asserted (i.e. by Sachs, or Branson and Rotemberg).[1]   He points out, for example, that the Federal Republic of Germany (FRG), Austria, and Italy show a flexibility similar to that of the US and builds on the study by Coe and Gagliardi.[2] But they, in fact, show greater real wage rigidity, at least for the FRG and UK, than for the United States.

However, the conclusions of Coe and Gagliardi should in general be taken with some caution because the non-acceleration inflation rate of unemployment (NAIRU), which is used to "construct" the short-run real wage rigidity, seems to be an insufficient indicator of real wage flexibility. Differences in the NAIRU reflect not only differences in real wage flexibility but also differences in other factors influencing labour market flexibility: for example, institutional or legislative conditions, or the mismatch between vacancies and the unemployed.   So the NAIRU is, if anything, only an indicator of flexibility as a whole and not of real wage flexibility in particular.

Movements in the estimated NAIRU are strongly associated with movements in unemployment. The NAIRU therefore also reflects changes in labour supply. If labour force trends differ considerably, as in the 1970s and 1980s (e.g., in the US the labour force increased much more than in the European countries), there seems to be a great danger that cross-country comparisons of flexibility based on unemployment figures will be distorted unless unemployment rates are "corrected" for changes in the labour supply.   For example, unemployment rates reflect only insufficiently the fact that in the United States the rise in unemployment was accompanied by a considerable increase in employment, while in most of the European Community (EC) countries it was accompanied by a slow-down.

Against this background, it seems to me that the Coe-Gagliardi results do not refute the thesis that real wages are relatively flexible in the United States and that this has contributed significantly to the better employment performance in that country. The results probably would have been different if, instead of the rise in unemployment, changes in employment or in unemployment "corrected" for variations in labour supply had been used. Another observation period, for example 1973-83 instead of 1975-82, would also probably have modified the results, at least for some countries.

Corporatism, consensus, and economic performance

Metcalf points out the close connection between corporatism, consensus, and macroeconomic performance. His conclusion is that corporatism seems to be an important factor for a favourable macroeconomic development. He quotes evidence from Bean, Layard, and Nickell,[3] according to which more corporatist economies display a greater response of wage change to unemployment in both the short and the long run. It is also claimed that in these countries there is less real wage resistance, and that both the increase in unemployment in the last two decades and the level of unemployment in the 1980s were lower than in less corporatist economies. The last statement is not, however, correct for *all* corporatist economies. In France, the FRG, and UK — countries characterized as being more corporatist — unemployment since 1973 has risen on average much more than in the less corporatist United States and the unemployment rate in the 1980s has been higher. Obviously the connection between corporatism and economic performance is less close than Metcalf claims.

There also seem to be certain inconsistencies between some of the findings reported by Metcalf. In his discussion of the real wage/employment association, Metcalf states that countries where real wages are most rigid tend to experience the biggest rise in unemployment, and vice versa. According to Figure 1, which stems from Coe and Gagliardi, several European countries exhibit these characteristics: above all the UK, France, and the Netherlands. This would also apply to the FRG if the period 1973-83 were taken instead of 1975-82, or if changes in employment or in unemployment "corrected" for variations in the labour supply were considered instead of the rise in unemployment. According to the classification by Bruno and Sachs,[4] all the countries quoted here are corporatist economies. Following Bean, Layard, and Nickell, these countries should have displayed relatively low real wage resistance and a below average increase in unemployment. These findings seem to contradict each other.

But this is not my main point of criticism on this topic. Rather it concerns the relationship between corporatism, consensus, and economic performance. The experiences of the 1970s in many European countries raise considerable doubts that it is corporatism *per se* which produces good economic performance. Rather, they point out that consensus is the necessary condition. This must include both economic policy targets and measures. Several European countries in the 1970s tried to reach a greater consensus, for example the FRG with the so-called concerted action, or the UK with its incomes policy. But these attempts failed in the end because of divergent ideas about both policy targets and measures, and because no consensus could be reached about wage behaviour. Only corporatist Sweden shows a high degree of consensus which lasted for a long time. That explains the more favourable development of employment there than in other European countries, and the lower unemployment consequences of real shocks ascertained by Newell and Symons.[5]

Consensus also improves economic performance in *non-corporatist* economies. This is shown, for example, by Switzerland, where a relatively high degree of consensus exists both on the macroeconomic and the microeconomic levels. Real wage flexibility there is relatively high and unemployment low. The same applies with some restrictions to the United States. Therefore it is not corporatism but consensus that appears to be the decisive factor for better economic performance. My conclusion is that consensus can improve performance without corporatism, but corporatism cannot do so without consensus. One must also take into account that there are interrelations between consensus and performance: consensus improves economic performance, but a good performance also makes it easier to reach a consensus.

External versus internal mobility

I agree with the OECD Group of Experts (Dahrendorf *et al.*)[6] that a connection does exist between external and internal mobility. If external mobility is low because, for example, labour contracts or social and labour legislation impair labour market flexibility, or because there is a low propensity to migrate for institutional or sociological reasons, internal mobility can compensate for this and improve the allocation of resources. The form of mobility is determined to a high degree by the organization of the labour market and the general economic framework of each country; these in turn are determined by historical, social, and political developments. In the US, high external mobility seems favourable to economic performance. Under the special conditions of Japan, high internal mobility seems to compensate for the lack of external mobility. But it makes great demands on the individual employee; for example, he must be prepared to change his place of residence and even to go abroad. Hence indeed it can be said that flexibility is needed for good labour market performance, but it cannot be said a priori which form of flexibility will be appropriate. That depends on the particular historical, economic, and social conditions of each country.

In the FRG external mobility was relatively high in the 1950s, although it was still lower than in the US. Since then it has been reduced significantly by social and labour legislation, as well as institutional and economic factors. This is demonstrated, for example, by the development of hirings and dismissals, which show distinct downward trends since the 1960s. A certain compensation was provided by increasing internal mobility, shown by the large number of job changes within firms. But the same factors which reduced external mobility also limited internal mobility. For example, job changes within firms requiring a shift in place of residence are relatively rare in the FRG; most job changes take place within the same town. Mobility as a whole has diminished in the FRG, and that has had consequences for employment. Similar tendencies seem to have occurred in other EC countries too.

Relative wages and relative employment

Metcalf's findings suggest an association between the industrial wage structure and the productivity structure. If we ask what impact this association has had on employment, we have to take into account that there are interrelations between the development of wages and productivity. If labour becomes more expensive relative to capital, there will be an incentive to substitute capital for labour and such substitution increases productivity. Adjustment processes between wages and productivity therefore take place in both directions.

The influence of wages on productivity at the macroeconomic level can be measured approximately by the "substitution component" of the productivity increase, i.e. the part attributable to changes in the labour/capital input ratio.[7] Our estimates for the period 1973-83 for the United States as well as the EC countries show increases in productivity caused by substitution throughout the economy, but they were distinctly higher in the EC than in the US. Since real wages in the United States rose only moderately in the period 1973-83, the impulse to substitute capital for labour — and therefore the increase in productivity due to substitution — was low. In the EC countries, on the contrary, real wages rose strongly and the pressure to substitute capital for labour was considerable. The increase in productivity caused by substitution was therefore relatively high. That could suggest that in the EC productivity adapted to wages more than in the United States.

The above discussion relates to the economies as a whole, but a similar reasoning can be pursued as to the link between productivity and wage structure. Thus, similar relationships between wage structure and productivity structure in the United States and the EC countries does not necessarily mean that the consequences for employment were the same.

Finally, I think it is worth noting the relationships that exist between the macroeconomic real wage level, the wage structure, and the bargaining process. If wage settlements vary in accordance with the specific situation in each sector, the aggregate real wage could be higher without negative consequences for employment than in the case of rigid wage structures. Highly centralized bargaining processes that result in uniform wage increases across the economy therefore diminish the scope for real wage rises. It seems to me that these interrelations have not received enough attention from wage-setters in the EC countries.

Concluding remarks

Metcalf's paper shows that in examining the connections between flexibility and employment many factors have to be taken into account: the wage-employment association as well as the broad field of industrial relations and social and labour legislation. There is distinct interdependence between these factors. Often the importance of individual factors can hardly be identified because they have both direct and indirect effects, and the direct ones could be less significant. Some factors could also be less important in the short run, but of great importance in the long run. That applies, for example, to changes in labour and social legislation. The results in the long run may also stand in contrast to those in the short run. Moreover, the unsatisfactory statistical base makes it very difficult to test connections empirically.

Metcalf's paper also shows that macroeconomic approaches alone do not do justice to the multiple relationships between flexibility and employment. Macroeconomic approaches like that associated with the NAIRU only display a rough picture of the connection because of the high degree of aggregation, and therefore require in addition a microeconomic or "mesoeconomic" foundation. This topic presents a broad field for further research.

Notes and sources

1. J. Sachs, "Wages, Profits and Macroeconomic Adjustment: A Comparative Study", Brookings Papers on Economic Activity, No. 2, Washington DC, 1979, pp. 260-333; and W. Branson and J. Rotemberg, "International Adjustment with Wage Rigidity", European Economic Review, May 1980, pp. 309-332.

2. D. Coe and F. Gagliardi, "Nominal Wage Determination in Ten OECD Economies", Working Paper 19, Economics and Statistics Department, OECD, Paris, March 1985, paras. 60 and 70.

3. C. Bean, R. Layard, and S. Nickell, "The Rise in Unemployment: A Multi-Country Study", Economica, Vol. 53, No. 210(S), 1986, pp. S1-22.

4. M. Bruno and J. Sachs, The Economics of Worldwide Stagflation, Basil Blackwell, Oxford, 1985.

5. A. Newell and J. Symons, "Corporatism, Laissez-faire and the Rise in Unemployment", Working Paper No. 853, Centre for Labour Economics, London School of Economics, 1986.

6. R. Dahrendorf, et al., Labour Market Flexibility, OECD, Paris, June 1986, para. 45.

7. For the estimation of the "substitution component" of productivity increase, see E. Wohlers and G. Weinert, Unterschiede in der Beschäftigungsentwicklung zwischen den USA, Japan und der EG, Verlag Weltarchiv, Hamburg, 1986, pp. 101-104.

Hysteresis, Persistence, and the NAIRU: An Empirical Analysis for the Federal Republic of Germany

Wolfgang Franz

The author is grateful to W. Smolny, H. Böhm, H. Dolejsky, and M. Ginter, for able research assistance, and to L. Calmfors for his valuable suggestions for this paper. He is also indebted to C. Wyplosz and P. Van Rompuy for their detailed comments, and to H. Bloom, T. Palm, C. Schnabel, and the participants of the CEPS Macroeconomic Workshop for helpful discussions.

A natural rate that hops around from one triennium to another under the influence of unspecified forces, including past unemployment rates, is not "natural" at all. "Epiphenomenal" would be a better adjective; look it up.

R.M. Solow[1]

I. Introduction

One of the obstacles to using expansionary demand management to lower unemployment is the fear of inflation. Influential policy-makers and economists are united in the view that such a cure might rekindle inflation.

A common method of evaluating the scope for demand expansion is to try to estimate a threshold rate of unemployment above which policies of demand stimulus are non-inflationary. This has been done in a number of studies.[2] However, this non-accelerating inflation rate of unemployment (NAIRU) seems to have been anything but stable over the past decade. More ironically, it appears to follow the actual unemployment rate rather closely, so that, by and large, actual unemployment is always natural. If so, the chances that a rapid recovery will reduce unemployment substantially may be quite limited.

While empirical research seems to indicate that the rise in the NAIRU in the 1970s can be attributed to various supply shocks, such as OPEC and a (resulting) productivity slow-down,[3] these determinants are less promising candidates as explanations for the development in the 1980s. In the absence of major shocks it is an increasingly popular argument that the NAIRU itself depends on the time-path of previous actual unemployment. This effect has been christened "hysteresis" and is the subject of this study.

Concentrating on data for the Federal Republic of Germany (FRG), we find that the rise in long-term unemployment may contribute substantially to an explanation of the recent upwards shift in the NAIRU. Our analysis shows the importance of distinguishing between the contemporaneous and the steady-state NAIRU when evaluating the scope for demand management.

While our calculations are still tentative, they already show that the concept of the NAIRU is not a straightforward guide for economic policy. Thus the study does *not* support the view that our policy options have to be constrained by a high equilibrium rate of unemployment. Once an increase in employment comes under way, the contemporaneous NAIRU will fall. This should open possibilities for a future fall in unemployment that would *not* have to be accompanied by rising inflation.

Part II of the paper provides a brief survey of various channels through which hysteresis effects may operate and discusses their relevance in the context of the FRG. Part III contains an empirical attempt to test the screening hypothesis of hysteresis through an economic analysis of structural/frictional unemployment built around the Beveridge curve, which relates vacancies and unemployment. Part IV investigates econometrically whether hysteresis can contribute to an explanation of the increase in the NAIRU. Part V summarizes our findings, doubts, and caveats.

II. Channels of hysteresis and unemployment persistence and their relevance to the FRG

According to the literature, a dynamic system is said to exhibit hysteresis if its stationary equilibrium depends on initial conditions. Formally, in a system of linear differential equations with constant coefficients, $\dot{x} = Ax - z$, hysteresis occurs if the transition matrix A is singular, so that the solution to $A\bar{z} - \bar{x} = 0$ (where a bar denotes a steady-state value) is indeterminate.[4] This indeterminacy stems from the fact that if the stability conditions are satisfied, a unique stationary equilibrium exists for any set of initial conditions.

More specifically, *unemployment* exhibits hysteresis when actual unemployment depends on past values with coefficients summing to one. Hysteresis can be distinguished from *persistence*.[5] In the latter case, the coefficients still indicate a causal relationship running from previous values to the current one, but the coefficients do not sum to one. Although this distinction has policy implications, it is not always applied in the literature. For example, Blanchard and Summers[6] use the term hysteresis "more loosely to refer to the case where the degree of dependence on the past is very high, where the sum of coefficients is close but not necessarily equal to one."

An early example of a model in which "the time path to equilibrium partially shapes that equilibrium" is Phelps.[7] In his model a temporary boom phase may have permanent effects on the attitudes of workers, so that a departure from the equilibrium produces effects which may persist even after returning to equilibrium. Hence, the equilibrium natural rate of unemployment is not invariant to the adjustment path towards that equilibrium.

More formally, hysteresis and persistence can be introduced into the NAIRU framework in the following way. Let p_t be the instantaneous inflation rate and p_t^* its expected value. Inflation is determined by p_t^* and by the deviation of actual unemployment U_t from the contemporaneous NAIRU U_t^*.

(1) $p_t = p_t^* - \gamma (U_t - U_t^*)$.

Assume, for the sake of simplicity, that

(2) $U_t^* = \alpha U_{t-1} + \beta Z_t$,

where Z_t denotes a vector of other explanatory variables. The steady-state NAIRU is then defined as the situation in which $p_t = p_t^*$ and $U_t = U_{t-1}$, and is given by $\beta Z_t/(1 - \alpha)$. True hysteresis requires that $\alpha = 1$, so that the stationary equilibrium depends only on initial conditions, whereas persistence of unemployment means $0 < \alpha < 1$. In the latter case the NAIRU evolves towards its steady-state level. The speed of this adjustment depends on the magnitude of α. Equation (2) may be extended in several ways, such as

(2a) $U_t^* = f [\sum_{s = -\infty}^{t} (U_s - U_s^*); Z_t]$

i.e., changes in the NAIRU are determined by a (long) history of the deviations of actual unemployment from the contemporaneous NAIRU. This is basically the formulation in Buiter and Gersovitz, Hargreaves Heap, and Sachs.[8]

In the literature the discussion of persistence has followed two main routes. The first has focused on the individual's experience with unemployment. Using microeconomic data about unemployed persons, researchers have found state-dependence effects, i.e., that the present probability of leaving the unemployment register is affected both by the duration of the current spell of unemployment and by the length and/or number of previous spells of unemployment (lagged duration dependence and occurrence dependence, respectively).

Examples of this type of work include Heckman and Borjas[9] and, for the FRG, Franz.[10] Using the hazard function — which relates the success-rate of leaving unemployment to the length of time in the unemployment pool — the latter study identified a log-normal shaped curve for youths, indicating that the individual's chance of escaping from unemployment tends to decrease after a rather short period of joblessness. When Clark and Summers took into account multiple spells of unemployment for a given person, interrupted only by short periods of employment, they found that a hard core of people bear the major burden of unemployment in the US.[11]

The second approach to persistence is macroeconomically oriented and takes its starting point from unexplained movements of the NAIRU. For instance, Solow[12] has found it striking that the estimated equilibrium rates of unemployment within countries vary widely from sub-period to sub-period and, we might add, follow the actual unemployment rate closely. Leaving aside the (semantic?) question of whether an equilibrium unemployment rate which changes over time is a paradox, the basic problem still remains: *why* is the current equilibrium level of unemployment dependent on the past history of unemployment?[13]

Below we discuss three major types of explanation as to why unemployment may exhibit hysteresis or persistence.

II.1. Depreciation of human capital

The general idea is that prolonged unemployment is likely to depreciate the skills of the unemployed worker. One possible application of this argument can be illustrated by referring to search theory. The search process should be seen from the viewpoints of both the employer and the unemployed person. In a screening process the firm has to identify the unknown productivity of the applicant for a job. If firms use unemployment experience itself as a screening device, then applicants with a long duration of unemployment are viewed as the less promising candidates. This criterion is more likely to be applied the easier it is for firms to fill job openings. Moreover, this "unemployability" effect does not necessarily depend on whether the human capital of the unemployed person has in fact depreciated; firms need only *believe* that this is the case.

It has been argued[14] that employers sometimes have erroneous prior beliefs about the distribution of the unemployed with respect to their qualifications. When firms expect members of a "superior" group to be readily available due to, say, adverse labour market conditions, then their expected search time and costs of finding qualified persons are lower and the tendency to reject less qualified applicants becomes greater. Although this misperception will tend to fade after a recognition lag, those unemployed persons not considered for the job in question will already have been relegated to the pool of long-term unemployed, thus creating persistence.

Turning to the applicants' side of the search process, long-term unemployment may reduce the search intensity of workers due to discouragement, because they have been rejected so often by employers. If they run out of unemployment benefits, they may drop out of the labour market entirely. Such decisions can lead to an irreversible reduction in the labour supply if skills are depreciated at a high rate.

Finally, if skills are acquired not only through on-the-job training but also through changing jobs, then high unemployment also causes a deterioration in skills because it reduces job mobility. Thus once workers become unemployed they are faced with greater difficulties in acquiring skills and in finding a job.[15]

II.2. Wage bargaining

A second mechanism which can possibly generate hysteresis stems from the role of the unemployed in the wage bargaining process. More specifically, past unemployment may raise today's unemployment level because the unemployed exert small influence on wage-setting. This argument rests basically on two premises:

• Unions care less about the unemployed "outsiders" than about the welfare of their employed members, the "insiders".

• Unemployed workers cannot find jobs at lower wages outside the unionized sector either because firms do not accept underbidding or because there is no sector that is not covered by collective bargaining.

The theory usually rests on the assumption that wages are set by unions acting in the interests of their median members.[16] If members differ with respect to the probability of becoming unemployed in the case of adverse employment shocks (e.g. because of seniority rules), they will have different wage objectives. To the extent that a rise in unemployment leads to a fall in membership, the new median members will face a smaller unemployment risk and hence a higher wage goal will be chosen. Any rise in unemployment because of temporary shocks will therefore cause a wage increase that also reduces future employment, i.e., (un)employment will be serially correlated. The degree of persistence will depend directly on the sensitivity of membership to past employment.

What happens with the outsiders in the face of increasing demand? Will firms enlarge the pool of insiders by hiring outsiders?[17] In a theoretical model Solow[18] shows that this may be unlikely. The reason is that the expected utility of employed workers decreases with the number of union members: the unemployment risk of employed workers would increase and/or a setting of lower future wages would be necessary in order to avoid loss of jobs.

It is difficult to judge the relevance of these arguments for the FRG. In general, outsiders do not seem to succeed in gaining employment through underbidding. One "formal" explanation is that there is a legally required extension of the union wage to cover all workers in the field, regardless of whether they are unionized. These restraints are based on the constitutional principle of the freedom of negative coalition. Another explanation has been given by Lindbeck and Snower.[19] They argue convincingly that besides bowing to social norms, according to which underbidding is viewed as an improper form of social behaviour, employers may refuse to accept such bids for other reasons. The costs of hiring underbidders may still be high due to the hiring, training, and firing process and due to the possibility that the remaining job holders might withhold cooperation from these entrants, thus lowering their productivity.

On the question of the extent to which unions take the unemployed into account when setting the aggregate wage (for both insiders and outsiders), formal rules and actual behaviour seem to differ. With few exceptions, unions in the FRG do not accept unemployed people as new members because they are considered to be "free riders" and because of the fear that the unemployed would vote negatively on strike questions. Only very recently have these barriers to entry been lowered. However, the unemployed are still formally excluded from voting on strike activities. More important for the discussion here, the unemployed are not even passively involved in wage bargaining. Union acceptance of the outcome of negotiations is decided by a commission which is composed mainly of the leaders of workers' councils of the larger firms, which in turn are dominated by union members.[20] It thus appears that formal rules support the view that the interests of the unemployed are not taken into account in wage bargaining.

This, however, may be a somewhat hasty conclusion. What matters is not formal rules but actual behaviour, and this indeed seems to pay attention to outsiders as well. For example, the major claim and goal of the unions during the metal industry strike of the summer of 1984 — one of the longest and most costly in recent FRG history — was to create more jobs for the unemployed by reducing the level of weekly hours worked.[21] Although the reduction might also have met the preferences of the employees, it seems reasonable to argue that the costly strike and moderate wage increase awarded (the price for partial success in reducing working time) demonstrated that the unions did care about the unemployed. Another example is the unions' repeated criticism of the practice of continual overtime hours and their proposed legal restrictions on working hours. Against this background one must remain sceptical about the importance of the insider-outsider theory.

II.3. Capital shortage

The third approach to explaining hysteresis or persistence effects stresses the role of the capital stock. The basic idea[22] is that the

NAIRU depends on the capital stock and that a decline in the capital stock can be treated analytically as a supply shock. Since investment depends on factor prices as well as the state of demand in the economy, running the economy at unemployment rates higher than the NAIRU will reduce investment. That, in turn, will eventually increase the NAIRU. In the FRG, the argument that the existing capital stock is inadequate to provide jobs for the unemployed has been emphasized, for example, by Giersch.[23]

Figure 1 shows FRG capacity utilization rates of the existing capital stock and of the labour supply. The source of the first series is the FRG council of economic advisers (CEA). These calculations are based on fitting trend lines for the capital/output ratio. The data on the utilization rate of labour were calculated by the author. The underutilized labour in this series includes the officially registered unemployed plus discouraged workers,[24] and allows for a possible increase in structural/frictional unemployment of up to 4% in 1984.

The figure shows that utilization rates of the capital stock nearly reached "normal utilization", i.e., 97.25% according to the definition of the CEA. On the other hand, utilization of labour is far below "normal", with the *under*utilization rate being about 10% in the last three years. We have also plotted capacity utilization rates for the manufacturing sector calculated by the Institut für Wirtschaftsforschung (IFO). These figures are based on a questionnaire to employers rather than derivations from production functions. As can be seen, the CEA and IFO series move closely together and in 1985 nearly regain the pre-recession levels of 1973.

Does this data indicate that expansion is hampered by a capital shortage? To some extent the answer depends on the nature of the production function. The greater the possibilities for substituting labour for capital, *ex ante* and *ex post*, the more unlikely it is that the capital stock is really a constraint. When product demand increases and firms find it profitable to increase capacity, they can, in the short run, employ more labour with the existing capital stock, for example through extended shift work. Unless there is a high degree of inflexibility in the production process and limits on expanding the capital stock (such as environmental restrictions or high user costs of capital), one should not expect the problem of a possible capital shortage to be significant during periods of higher aggregate demand. It is, of course, possible that a *strong* increase in aggregate demand may be necessary if expanding capacities requires building new factories rather than enlarging present plants or reopening old factories.

It is well known that in the 1930s and during World War II, considerable disinvestment and reduction in the size of the

Figure 1. Capacity utilization rates and investment
(FRG: 1970-85)

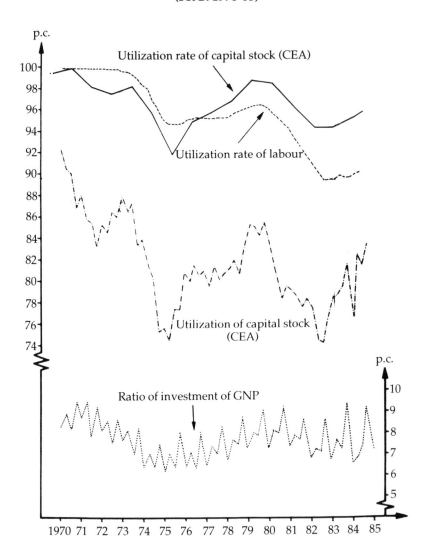

100

civilian capital stock took place. But it did not prevent many economies from attaining full employment shortly afterwards.[25] A more thorough empirical test, however, requires production function estimates evaluating *ex ante* and *ex post* substitutability.

III. Econometric analysis of the Beveridge curve

The conclusion from the above discussion is that the screening hypothesis is likely to be the most important channel through which hysteresis and persistence effects may arise. Ideally one should set up a framework that allows a test of all the various possibilities. This is, however, beyond the scope of the present paper. Instead we concentrate on the screening hypothesis, using the so-called Beveridge curve, which relates vacancies to unemployment.

For any given structure of the labour market, vacancies and unemployment will be related in the manner indicated by the stylized curve B_0B_0 in Figure 2. The basic idea behind the curve is that the chance of creating employment by matching the unemployed and vacancies is positively related both to the number of unemployed and the number of vacancies. When there are vacancies, for any given unemployment rate, the matching process is easier; hence, more job matches take place. In other words, the more vacancies, the higher the flows out of unemployment. A higher outflow rate implies a lower unemployment rate. Hence, there is an inverse relation between vacancies and unemployment.[26] The position of the curve can be seen as a measure of the degree of mismatch between job applicants and available jobs. To the extent that this mismatch increases, the curve will shift outwards as indicated.

More formally, the Beveridge curve can be written as

$$(3) \quad UR_t = a_0 + a_1 VR_t^{-1} + a_2 A_t$$

where UR and VR denote the unemployment and vacancy rate, respectively. The variable A is designed to capture all sources of a possible shift of the Beveridge curve.

The basic hypothesis of our testing strategy is simple. If firms use unemployment as a screening device and reject applicants with an above average unemployment experience, one should expect a given number of vacancies to be associated with higher unemployment if the share of long-term unemployment increases. This phenomenon can therefore be viewed as a type of mismatch on the aggregate level between labour supplied and demanded. An increase in long-term unemployment will thus cause an outward shift of the Beveridge curve.

Figure 2. A stylized Beveridge curve

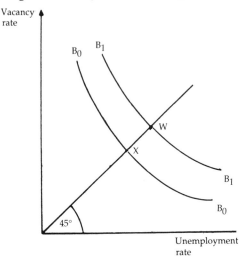

explain shifts in the Beveridge curve. An increased mismatch can also be due to a higher possibility that the unemployed and the vacancies suitable for them are in different regions, or that the skills of the unemployed do not meet the requirements of the jobs in question. Moreover, unemployed workers may reduce their search intensity if they receive a more generous unemployment compensation.

In what follows we attempt to identify econometrically the nature of the Beveridge curve. We also investigate whether the unemployment/vacancy relationship has shifted and, if so, which factors have determined the movement. Before this can be done, however, a brief analysis of the data on unemployed persons and on vacancies is in order.

Official figures on unemployed persons and vacancies include only those registered at the labour office. There is every reason to argue that these data are incomplete and biased. Therefore in addition to the official figures we also use corrected data.

The corrected unemployment figures include discouraged workers and people on training programmes.[27] We include the latter group because these programmes are financed by the labour office for workers who would otherwise be unemployed. For discouraged workers we estimated a labour supply function which uses the state of the labour market as one of the explanatory variables. This regression was then used to calculate a labour force for a full employment situation. The difference between the latter figure and the originally estimated labour force gives a rough idea of the number of discouraged workers (net of additional workers).

Official vacancy data have been corrected by dividing them by the fraction of new hirings created through intervention of the labour office. This fraction is defined as the ratio of cumulated new vacancies to cumulated new hirings during a year. This fraction is not constant over time but fluctuates around a declining trend from 1969.

For purposes of illustration, Figure 3 presents the evidence of the Beveridge curve using corrected data. We observe a curve approximating a hyperbola which may not be stable over the whole time-period. The suspicion is raised that a shift to the right might have taken place.

Figure 3. Beveridge curve with corrected data (1961-83)

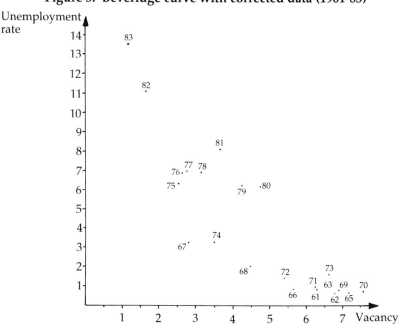

To check these visual impressions, Table 1 reports some estimates of the Beveridge curve using annual data for the period 1961-83. Columns (1) to (5) use official figures of unemployment and vacancy rates while the remaining columns use corrected data. (Lack of space prohibits us from presenting all attempts with different functional forms.) All equations are IV (instrumental variables) estimates.[28] We also ran the regressions with OLS estimates, but the results did not change significantly.

We start with the estimates of the Beveridge curve based on official data. The simple regression reported in column (1) is already capable of explaining 77% of the variance. Starting with this equation, the unemployment rate equals the vacancy rate at 1.9%. Inserting an unemployment rate of 9.1% (the 1983 figure) yields a corresponding vacancy rate of 0.36%. This is very close to the actual figure of 0.35%.

As a first tool to capture a possible outward shift of the Beveridge curve, we inserted dummy variables into the regression. This procedure should, of course, be seen more as a type of data analysis rather than as a testing of hypotheses. Dummy variable D1 allows for a shift during 1975-83, while dummy variable D2 takes into account a possible second shift during 1981-83. In columns (2) and (3) both dummy variables enter the regression as constants. This increases the value of the unemployment rate which the Beveridge curve is approaching as the vacancy rate (= vacancies/non-self-employed persons) becomes large. As can be seen, both dummy variables are significant but the major improvement in the explanatory power is due to the shift in the 1970s.

We now turn to the corresponding estimates based on corrected figures of unemployment and vacancies. Column (6) reveals that both dummy variables are highly significant, as is the inverse of the corrected vacancy rate. This implies — as do the estimates based on official figures — that the unemployment rate for any given vacancy rate increased in 1975 and again in 1981. Thus, even if the vacancy rate becomes very large, these estimates indicate that the unemployment rates prevailing before 1975 will not be reached again.

In order to capture possible clockwise loops in the unemployment /vacancy relation, we included the first difference of the inverse of the vacancy rate as an additional explanatory variable.[29] Columns (4) and (8) reveal that the coefficient of this variable is negative and highly significant. The inclusion of this variable not only leads to a considerable improvement of the standard error of estimate, but with one exception does not alter the significance of the dummy variables. Hence there is some evidence for loops around a long-run Beveridge curve, but they cannot serve as a substitute for its outward shift.

One possible way to illustrate the importance of the estimated outward shift of the Beveridge curve is to compute its impact on structural and frictional unemployment. This is reported in Table 2. The measures are equilibrium structural/frictional unemployment rates. They are calculated according to points where the unemployment rate equals the vacancy rate,[30] and correspond to points X and W, respectively, in Figure 2 (page 102). The calculations are made with both official and corrected data. In the latter case the corrected unemployment rates have been converted into official ones by multiplying them by the ratio of

Table 1. Estimates of the Beveridge curve 1963-83

Explanatory variables	Official unemployment rate					Corrected unemployment rate			
	(1)	(2)	(3)	(4)	(5)	(6)	(7)	(8)	(9)
1/VR	3.1226 (8.5)	1.9450 (5.9)	1.2211 (2.7)	2.4917 (6.8)	2.1105 (5.5)				
1/VRC						6.2272 (3.6)	4.7898 (9.9)	9.2140 (4.7)	8.5491 (4.6)
D1		2.3876 (5.3)	2.5124 (6.0)	1.8784 (6.5)	1.2538 (2.4)	4.3618 (8.4)	2.2226 (2.5)	3.8946 (8.0)	2.9485 (3.2)
D2			1.6410 (2.2)	0.5891 (1.2)	0.6656 (1.2)	2.5972 (3.2)		2.4304 (3.3)	1.2479 (2.0)
1/(VRC - 1.0)									1.3318 (3.4)
Δ(1/VR)				-1.2638 (5.4)	-1.1860 (4.9)				
Δ(1/VRC)								-3.9417 (2.6)	-3.3642 (2.3)
SLU.					0.1018 (2.3)				0.1612 (2.2)
constant	0.3103 (0.8)	0.2911 (1.2)	0.5909 (2.2)	0.0982 (0.5)	-0.2188 (0.6)	0.3096 (0.8)	1.1266 (4.1)	-0.1646 (0.4)	-1.2436 (1.6)
R^2	0.7656	0.8977	0.9143	0.9656	0.9660	0.9406	0.9384	0.9539	0.9593
DW	1.6351	2.2995	1.7596	1.9718	1.7864	2.1938	2.0759	2.0178	1.7430
SEE	1.1746	0.7758	0.7101	0.4539	0.4512	0.9213	0.9386	0.8142	0.7652

Notes: The dependent variable for the estimates is the unemployment rate. See the text for the various definitions of the unemployment rate. All equations are IV estimates; t-values in brackets.

Symbols: VR: vacancy rate   D2: 1 for 1981-83, 0 otherwise   SLU: share of long-term
VRC: corrected vacancy rate   Δ: indicates first difference   unemployment (see Table 3)
D1: 1 for 1975-83, 0 otherwise   SEE: standard error estimates

actual to corrected unemployment rates of the years under consideration. This has been done in order to allow a direct comparison. Taken at face value, the estimates do not differ very much whatever method is used, but they do seem to indicate that the Beveridge curve shifted during the past ten years.

Table 2. Equilibrium unemployment rates
(%)

	Estimates based on official data	Estimates based on corrected data converted into official figures
1974	1.4	1.9
1980	3.5	3.4
1983	5.0	5.5

It should be emphasized that the equilibrium unemployment rates measured in Table 2 do not necessarily imply that equality of unemployment and vacancies is optimal. A more careful analysis would require the evaluation of the marginal costs associated with another unemployed person (such as the output loss) and with an unfilled job (e.g. inflationary pressure).[31]

The next step is to test directly whether the outward shift of the Beveridge curve can be explained by a rise in the share of long-term unemployment. That such a rise has indeed occurred is confirmed by Table 3. In columns (5) and (9) of Table 1 the share of long-term unemployed (SLU) is included as an additional explanatory variable.[32] As can be seen, this variable is highly

significant in all versions of the equations. However, it does not tell the whole story, especially because dummy variable D1 still remains significant. Indeed, omitting the dummy variables leads to a considerably higher standard error of estimate. Therefore the suspicion may be raised that although persistence effects (as proxied by the SLU variable) are to a non-neglibible extent responsible for the outward shift of the Beveridge curve, especially in the 1980s, some other influences have also been at work.[33]

In order to clarify which factors these can be we have computed measures for regional and qualifications mismatch.[34] The problem with these measures is that sufficiently disaggregated and consistent time-series of unemployed persons and vacancies are not available prior to 1976. Hence, we could not introduce them as additional explanatory variables in Table 1. As has been shown elsewhere, however, these indicators are fairly constant so that they seem unlikely to be able to contribute to an explanation of the outward shift of the Beveridge curve.[35] The same argument holds

Table 3. Long-term unemployment: 1966-84[1]

Year	%	Year	%
1966	5.5	1976	17.9
1967	3.8	1977	18.6
1968	21.0	1978	20.3
1969	15.4	1979	19.9
1970	8.9	1980	17.0
1971	5.3	1981	16.2
1972	5.7	1982	21.3
1973	8.5	1983	28.5
1974	5.2	1984	32.8
1975	9.6		

Note: 1. Share of workers who have been unemployed for one year or more.
Source: Information given by the Institut für Arbeitsmarkt- und Berufsforschung.

for the unemployment benefit replacement ratio, which has fallen during the period 1974-83. Therefore, at this stage the share of long-term unemployed seems to be the only obvious candidate to explain the observed outward shift of the unemployment/ vacancies relationship.

IV. Persistence and the increase of the NAIRU

This part of the paper attempts to test whether the increase of the NAIRU in the 1980s can be explained by hysteresis or persistence effects. That such an increase seems to have occurred is confirmed by inspection of Figure 4, which shows the relation between the change in inflation and unemployment. (See Appendix for definition and measurement of the variables.) Stable inflation, i.e., $p_t=p_{t-1}$, seems to be associated with an official unemployment rate of about 1% in the 1960s. In the 1970s and the 1980s, however, the official unemployment rate seems to have increased to about 4% and 9%, respectively. Hence, the NAIRU seems to be anything but stable.

Since the empirical findings in the previous section gave some support for the screening hypothesis, the Beveridge relationship is included in the framework deriving the NAIRU in the analysis here. The model consists of three equations: standard price and wage equations, and a Beveridge curve linking unemployment and vacancies.

IV.1. Basic model

The theory on which we base our calculations is well known. We assume a pricing rule in which the product price (P) is a mark-up

107

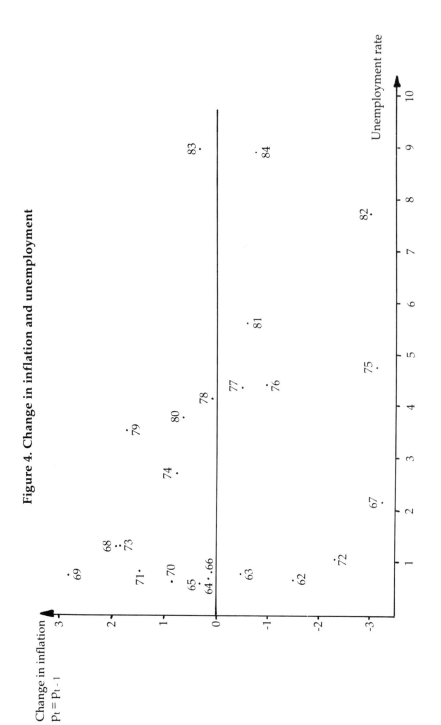

Figure 4. Change in inflation and unemployment

on a weighted average of domestic unit labour costs (W/Π, where W denotes the gross hourly wage rate and Π productivity), adjusted for a payroll tax factor (V^s) and the domestic currency value of import and agricultural prices (M). The mark-up factor (Z) depends on demand conditions (X) in the goods market, and V^{ind} is the indirect tax factor.[36]

(4) $\quad p_t = V_t^{ind} \cdot Z(X_t) \cdot [V_t^s \, W_t \, /\Pi_t]^\alpha \, M^{1-\alpha}.$

By taking the time derivative of the logarithmic version of equation (4), we obtain:

(5) $\quad p_t = \alpha \, (W - \pi)_t + (1 - \alpha)m_t + z(x_t) + v_t^{ind} + \alpha \, v_t^s,$

where lower case letters denote growth rates. In order to take into account possible price inertia, we add a distributed lag of past values of p to equation (5).

The following wage equation is used:

(6) $\quad w_t = \beta_1 \, p_t^* + \beta_2 \pi_t + \beta_3 \, UR_t + \beta_4 VR_t^{-1} \quad (\beta_1, \beta_2 > 0; \quad \beta_3, \beta_4 < 0)$

The argument for including both labour market variables — the unemployment rate (UR) and the vacancy rate (VR) — is that wage bargaining in the FRG takes place at industry level. So in some sectors (and/or regions) there may be an excess demand for labour while others suffer from unemployment. Since w refers to effective wages, we should take into account differences due to different labour market conditions. While UR_t and VR_t are truncated at zero values, inclusion of only one of these variables might not be sufficient to capture these different labour market conditions.

As the analysis in Part III shows, UR and VR are related through the Beveridge curve (see equation (3), page 101):

(7) $\quad UR_t = \gamma_0 + \gamma_1 \, VR^{-1} + \gamma_2 SLU_t \qquad\qquad (\gamma_1, \gamma_2 > 0)$

where SLU stands for the share of long-term unemployed. Since we are interested in the NAIRU, we solve equation (7) for VR_t^{-1} and insert this expression into the wage equation (6) which in turn is inserted into equation (5). We thus obtain the following reduced form of the process of wage and price determination.[37]

(8) $\quad p_t = a_1 + \sum_i \lambda_i p_{t-i} + a_2 \pi_t + a_3 z(x_t) + a_4 m_t$

$\qquad + a_5 v_t^{ind} + a_6 v_t^s + a_7 UR_t + a_8 SLU_t$

$\qquad (a_2 \gtrless 0, a_3, a_4, a_5, a_6, a_8 > 0, a_7 < 0)$

In reaching equation (8) we have made several simplifying assumptions. First, inflationary expectations are captured by the distributed lag of past inflation rates. Indeed, estimation of

109

equation (8) revealed that either p* (measured as an AR-process) or the distributed lag were significant, but not both variables. In accordance with other studies,[38] we want to stress that omitting p* is arbitrary. Second, due to the partial *ad hoc* character we did not consider parameter restrictions in equation (8). In particular, we do not restrict the sum of coefficients ∂ associated with lagged inflation to one.

IV.2. Empirical results

The empirical results are contained in Table 4. Column (1) refers directly to equation (8). As can be seen, all parameter values possess the sign expected theoretically and, with one exception, are highly significant at conventional standards.

The positive coefficient on x may be interpreted as a procyclical price mark-up. If so, this result contradicts the findings for major European countries reported by Gordon in 1986.[39] Although insignificant, the parameter value of trend productivity growth (π) seems implausibly high in absolute terms. The same holds for the parameter value of v^{ind}. In the latter case the suspicion may be raised that to some extent v^{ind} serves as a dummy variable, since it only has non-zero values at very few points in time.[40] The variable SLU (share of long-term unemployed) has the sign theoretically expected and is significant. Finally, the sum of coefficients associated with lagged p is less than one but very close to it. We use the Chow test to examine stability and divide the sample period at 1973/Q4. A comparison of the computed F-values with the theoretical ones reveals that stability cannot be rejected at either the 5 or 1% levels.

Since we do not want the NAIRU to depend on the change in demand conditions (x), this variable can either be set at zero (i.e., x = 0) or omitted, as has been done in column (2). As can be seen, the parameter values do not change very much. Indeed, evaluating the beta coefficients for column (1) (not reported) reveals that the explanatory power of x is not overwhelming. Moreover, the following calculations of the NAIRU will show that both procedures produce the same results.

In order to check the relevance of the SLU variable, column (3) reports results of an estimation where the unemployment rate (UR) has been replaced by the output ratio (Q). The major change is in the sum of lag coefficients and in the intercept. This makes it very clear that the estimates must be viewed with some care. While the short-run impact of SLU on p does not differ between the equations displayed in columns (1) and (3), the long-run impact is only one-third in column (3).

110

Table 4. Estimates of the Phillips curve: 1961/Q4 - 1984/Q4[1]
(dependent variable: p)

	(1)	(2)	(3)
$\sum \lambda_i$	0.9137 (7.5)	0.9190 (7.3)	0.7757 (7.0)
π	-0.4323 (0.8)	-0.4060 (0.7)	-0.1806 (0.4)
x	0.1039 (2.7)	–	0.0850 (2.1)
m	0.0620 (2.9)	0.0622 (2.8)	0.0631 (3.0)
v^{ind}	0.4797 (2.2)	0.3942 (1.8)	0.5030 (2.4)
v^s	0.1336 (2.1)	0.1123 (1.7)	0.1529 (2.4)
UR	-0.1175 (2.8)	-0.1472 (3.5)	–
SLU	0.0249 (2.1)	0.0331 (2.7)	0.0237 (2.1)
Q	–	–	0.0894 (3.1)
Constant	0.2335 (0.4)	0.2874 (0.5)	-8.8340 (3.2)
$\bar{R}^2$	0.6285	0.6000	0.6360
DW	2.2349	2.2048	2.2000
SEE	0.3302	0.3426	0.3268
Chow	1.27	1.33	1.52

(divided at 1973/Q4)

F (theor.)			
5%	1.93	1.97	1.93
1%	2.51	2.59	2.51

Note: 1. Q4 = fourth quarter.

These differences make it difficult to reach safe grounds for an evaluation of the NAIRU. At this stage we can only argue that we cannot reject the hypothesis that the growing share of long-term unemployment has implications for the NAIRU. To see this, refer to the reduced form equation for inflation given by columns (1) and (2).

We shall first calculate the NAIRU taking the share of long-term unemployed as given. The following assumptions are made:

(i)   The inflation rate is assumed to be stable, i.e., $p_t = p_{t-i}$ (i = 1,..,n) where n denotes the length of polynominal lag distribution of past inflation rates.

(ii)   It does not seem appropriate to offset wholly or partly the inflationary effects of exogenous shocks by demand management raising unemployment. In particular, we do not want to include the effects of "self-inflicted wounds" such as increased tax rates. We thus set $v^{ind} = v^s = 0$.

(iii) It is assumed that the amount of m which exceeds p can be treated as exogenous. Hence, we set m-p = 0.

(iv)   Since the sum of coefficients associated with lagged inflation is less than one (but close to this value in the specification chosen for the calculation of the NAIRU[41]), the NAIRU is dependent on p to a very small amount. We therefore have to choose a rate of inflation. We regard an annual rate of 3% as "tolerable", i.e., p is set equal to 0.75.

These assumptions give an estimate of a NAIRU which depends upon productivity growth and the share of long-term unemployed. This is called the contemporaneous NAIRU UR*. From column (1) of Table 4 we obtain (for x = 0):

(9) UR* = 1.83 - 3.68π + 0.21 SLU.

From column (2) of Table 4 we have:

(9a) UR* = 1.83 - 2.70π + 0.22 SLU.

As can be seen, both procedures yield approximately the same coefficient associated with SLU. In Table 5, column (2) displays computed values of UR* taken from equation (9a) and employing actual values of SLU and π. Moreover, column (3) of the table shows calculated values of UR* which differ from those reported in column (2), in that actual values of π are replaced by a constant value of $\pi = 0.5\%$.

Taken at face value, these estimates of the contemporaneous NAIRU are, for 1985/86, in close agreement with actual

Table 5. Estimates of the NAIRU[1]

(%)

Time period	Official unemployment rate (1)	"NAIRU" (2)	"NAIRU"[2] (3)
1970-74	1.3	0.7	1.9
1975-79	4.4	3.5	4.2
1980	3.7	3.8	4.1
1981	5.3	3.8	4.0
1982	7.6	5.1	5.1
1983	9.3	6.9	6.3
1984	9.3	8.0	7.6
1985[3]	9.3	8.1	8.1
1986[3]	9.2	8.8	8.8

Notes: 1. See text for details.
2. Calculated for $\pi = 0.5$.
3. Forecast estimates for $\pi = 0.5$ in 1985 and 1986, SLU = 35.0 in 1985, and SLU = 38.0 in 1986.

unemployment. In addition, the estimates displayed in columns (2) and (3) are largely in agreement with other studies, such as Coe.[42] However, the share of long-term unemployed cannot, of course, be regarded as an exogenous variable. Indeed, the whole point of the argument is that the value of the NAIRU depends upon the history of unemployment. In the presence of persistence these values may overestimate the threshold unemployment rate, above which expansionary demand measures result in an accelerating inflation. (Thus we have labelled columns (2) and (3) "NAIRU" because we feel that the calculations give misleading figures.)

In order to take into account this argument, Table 6 reports an attempt to gain insight into the dynamic structure of how previous unemployment rates determine the present share of long-term unemployment. Using the ALMON-technique, the share of long-term unemployed has been regressed on current and past values of unemployment rates. The regression with the lowest standard error of estimate displays the lag structure presented in Table 6.

Inserting the equation from Table 6 into equation (9a) and imposing a stable rate of unemployment (i.e., setting $UR_{t-1} = UR_{t-2} = ... = UR_{t-11} = UR$) gives the steady-state NAIRU UR discussed in Part II,[43] to distinguish it from the contemporaneous NAIRU. The share of long-term unemployment has thus been adjusted to a long-run equilibrium which is consistent with stationary equilibrium. More precisely, from equation (9a) and Table 6 the following expression is obtained:

(10) $UR^* = 2.89 - 2.70\,\pi + 0.73\,\overline{UR}.$

Table 6. Regression results of $SLU_t = a_0 + \sum_{i=0}^{11} \lambda \ UR_{t-i}$

(t-values in brackets)

λ_0 = -1.094 (5.1)	λ_6 = 0.766 (11.6)
λ_1 = -0.228 (3.2)	λ_7 = 0.583 (14.0)
λ_2 = 0.361 (5.6)	λ_8 = 0.368 (6.9)
λ_3 = 0.714 (6.9)	λ_9 = 0.161 (2.1)
λ_4 = 0.873 (7.7)	λ_{10} = 0.004 (0.1)
λ_5 = 0.876 (9.0)	λ_{11} = -0.06 (1.0)

$\sum_i \lambda_i$ = 3.321 (29.7); a_0 = 4.830 (12.6); $\overline{R}^2$ = 0.930; SEE = 2.294

Recalling equation (2) from Part II and the distinction between persistence and hysteresis discussed there, equation (10) indicates persistence but not hysteresis, since the coefficient associated with $\overline{UR}$ is considerably less than one. Moreover, for $UR^* = \overline{UR}$ and assuming a 0.5% value for π again, we obtain a steady-state NAIRU of 5.7% from equation (10). This value for 1986 is considerably lower than the value calculated in column (3) of Table 5.[44]

Although there is considerable uncertainty with respect to this lower figure, it still may be able to indicate that an evaluation of the NAIRU should take into account the possibility of persistence. Unless this is done, there is at present a serious risk of overestimating the NAIRU. This will give misleading information to policy-makers if they use the NAIRU as a guide and/or an indicator for their policy.

V. Conclusions

This paper deals with the persistence effects of high unemployment. The literature surveyed in this paper offers several explanations for persistence, but the paper argues that the most plausible candidate is that employers use (long) unemployment experience as a screening device. Using the Beveridge curve framework, some support for this channel is found.

The paper also attempts to evaluate the impact of persistence on the NAIRU. Employing a reduced form of a price, a wage, and a Beveridge curve equation, we found that the rise in long-term unemployment may in fact contribute substantially to an explanation of the recent shift in the NAIRU. The analysis shows the importance of distinguishing between the contemporaneous NAIRU (i.e., the NAIRU given the share of long-term unemployed and, hence, the history of unemployment) and

114

the steady-state NAIRU (i.e., the NAIRU sustainable in the long-run equilibrium, when endogenous responses of the contemporaneous NAIRU to past unemployment are taken into account).

It should be emphasized that the calculations are tentative due to several imperfections. If anything can be learned from them, it is that the concept of the NAIRU is not a straightforward guide for economic policy. Thus it is difficult to conclude with policy implications. This study, however, does not support the view that we have to be stuck with a high equilibrium rate of unemployment. Once an increase in employment comes under way, the contemporaneous NAIRU will fall. This would seem to open possibilities for a future fall in unemployment that would *not* have to be accompanied by rising inflation.

The empirical results of this paper therefore do not agree with the belief held by the public that a policy of expansion would only rekindle inflation. It seems as misleading to argue that we are stuck with a much higher non-inflationary threshold unemployment rate, as to argue that, by and large, current unemployment is required in order to stabilize inflation.

Appendix: Symbols, description, and sources of data used in the analysis in Part IV

List of symbols used in the analysis in Part IV

M	domestic currency value of import and agricultural prices
P	product price
P*	expected product price
Q	output ratio
SLU	share of long-term unemployed persons
t^m	value added tax rate ("Mehrwertsteuer")
t^v	employer's contribution to social security divided by gross labour
UR	official unemployment rate income
URC	corrected unemployment rate
V^{ind}	indirect tax factor
V^s	payroll tax factor
VR	official vacancy rate
VRC	corrected vacancy rate
W	gross hourly wage rate
X	demand conditions on the goods market
Z	mark-up factor on prices
Π	productivity of labour

m, p, p*, v^{ind}, v^s, w, x, z, and π are rates of change of the respective variable with capital letters.

Description of data used in Section IV.2

(All variables except Q, UR, and SLU are quarterly rates of change defined as $x_t = (X_t - X_{t-1})/X_{t-1} \bullet 100$ and are seasonally adjusted.)

p   Rate of change of the fixed weight deflator of final domestic demand (weights as of 1980).

π   Trend productivity growth per person; excluding the agricultural and governmental sectors and private households, the trend equation is $\pi = 3.4 + 0.04t - 0.0007\, t^2$.

m   Rate of change of a weighted average of import and agricultural prices.

v^{ind} Rate of change $1 + t^{ind}$, where t^{ind} is the indirect tax rate.

v^s Rate of change of $1 + t^v$, where t^v is the ratio of employers' contributions to social security to gross labour income.

z(x)   Rate of change of real final domestic demand.

UR   Official unemployment rate.

SLU   Ratio of unemployed persons who have been unemployed for one year and more to all employed x 100.

Q   Output ratio, defined as the ratio of actual output to full
            employment output. Full employment includes employed
            persons plus official unemployed plus discouraged workers,
            minus structural/frictional unemployed; this sum is multiplied by
            lagged productivity. (For details, see W. Franz, "Zur Evaluierung
            der Kosten einer monetären Disinflationspolitik", mimeo, paper
            presented at the meeting of the "Theoretischer Ausschuss des
            Vereins für Sozialpolitik" in May 1986.)

Sources of data used in Section IV.2

$p, v^{ind}, v^s, z(x)$ Deutsches Institut für Wirtschaftsforschung (DIW),
            Lange Reihen der vierteljährlichen volkswirtschaftlichen
            Gesamtrechnung für die Bundesrepublik Deutschland;
            saison - und arbeitstäglich bereinigte Werte, Berlin,
            October 1985.

UR, SLU   Amtliche Nachrichten der Bundesanstalt für Arbeit
            (ANBA); Institut für Arbeitsmarkt - und Berufsforschung
            der Bundesanstalt für Arbeit.

m   Import prices: Statistisches Bundesamt, Fachserie M,
            Reihe 1; Jahresgutachten des Sachverstän-digenrates.

            Agricultural prices: Statistisches Bundesamt, Wirtschaft
            und Statistik.

π Jahresgutachten des Sachverständigenrates.

Notes and sources

1. R.M. Solow, "Unemployment: Getting the Questions Right", *Economica*, Vol. 53, No. 210 S, pp. S23-34, 1986. For the sake of convenience, Webster's *New Collegiate Dictionary* (1979) defines an epiphenomenon as a "secondary phenomenon accompanying another and caused by it".

2. See, for instance, the survey by D. Metcalf, "Labour Market Flexibility and Jobs: Evidence from OECD Countries with Special Reference to Europe", in this volume.

3. The standard reference is M. Bruno and J.D. Sachs, *Economics of Worldwide Stagflation*, Harvard University Press, Cambridge, (Mass.), 1985. See also *Economica*, Vol. 53, for detailed country studies.

4. See F. Giavazzi and C. Wyplosz, "The Zero Root Problem: A Note on the Dynamic Determination of the Stationary Equilibrium in Linear Models", *Review of Economic Studies*, Vol. 52, No. 169, 1985, pp. 353-357.

5. I owe this point to Charles Wyplosz, who explains it in more detail in his comments on my paper in this volume.

6. O.J. Blanchard and L.H. Summers, "Hysteresis and the European Unemployment Problem", in S. Fischer (ed.), *NBER Macroeconomic Annual 1986*, MIT Press, Cambridge (Mass.).

7. E.S. Phelps, *Inflation and Unemployment Theory*, Macmillan, London, 1972, p. 78.

8. W.H. Buiter and M. Gersovitz, "Issues in Controllability and the Theory of Economic Policy", *Journal of Public Economics*, Vol. 15, 1981, pp. 33-43; S.P. Hargreaves Heap, "Choosing the Wrong 'Natural' Rate: Accelerating Inflation or Decelerating Employment and Growth?", *Economic Journal*, No. 90, 1980, pp.611-620; J.D. Sachs, "High Unemployment in Europe: Diagnosis and Policy Implications", Working Paper No. 1830, National Bureau of Economic Research, Cambridge (Mass.), 1986.

9. J.J. Heckman and G. Borjas, "Does Unemployment Cause Future Unemployment? Definitions, Questions and Answers from a Continuous Time Model of Heterogeneity and State Dependence", *Economica*, Vol. 47, 1980, pp. 247-283.

10. W. Franz, *Youth Unemployment in the Federal Republic of Germany: Theory, Empirical Results, and Policy Implications. An Economic Analysis*, Mohr und Siebeck, Tübingen, 1982.

11. K.B. Clark and L.H. Summers, "Labour Market Dynamics and Unemployment: A Reconsideration", *Brookings Papers on Economic Activity*, Vol. 1, 1979, pp. 13-60. For an overview of these aspects of the youth labour market, see J.M. Evans, W. Franz, and J.P. Martin, *Youth Labour Market Dynamics and Unemployment. An Analysis*

for *Policy-Makers*, OECD, Paris, 1984.

12. R.M. Solow, op. cit., note 1.

13. For examples of studies which deal with this question empiricially using a macroeconometric framework see Blanchard and Summers op. cit., note 6; D.T. Coe, "Nominal Wages, the NAIRU, and Wage Flexibility", *OECD Economic Studies*, Vol. 5, 1985, pp. 87-126; R.J. Gordon, "Productivity, Wages, and Prices Inside and Outside of Manufacturing in the US, Japan, and Europe", mimeo, paper presented to the International Seminar on Macroeconomics, 23-24 June, 1986; J.D. Sachs, op. cit., note 8. A partial survey of causes for hysteresis is provided by S.P. Hargreaves Heap, op. cit., note 8.

14. R.L. Peterson, "Economics of Information and Job Search: Another View", *Quarterly Journal of Economics*, Vol. 86, 1972, pp. 127-131.

15. S.P. Hargreaves Heap, op. cit., note 8, p. 614.

16. The first models of this type were G. Grossman, "Union Wages, Temporary Layoffs and Seniority", *American Economic Review*, Vol. 73, 1983, pp. 277-290; and D. Blair and D. Crawford, "Labour Union Objectives and Collective Bargaining", *Quarterly Journal of Economics*, Vol. 99, 1984, pp.547-566. Later examplea are N. Gottfries and H. Horn, "Wage Formation and the Peristency of Unemployment", Seminar Paper No. 347, Institute for International Economic Studies, University of Stockholm, 1986; and O.J. Blanchard and L.H. Summers, op. cit., note 6. A survey of some aspects of this topic is provided by L. Calmfors, "Trade Unions, Wage Formation and Macroeconomic Stability — An Introduction", *Scandinavian Journal of Economics*, Vol. 87, 1985, pp. 143-159.

17. Outsiders may include not only unemployed persons but also people holding bad jobs in the terminology of the dual labour market theory.

18. R.M. Solow, "Insiders and Outsiders in Wage Determination", *Scandinavian Journal of Economics*, Vol. 87, 1985, pp. 411-428.

19. A. Lindbeck and D.J. Snower, "Wage Setting, Unemployment and Insider-Outsider Relations", Paper and Proceedings, *American Economic Review*, Vol. 76, 1986, pp. 235-239.

20. See J. Bergmann, "Gewerkschaften — Organisationsstruktur und Mitgliederinteressen", in G. Endruweit *et al.* (eds.), *Handbuch der Arbeitsbeziehungen*, de Gruyter, Berlin, 1985, pp. 89-108.

21. For a survey and economic analysis of reductions in working time in the FRG, see W. Franz, "Is Less More? The Current Discussion About Reduced Working Time in Western Germany: A Survey of the Debate", *Zeitschrift für die gesamte Staatswissenschaft*, Vol. 140, 1984, pp. 626-654.

22. This is elaborated in J.D. Sachs, op. cit., note 8.

23. H. Giersch, (ed.), *Capital Shortage and Unemployment in the World Economy*, Mohr, Tübingen, 1977.

24. For details, see Section III, p. 101.

25. O.J. Blanchard and L.H. Summers, op. cit., note 6.

26. For an example of a detailed theoretical derivation of this verbal illustration, see W. Franz, "Match or Mismatch? The Anatomy of Structural/Frictional Unemployment in Germany: A Theoretical and Empirical Investigation", mimeo, paper presented at the VIth Conference of the Latin American Econometric Society at Cordoba (Argentina), 1986; and R. Jackman, R. Layard, and C. Pissarides, "On Vacancies", Discussion Paper No. 165, Centre for Labour Economics, London School of Economics, 1983. A description of various types of mismatch is also contained in A.J. Brown, "UV Analysis", in G.D.N. Worswick (ed.), *The Concept and Measurement of Involuntary Unemployment*, Allen and Unwin, London, 1976, pp. 134-145.

27. For a more detailed description, see W. Franz, "Challenges to the German Economy 1973-1983. Supply Shocks, Investment Slowdown, Inflation Variability and the Underutilisation of Labour", *Zeitschrift für Wirtschafts- und Sozialwissenschaft*, Vol. 105, 1985, pp. 407-430.

28. VR and VRC have been calculated using lagged values, GNP, M1, and a time trend.

29. These loops have been analyzed theoretically by B. Hansen, in "Excess Demand, Unemployment, Vacancies, and Wages", *Quarterly Journal of Economics*, Vol. 84, 1970, pp. 1-23. For a similar empirical procedure, see F. Reid, and N.M. Meltz, "Causes of Shifts in the Unemployment Vacancy Relationship: An Empirical Analysis for Canada", *Review of Economics and Statistics*, Vol. 61, 1979, pp. 470-475.

30. The calculations are based on the estimates displayed in columns (3) and (6) of Table 1.

31. See, for example, K.G. Abraham, "Structural/Frictional vs. Deficient Demand Unemployment: Some New Evidence", *American Economic Review*, Vol. 73, 1983, pp. 708-724.

32. It should be clear, however, that the share of long-term unemployed (SLU) is a poor proxy for persistence of the type in question. Moreover, the estimates are plagued by the fact that the unemployment rate and the SLU variable are, by definition, related via the probability of leaving the unemployment register. Lack of reliable data prohibits us from taking into account proxies for persistence other than the share of long-term unemployed.

33. This is consistent with a recent study for the UK by A. Budd, P. Levine, and P. Smith, "Unemployment, Vacancies, and Long-Term Unemployment", Discussion Paper No. 154, Centre for Economic Forecasting, London Business School, 1985. The authors show that the observed outward shift of the UK Beveridge curve is due, in part, to the rise in the proportion of unemployment which is long term.

34. For details, see W. Franz and H. König, "Nature and Causes of Unemployment in the Federal Republic of Germany since the Seventies: An Empirical Investigation", *Economica*, Vol. 53, No. 210 S, 1986, pp. S219-244.

35. See W. Franz, op. cit., note 26.

36. The indirect tax factor (V^{ind}) is defined as $1+t^m$, where t^m is the value added tax rate ("Mehrwertsteuer"). The payroll tax factor V^s is defined in a similar fashion, namely $V^s = 1+t^v$ where t^v is the payroll tax rate. For an application of a similar hypothesis of pricing behaviour for the US, Japan, and Europe, see R.J. Gordon, op. cit., note 13.

37. Another possibility is, of course, to estimate all three equations separately. Following the arguments outlined by R.J. Gordon, in "Inflation, Flexible Exchange Rates, and the Natural Rate of Unemployment", in M.N. Baily (ed.), *Workers, Jobs, and Inflation*, Brookings Institution, Washington, DC, 1982, pp. 88-155, we use the reduced form approach, since our goal is only the evaluation of the NAIRU rather than a detailed description of the structure of wage and price determination.

38. See, for instance, R.J. Gordon, "Understanding Inflation in the 1980s", Brookings Papers on Economic Activity, No. 1, 1985, pp. 263-299.

39. R.J. Gordon, op. cit., note 13.

40. We have experimented with various measures of the influences of tax rates on p, such as different measures of a tax wedge. Following the study by J. Sachs and C. Wyplosz, "The Economic Policies of President Mitterand", *Economic Policy*, Vol. 2, 1986, pp. 261-322, we have also used a log tax wedge, but this variable lacked significance.

41. As can be seen from other estimates in Table 4, this is not common to all estimates. Indeed, other studies for the FRG found coefficients significantly less than one. See, for example, D.T. Coe, op. cit., note 13, Table 1.

42. D.T. Coe, op. cit., note 13.

43. Another possible way to evaluate the long-run equilibrium NAIRU is to introduce a distributed lag of past unemployment rates directly into the Phillips curve. This procedure, however, causes difficulties due to the presence of the distributed lag of past inflation rates, which take into account adaptive expectations and price inertia.

44. Moreover, more optimistic but still realistic assumptions about (future) trend productivity growth yield lower long-run equilibrium NAIRUs such as 4.5% for an annual rate of π of 2.5%. Reviewing economic forecasts, $\pi = 2.5\%$ does not seem to be an unlikely figure. Since the productivity effect on inflation is uncertain from Table 5, we do not pursue this issue here.

Additional references

Franz, W., "The Reservation Wage of Unemployed Persons in the Federal Republic of Germany: Theory and Empirical Test", *Zeitschrift für Wirtschafts- und Sozialwissenschaften*, Vol. 102, 1982, pp. 29-51.

Franz, W., "The Past Decade's Natural Rate and the Dynamics of German Unemployment: A Case against Demand Policy?" *European Economic Review*, Vol. 21, 1983, pp. 51-76.

Pissarides, C.A., "Short-run Equilibrium Dynamics of Unemployment Vacancies, and Real Wages", *American Economic Review*, Vol. 75, 1985, pp. 676-690.

Tobin, J., "Unemployment in the 1980s: Macroeconomic Diagnosis and Prescription", in A.J. Price (ed.), *Unemployment and Growth in the Western Economics*, Series: Europe/America 2, Council on Foreign Relations, New York, 1984, pp. 79-112.

Comments

by Charles Wyplosz

With considerable courage, Franz squarely engages one of the most crucial and difficult issues of the day: the apparently inexorable rising tide of unemployment which has swept over much of Europe since the 1970s. The result is a paper which makes an interesting contribution to the very active current effort to sort out competing hypotheses. The issue at stake is that according to a number of empirical studies, the equilibrium rates of unemployment (the NAIRUs) have risen substantially in most European countries and are usually found to stay uncomfortably close to the actually observed rates of unemployment.

Many economists, such as Solow,[1] have reacted to these findings by expressing scepticism towards these numbers (typically believing that they are too high), and questioning the estimating procedures as well as the NAIRU concept itself and the associated Phillips curve. Certainly, since its initial discovery, the Phillips curve has been a statistical regularity in search of a theory. Almost three decades and several innovations later, there is still no generally accepted theory behind it. We have several theories which can be made to generate a Phillips curve, so that one or another version of the curve is acceptable to most economists. But the econometrician still faces the problem of an excess of bounties in formalizing an empirical Phillips curve. One major problem is that many of the variables that ought to figure in the intersection of most theories are unobservable; that is the case of expected inflation and the reservation wage, among others. As a result, even a narrowing down of theoretical disagreements will not dispel scepticism towards the empirical results.

But the striking fact is that with such a diversity of theories and econometric applications, estimated NAIRUs do not differ much from one study to another: we always find that it has grown in parallel to the observed rate of unemployment. Consequently, many authors have attempted to explain this evolution.

Development of hypotheses

A first explanation has emphasized the role of adverse supply shocks, as in Bruno and Sachs.[2] This view is quite helpful up to the beginning of the 1980s, but leaves us rather helpless to cope with the unabating rise of the NAIRU in the current decade. It is not surprising therefore that many have turned to an explanation based on a purported increase in labour market rigidities.

A series of papers presented at a conference in Chelwood Gate and published in 1986 in a special issue of *Economica*[3] were designed to explore this hypothesis. For a variety of European countries, authors have built mismatch indicators. By and large, the general impression is that there is no evidence that these indicators have risen, and their explanatory power in the Phillips curves regression is nil.

The next line of investigation has taken up the possibility that increasing distortions introduced by various labour market regulations would account for at least part of the rise of the NAIRU. The purported culprits are minimum wage legislation, labour taxes and income taxes (the tax wedge), unemployment benefits, etc. These attempts have been partially successful, but the area remains a controversial one.

Such an unsatisfactory state of affairs implies two things: first, a growing frustration with the NAIRU concept and, second, fertile ground for a new theory. Quite recently several authors (Sachs, Blanchard and Summers, Lindbeck and Snower, and Gottfries and Horn) have brought up the so-called hysteresis hypothesis, initially advanced by Kemp and Wan, and Hargreaves Heap.[4] This hypothesis fits the bill: it is new (therefore exiciting!) and it implies that there is no such thing as a NAIRU; furthermore, it has striking policy implications. It also fits in nicely with another recent innovation, the insider-outsider theory proposed by Solow, and Lindbeck and Snower.[5] Quite normally, the hysteresis hypothesis has attracted immediate and widespread interest. We therefore need to know whether it has empirical relevance. It is Franz's objective to submit this theory to data from the Federal Republic of Germany (FRG).

Definition of hysteresis

Formally, hysteresis occurs when, in discrete time, the system of differential equations posseses a unit root. (For a detailed discussion, see Giavazzi and Wyplosz.[6]) Consider a simple, one-dimensional case, where a variable X_t follows a law of motion:

(1) $X_t = a \cdot X_{t-1} - Z_t$.

If $a \neq 1$, in the steady state defined by $X_t - X_{t-1} = 0$, we have $\bar{X} = \bar{Z}/(a-1)$, (where a bar denotes the steady-state value). $\bar{X}$ is then unique and independent of the path followed by the exogenous variable Z_t; only its steady-state level $\bar{Z}$ matters. But if $a = 1$, we have the case of *hysteresis*. Then, provided that the existence condition $\bar{Z} = 0$ is satisfied, the steady-state value of X is not unique. Any value is possible and $\bar{X}$ will actually depend upon the path of Z_t, as the solution to (1) is now $\bar{X} = X(0) + \sum_{t=0}^{\infty} Z_t$. Put another way, any *temporary* disturbance to Z will have a *permanent* effect on X.

A general formulation of the Phillips curve is as follows:

(2) $\pi_t = \pi_t^* - \alpha(U_t - U_t^*)$,

where π and π^* are, respectively, the actual and expected rates of inflation, and U is the rate of unemployment. The NAIRU corresponds to the steady-state situation when $\pi = \pi^*$, so that $U = U^*$. A given theory of the labour market will provide a theory of the determinants of U_t^*, for example $U_t^* = bZ_t$, where Z_t is a vector of relevant variables.

The possibility of hysteresis arises when U_t^* is also a function of past unemployment rates, as:

(3) $U_t^* = a\, U_{t-1} + bZ_t$.

(A more general formulation would involve a distributed lag of past U_{t-i} with weights a_i. All of the following discussion applies with $a = \Sigma a_i$.) Substituting (3) in (2) we have:

(4) $\pi_t = \pi_t^* - \alpha\,(U_t - aU_{t-1}) + \alpha bZ_t$.

Hysteresis occurs when $a = 1$. When we impose the steady-state conditions $\pi = \pi^*$ and $U_t = U_{t-1}$, we obtain the existence requirement $Z_t \to 0$ as $t \to \infty$, and no further restriction on U; there is no longer a unique NAIRU. If $a = 0$, we have the standard case where the NAIRU is $\overline{U}^* = b\overline{Z}$. For values of a between 0 and 1, the NAIRU still exists: $\overline{U}^* = b\overline{Z}/(1-a)$.

The importance of "a"

The value of a is seen to have policy implications. Indeed, $a = 1$ means that a high level of unemployment rate today results in a high NAIRU tomorrow, the stylized fact discussed earlier. If we accept that the European NAIRUs are currently high because of the recent experience of high unemployment rates, we see that a strong demand expansion which reduces the rate of unemployment would also reduce the NAIRU by the same amount, no matter what other, possibly structural, forces are at work, as captured by some of the components of vector Z_t. Of course, such a policy may have temporary inflation effects. On the contrary, if $a = 0$, an expansion will leave the NAIRU unaffected and equal to bZ, only temporarily reducing unemployment and simultaneously building up inflation.[7]

The case $0 < a < 1$ is interesting. There is no hysteresis anymore as $\overline{U}^* = b\overline{Z}/(1 - a)$, but the NAIRU evolves slowly (if a is large) towards its steady-state level. A temporary expansion *may not* be advisable — even in the short run — because of its inflationary implications. It is quite crucial to distinguish this case of *persistence* from the case of hysteresis, which strictly occurs only when a = 1.

According to equation (4), it is clear how to test the hysteresis and persistence hypotheses. If the coefficient of U_{t-1} (or a distributed lag on U) is not significantly different from zero, both hypotheses are rejected. If this coefficient is equal but of opposite sign to that of U_t, we cannot reject the hysteresis hypothesis.

Alternative interpretation of Franz

Franz reviews the reasons which have been advanced recently as to why hysteresis might occur, discusses how they might apply to the FRG, and then focuses on the hypothesis of a (perceived and/or actual) depreciation of human capital. His approach is largely atheoretical so that it is not always clear how to construe his observations. Here I wish to offer an alternative interpretation based on the insider-outsider view, according to which some unemployed workers become outsiders to the bargaining process and therefore play no part in the Phillips curve equation. This means that the NAIRU ought to include only the insiders. If one argues, following Gregory,[8] that the long-term unemployed workers make up the population of outsiders, it is the rate of short-term unemployment, $U^{ST} = U - U^{LT}$, which ought to enter the Phillips curve:

(5) $\quad \pi_t = \pi_t^* - \alpha(U_t - U_t^{LT} - bZ_t).$

Assume now that of those who lost a job last year, a fraction γ still remain unemployed and therefore become long-term unemployed:

(6) $\quad U^{LT} = U_{t-1}^{LT} + \gamma (U_{t-1} - U_{t-2}),$

so that, for a given base period t = 0 (i.e. before unemployment started its secular rise),

(7) $\quad U_t^{LT} = \gamma U_{t-1} + U_0^{LT} - \gamma U_0.$

Inserting (7) in (5) yields:

(8) $\quad \pi_t = \pi_t^* \, \alpha(U_t - \gamma U_{t-1} - b'Z'_t),$

where $b'Z'_t = bZ_t + U_0^{LT} - \gamma U_0.$

Equations (5), (6), and (8) indicate the two crucial assumptions that Franz needs to test:

- that all long-term unemployed workers are outsiders, i.e. that U^{LT} enters equation (5) with a coefficient α, which is the same as for U but of opposite sign.

126

- that since t = 0, the number of long-term unemployed workers has increased by the same amount as the total number of unemployed workers; i.e., that $\gamma = 1$. Indeed, only if $\gamma = 1$ do we observe hysteresis in equation (8).

Of course, he could (should) also test directly for the coefficient of U_{t-1} in equation (3), as discussed earlier.

Franz's case

Instead, Franz chooses to build up his case in two steps. First, he argues that an increase in U^{LT} should shift out the Beveridge curve. The Beveridge curve shares with the Phillips curve a rather fuzzy theoretical basis, so the proposition that an increase in long-term unemployment should shift the curve needs to be explained better. (It could well shift it in; for example, if long-term unemployment results from better screening, so that most firms are happy with their labour force and vacancies are reduced.) But Franz confirms that in the FRG, as in several other countries, the Beveridge curve has shifted out, and he is able to attribute part of the cause to the rise in long-term unemployment. Thus, his dummy variables indicate a total upwards shift ranging from 4 to 7 percentage points in the rate of unemployment, while long-term unemployment has contributed to an increase in total unemployment of about 2 percentage points since 1980.

This result, if confirmed, is important. It establishes that a rise in the share of long-term unemployment in total unemployment impairs the functioning of the labour market through a less efficient job-search process, as captured by the Beveridge curve. But, in line with Franz's original purpose, the result does not establish the existence of hysteresis. If the Beveridge curve is of any use on this issue, it must be because of the unstated assumption that it is parameterized by the NAIRU, or more exactly, that it is shifting upwards proportionately to increases in the NAIRU. As stated above, hysteresis requires two conditions. The second one ($\gamma = 1$) cannot be tested with the Beveridge curve. But the first condition would imply that the upward shift of the Beveridge curve exactly matches the 2 percentage points that long-term unemployment contributed to total unemployment. The shift falls well short of it. This can be interpreted in two ways: first, that there is no hysteresis; second, that other factors than hysteresis have been at work. We are left wondering.

Finally, Franz deals directly with the Phillips curve, unfortunately introducing SLU = U^{LT}/U instead of U^{LT} among his regressors. His equation, which otherwise resembles (8), does not allow for a direct test of the hypothesis that $\gamma = 1$. The fact that the coefficient of SLU is significantly different from zero and positive suggests that indeed the long-term unemployed do not "weigh" as much as the short-term unemployed. His further evidence that SLU is related to U (Table 6, page 114) via a distributed lag opens up the possibility that persistence exists in the FRG. But, given the very crucial distinction between hysteresis and persistence, we would like to have a more definitive answer.

There are some other difficulties in interpreting Tables 5 and 6 (pages 113 and 114). First, failure to impose the restriction that the sum of the coefficients of the distributed lags on past inflation add up to unity amounts to not specifying a long-run vertical Phillips curve, i.e. to rejecting the hypothesis that there exists such a thing as a NAIRU. This is quite unfortunate as his regressions actually support the assumption. Indeed, plugging *his* equations Thus from regression (2) in Table 5 it appears that α is observed (5) and (6) into *his* equation (4) yields (his notations):

$$(9) \quad p = \alpha\ \beta_1 p^* + \alpha(\beta_2 - 1)\ \pi + \alpha(\beta_2 + \frac{\beta_4}{\gamma_1})\ U - \frac{\alpha\beta_4}{\gamma_1}\gamma_0$$

$$- \frac{\alpha\beta_4\gamma_2}{\gamma_1}\ SLU + (1 - \alpha)m + Z(x) + V^{ind} + \alpha V^s.$$

from the coefficient of m: $\alpha = 0.94$. The coefficient of p^* is $\Sigma\lambda_i$ and should be equal to α if the restriction $\beta_1 = 1$ is indeed accepted. With $\alpha\beta_1 = 0.92$, it seems likely that $\beta_1 = 1$ would not be rejected under any reasonable significance level. Note also that if, as is reasonable, $\beta_2 = 1$, the coefficient of π should be zero, which is accepted by the regression. On the other hand, the coefficient of V^{ind} should be 1 and that of V^s should be α: these restrictions do not seem to be accepted

Finally, I cannot understand why the "self-inflicted wounds" created by the wedge V^s are excluded from the NAIRU calculations. Wounds are wounds, and may well increase the NAIRU. Indeed, most of the other explanations for the rise of the NAIRU are based on labour market distortions due to other "self-inflicted wounds". It would be nice, on the contrary, to show the responsibility of V^s in the NAIRU, if only because it allows for an immediate policy implication.

Emerging verdict on hysteresis hypothesis

In conclusion, we must ask what the emerging verdict is on the hysteresis hypothesis. So far, Franz's results for the FRG seem to make a case for the existence of some persistence, while casting serious doubts on hysteresis. This is in line with the work of Coe and Gagliardi,[9] who only found hysteresis in the case of Australia. (Curiously, this is the case described by Gregory!)

128

Only Blanchard and Summers[10] so far claim support for the hysteresis hypothesis in their work on the FRG, France, and the UK. Could their results be spurious?

In earlier work with Sachs,[11] we tried hard to find some evidence of hysteresis, or at least persistence, in the French case. We derived a theory of the Phillips curve whereby the NAIRU would be a function of the reservation wage, proxied by a time trend, and the difference between (the log of) the labour tax wedge and (the log of) labour productivity measured at full employment, i.e. the variable denoted by ψ in Table 1. In addition, we used a dummy capturing the particular effects of price controls and the ratio π^m/π of imported price inflation to domestic inflation (measured by the value-added deflator). In Table 1, regression (1) is the simplest specification of the Phillips curve and attributes a significant effect to the unemployment rate U. However, when the change in the rate of unemployment is introduced in regression (2), we obtain the pure hysteresis result of Blanchard and Summers: all that matters is the *change*, not the *level* of unemployment. But the next three regressions, which include all the variables suggested by our theory [and especially regression (5)] show that this is spurious. Indeed, we reject both the hysteresis and the persistence hypotheses.

There is thus some mounting evidence against hysteresis as an explanation of the rise of NAIRUs in Europe. More work will be needed to reach a firm conclusion, of course. But we should agree on the procedures. I believe that the following is true.

• Insider-outsider theories do not necessarily imply hysteresis. (Indeed, the work of Blanchard and Summers seems to indicate that we need the assumption that insiders lose their status after one period of unemployment and that outsiders become insiders after one period of employment.) But they do imply persistence. Rejecting the persistence hypothesis would mean rejecting the insider-outsider theory. However, the power of the test is weak, as failure to reject persistence is not a failure to reject the insider-outsider theory.

• Job-screening theories argue that an increase in long-term unemployment should lead to an outward shift of the Beveridge curve and to an increase of the NAIRU. In this view, rejecting the significance of the long-term unemployment rate in Phillips curve equations amounts to rejecting the assumption that the long-term unemployed have become outsiders. But failure to reject the long-term unemployment effect is not a failure to reject the hysteresis hypothesis.

Table 1. Phillips curve for France: 1963-84
(dependent variable: $\pi - \pi_{-1}$)

	c	$\pi_{-1} - \pi_{-2}$	$(\pi^m/\pi)_{-1}$	U	$U - U_{-1}$	t	ψ	Price controls dummy	DW	$\bar{R}^2$
(1)	1.30 (2.07)	-0.14 (-0.78)	0.07 (1.54)	-0.25 (-1.99)				1.53 (2.59)	1.78	0.45
(2)	1.30 (2.32)	-0.12 (-0.79)	0.13 (2.58)	-0.02 (-0.09)	-2.38 (-2.21)			1.61 (3.04)	1.63	0.56
(3)	0.49 (0.82)	-0.26 (-1.74)	0.11 (2.57)	-1.05 (-2.33)	-1.40 (-1.37)	0.40 (2.41)		1.27 (2.63)	1.47	0.66
(4)	-25.50 (-1.62)	-0.22 (-1.37)	0.12 (2.62)	-0.39 (-1.48)	-1.85 (-1.74)		-5.43 (-1.70)	1.29 (2.42)	1.55	0.61
(5)	271.29 (5.81)	-0.35 (-4.23)	0.04 (1.60)	-5.28 (-6.86)	0.74 (1.10)	3.54 (6.45)	56.19 (5.80)	1.89 (6.62)	2.24	0.90

Notes: π = inflation rate (GDP deflator); π^m= rate of growth of impact prices; U = unemployment rate; y = log of labour productivity log of wedge, where wedge is the ratio of labour costs to net take-home pay; t is a time trend; the price control dummy is -1 in 1964, 1965, 1974, 1976, 1983, and +1 in each preceding year; t - statistics are in parentheses.
Source: INSEE.

Notes and sources

1. R.M. Solow, "Unemployment: Getting the Questions Right", *Economica*, Vol. 53, No. 210(S), 1986, pp. S23-34.

2. M. Bruno and J.D. Sachs, *Economics of Worldwide Stagflation*, Harvard University Press, Cambridge (Mass.), 1985.

3. Unemployment Supplement, *Economica*, Vol. 53, No. 210(S), 1986.

4. J.D. Sachs, "High Unemployment in Europe: Diagnosis and Policy Implications", Working Paper No. 1830, National Bureau of Economic Research, Cambridge (Mass.), 1985; O.J. Blanchard and L.H. Summers, "Hysteresis and the European Unemployment Problem", in S. Fischer (ed.), *NBER Macroeconomic Annual 1986*, MIT Press, Cambridge (Mass.); A. Lindbeck and D.J. Snower, "Wage Setting, Unemployment and Insider-Outsider Relations", Paper and Proceedings, *American Economic Review*, Vol. 76, 1986; N. Gottfries and H. Horn "Wage Formation and the Persistency of Unemployment", Seminar Paper 347, Institute for International Economic Studies, Stockholm, 1986; M.C. Kemp and H.Y. Wan, "Hysteresis of Long-Run Equilibrium from Realistic Adjustment Costs", in G. Horwich and P.A. Samuelson (eds.) *Trade, Stability and Macroeconomics*, Academic Press, New York, 1974; S.P. Hargreaves Heap, "Choosing the Wrong 'Natural' Rate: Accelerating Inflation or Decelerating Employment and Growth?", *Economic Journal*, No. 90, 1980, pp. 611-620.

5. R.M. Solow, "Insiders and Outsiders in Wage Determination", *Scandinavian Journal of Economics*, Vol. 87, 1985, pp. 411-428; A. Lindbeck and D.J. Snower, op.cit., note 4, pp. 235-239.

6. F. Giavazzi and C. Wyplosz, "The Zero Root Problem: A Note on the Dynamic Determination of the Stationary Equilibrium in Linear Models", *Review of Economic Studies*, Vol. 52, No. 169, 1985, pp. 353-357.

7. This model is complete and would require a theory of expected inflation. In the simple case where $\pi^{*}_{t} = \pi_{t-1}$ the inflation rate itself is determined by hysteresis: a temporary increase in inflation leads to a permanently higher inflation rate.

8. R. Gregory, "Wages Policy and Unemployment in Australia", *Economica*, Vol. 53, No. 210(S), 1986, pp. S53-74.

9. D. Coe and F. Gagliardi, "Nominal Wage Determination in Ten OECD Countries", OECD Working Paper No. 19, Paris, 1985.

10. O.J. Blanchard and L.H. Summers, op. cit., note 4.

11. J. Sachs and C. Wyplosz, "The Economic Consequences of President Mitterand", *Economic Policy*, No. 2, 1986, pp. 262-322.

131

Comments

by Paul Van Rompuy

In this paper, the hypothesis of hysteresis which has recently been suggested as a plausible explanation of the persistently high unemployment in Europe,[1] has been carefully examined and empirically tested in the case of the Federal Republic of Germany (FRG).

Franz evaluates, from both a theoretical and an empirical point of view, three alternative theories explaining the persistence of unemployment: employers' screening policies based on the observed spell of unemployment, restrictive union policies in which insiders play a decisive role in the bargaining process, and the capital shortage theory.

In view of the empirical results and the institutional framework that characterizes the FRG labour market, Franz accepts the screening assumption in his search for a plausible explanation of shifts of the Beveridge curve and of the substantial increase in the average length of unemployment.

He then derives NAIRU estimates (taking persistence effects into account), from a three-equation model based on a price and a wage equation and a Beveridge curve relationship. The author concludes that the NAIRU adjusted for hysteresis is less than one-half of the unemployment rate observed during recent years, and that this offers hopeful perspectives for a non-inflationary demand expansion in the FRG.

My comments on this interesting paper concentrate on two points, namely the acceptance of the screening assumption as the key factor in explaining unemployment persistence, and the alternative explanation of hysteresis by means of the insider-outsider theory.

Acceptance of the screening hypothesis

The capital shortage assumption

The capital shortage assumption, as stated, for example, by Bruno and Modigliani et al.,[2] stresses that profitability of investment has been reduced because of adverse demand or supply shocks. This leads to a downwards adjustment of the growth path of the capital stock and to a simultaneous increase in unemployment.

It is however difficult to see, *without relying on labour market rigidities and capital market imperfections*, how the relatively high degree of actual capital utilization in the FRG and elsewhere in Europe can create a source for unemployment persistence. Indeed, in the short run, increases in output can to some extent be met by higher degrees of capital and labour utilization without building up inflationary pressures. If demand expansion is considered to be permanent, new capacity will be installed embodying capital/labour ratios that are consistent with expected relative factor prices. Unless real wages rise relative to the cost of capital during the recovery, there is no reason to expect capital/labour ratios to increase in an endogenous way.

It may also be the case that the initial real wage is still substantially above the full-employment labour productivity level, so that a "real wage gap" exists as a starting condition. If so, the profitability of investment can only be increased by using less labour-intensive vintages to meet the higher demand for output.

My point here is that the capital shortage assumption, in order to be relevant, has to be linked with the labour market rigidities that are the subject of the explanation of unemployment persistence based on insider-outsider antagonism in the wage-bargaining process.

Shifts of the Beveridge curve

After discarding the capital shortage assumption, Franz concentrates on the screening hypothesis, according to which firms rely on unemployment experience as a negative indicator of the quality of job applicants. The hypothesis is examined by testing for the stability of the Beveridge curve. Of course, the best test of the screening hypothesis would make use of longitudinal data on unemployment experience. The use of aggregate time series on unemployment and vacancies is only a second-best procedure. Moreover, since the shift of the Beveridge curve plays such a decisive role in the paper, one wonders why the author relies so much on dummy variables to test for shifting, instead of introducing explicit mismatch variables that capture the sectoral, regional, or professional disequilibrium between vacancies and unemployment categories. One must also ask why unemployment benefits are not introduced explicitly beside the share of long-term unemployed as an explanatory variable.

The screening hypothesis taken in isolation as an explanation of unemployment persistence leads to some unanswered questions. If screening takes place in the way described in the paper, the wage structure has to be assumed as exogenously given. As the number of long-term unemployed queuing up for the given number of vacancies increases and the average spell of unemployment rises, one may assume a gradually declining reservation wage and underbidding by the unemployed. If skills indeed depreciate as spells of unemployment become longer and if the reservation wage declines as well, one can suppose that newly hired workers would be willing to bear an increasing share of the hiring and training costs, at least if there is no institutionalized minimum wage.

This increased willingness to absorb hiring and training costs would hold in particular for the unemployed youths, who are not handicapped by relatively high wage expectations based on previous job experience, e.g. in manufacturing industries. So if the wage structure were flexible downwards, inexperienced newcomers would be hired first and trained, eventually replacing better paid older workers.

The observation that the youth unemployment rate rose substantially in the European Community from 1981 to 1985 (e.g., from 6.5 to 9.5% in the FRG), and in most countries by even more than the rise in the overall unemployment rate, suggests that the screening hypothesis has to include other ingredients.[3] The downward rigidity of the wage structure and the provision of severance payments that increase with pay and tenure are additional factors in the explanation of the increasing persistence of both employment and unemployment. So labour turnover costs and downward rigid wages are additional explanatory variables in the human capital approach to unemployment hysteresis. This finding again points to the crucial importance of the insider-outsider hypothesis for wage bargaining.

Insiders and outsiders in wage bargaining

As has been stressed by Lindbeck and Snower,[4] labour turnover costs lead to employment stability in the face of random output shocks and to a wage rental, i.e. a wage above the reservation wage of the unemployed. The attractiveness of the insider-outsider theory lies in its ability to give a rationale for the organization of workers into a union and to explain employment persistence. It has a more general scope than the efficiency wage theory, which relies on the incentive value of wages and on unobservable productivity differences among workers. Moreover, in the efficiency wage theory, wages are assumed to be set by the firm, whereas wage bargaining at the industry or firm level reflects the European wage determination process better.

In order to move from employment stability (as compared to the variability of output shocks) to unemployment persistence, a union has to be brought in formally by means of a utility function representing its preferences with respect to wages and employment. As has been shown in the rather scarce economic literature on union decision-making under uncertainty in a dynamic setting (e.g. by Gottfries and Horn[5]) in the case of negative demand shocks, it is sufficient to assume that the majority of the union members remain employed under a majority-rule voting system for employment to decrease permanently and nominal wages to rise.

If the bargaining power of the union is not related to membership size but to the level of the turnover costs, the same results will obtain in a Nash bargaining solution, as has been shown recently by Lindbeck and Snower.[6] These results, obtained in recent contributions, suggest that under fairly general assumptions, workers in unionized firms may prefer less employment and higher wages when faced with independently distributed demand shocks.

One can, however, also point to a number of considerations that complicate the picture presented by the models noted above. *First*, a union organization entails costs financed by members' fees and time inputs. Some of the organizational costs are fixed and decline in per capita terms as union membership expands. The benefits of a wage increase for insiders therefore need to be corrected for the increase in union costs per member that must be covered in order to keep the union going.

Second, insiders and outsiders are linked together by means of unemployment benefits which are financed by social security contributions covered, at least partially, by a tax on wages. Assume, for example, that the unemployment fund pays the benefits out of current receipts. It is intuitively clear that the marginal utility to the union member of a wage increase will be reduced by the rise of the contribution paid into the unemployment fund in order to balance the budget. Hence, this effect tends to moderate wage increases. The magnitude of the effect will depend upon the wage elasticity of the demand for labour, the number of unemployed workers, and the replacement ratio. If, on the other hand, deficits of the unemployment insurance fund are financed by government subsidies, the burden of the increase in unemployment can be spread over all taxpayers and the negative effect of a wage increase on the member's utility will be weakened. However, massive unemployment and a high share of wage income in the tax base are expected to establish a rational link between insiders and outsiders.

Third, the threat of the union to the firm does not only relate to an increase in turnover costs. Strike activity and bargaining power are also related to the membership rate. It is therefore somewhat unrealistic to do away completely with membership size in relation to the work-force as a long-run target of a union. The short-run benefits of a wage increase and employment reduction have to be balanced against the long-run fall in membership. In contrast, in the usual insider-outsider models employment will shrink permanently in the case of successive negative demand shocks. The only constraint is the wage level at which labour costs hit the critical profitability level that determines the survival of the firm. Therefore, concern for the maintenance of future bargaining power will moderate the actual wage claims made by the union in an intertemporal setting.

The above discussion suggests an explicit formulation of a union wage determination model in order to test empirically the insider-outsider assumption.[7] Tests of more elaborate wage-employment models derived from optimizing behaviour by firms and unions are, however, still in an experimental stage. For example, Blanchard and Summers[8] test the insider-outsider model in an indirect way by introducing current and lagged employment in an aggregate wage equation. But no direct estimates of the parameters of the union's objective function are offered.

In my view, there is therefore a need for careful testing of union and wage-bargaining models. If estimates of the parameters of the union utility function can in principle be obtained, it should also be possible to derive the marginal rate of substitution between wages and employment. Changes over time in this marginal rate of substitution can eventually be detected by comparing subperiod parameter estimates, and this may shed light on the insider-outsider hypothesis.

The analysis above leads me to the conclusion that no convinving tests of the competing screening, capital shortage, and insider-outsider models have been offered in Franz's paper. In contrast with his approach, I wish to focus on the insider-outsider hypothesis. My reason is that the screening and capital shortage theories cannot stand on their own, but indeed presuppose wage rigidities of the type modelled in the insider-outsider approach. Since the latter has not been rejected in Franz's paper in a rigorous way, and since it can incorporate other features of the internal labour markets — such as seniority rules, differences in skill,[9] and turnover costs — it deserves a favourable prejudgement.

Concluding remarks

In the last section of his paper, Franz estimates the magnitude of hysteresis or persistence effects on the NAIRU. He finds that a temporary decrease in unemployment will indeed lower the long-run equilibrium NAIRU. This might lead one to the conclusion that a lower long-run unemployment level can be reached through a sufficiently strong and unexpected demand expansion that reduces short-run unemployment substantially.

I conclude by offering two comments on the possibilities of accomplishing an inflationary neutral demand expansion that will bring unemployment in a short period of time down to a steady-state NAIRU of say 4%.

First, the growth of output required to bring short-run unemployment down to the corrected NAIRU should be maintained for some successive years. It is therefore difficult to do this "by surprise" in order to avoid upwards-adjusting real wage claims by unions. The situation is further complicated if insiders set wages, a case which has not been rejected in a convincing way in this paper. Furthermore, it is unlikely that a quick move towards the corrected NAIRU can be realized without increasing non-wage labour costs. This will certainly be the case if skills really depreciate over long spells of unemployment (as the author assumes), forcing employers to increase their training costs.

Second, since the rate of capacity utilization is rather high in the FRG economy, the share of investment in GNP must increase substantially in order to arrive at the corrected NAIRU level. Since the profitability of investment in European Community countries has been caught in a downwards movement, it is hard to see how a boost in investment will spontaneously follow a strong demand expansion. A necessary condition for an investment boom seems to be a policy of real wage restraint — agreed upon by government, unions, and employers.

The caveats raised therefore serve as a warning against jumping from the hypothesis of unemployment persistence to the conclusion that an aggregate demand expansion will necessarily be able to lower long-run unemployment.

Notes and sources

1. For example, by O.J. Blanchard, and L.H. Summers, "Hysteresis and the European Unemployment Problem", in S. Fischer (ed.), *NBER Macroeconomic Annual 1986*, MIT Press, Cambridge, (Mass.).

2. M. Bruno, "Aggregate Supply and Demand Factors in OECD Unemployment, An Update", Working Paper No. 1696, National Bureau of Economic Research, Cambridge (Mass.), 1986; F. Modigliani, M. Monti, J. Drèze, H. Giersch and R. Layard, "Reducing Unemployment in Europe: the Role of Capital Formation", in this volume.

3. OECD, *Economic Outlook*, May, 1986, p. 31.

4. A. Lindbeck, and D.J. Snower, "Wage Setting, Unemployment and Insider-Outsider Relations", Papers and Proceedings, *American Economic Review*, May 1986, No. 76, pp. 235-239, and "Union Activity, Unemployment Persistence and Wage-Employment Ratchets", paper presented at the European Economic Association Congress, Vienna, 1986.

5. N. Gottfries and H. Horn, "Wage Formation and the Persistency of Unemployment", Seminar Paper No. 347, Institute for International Economic Studies, University of Stockholm, 1986.

6. A. Lindbeck and D.J. Snower, "Union Activity, Unemployment Persistence and Wage-Employment Ratchets", op. cit., note 4.

7. Research along these lines has been undertaken for single labour markets, as pointed out by J. Pencavel, "Wages and Employment under Trade Unionism: Microeconomic Models and Macroeconomic Applications", *Scandinavian Journal of Economics*. Vol. 87, No. 2, 1985, pp. 197-225.

8. O.J. Blanchard and L.H. Summers, op. cit., note 1.

9. See, for example, R. Solow, "Insiders and Outsiders in Wage Determination", *Scandinavian Journal of Economics*. Vol. 87, No. 2, 1985, pp. 411-428.

Work Sharing:
Why? How? How Not...

Jacques H. Drèze

I. Theory — why work-sharing?

I.1. Regular jobs

The distinction between the total number of hours worked and the number of persons employed is now part of any serious discussion of labour use and employment.[1] It has also found its way progressively into econometric practice.[2] The relevance of the distinction is brought out by the figures on hours worked per person, which reveal a steady decline both in the long run and in the recent past. (See Tables 1 and 2.)

The same distinction is relevant at the microeconomic level, both on the side of labour supply by households and on the side of labour demand by firms. At that level, it is also usefully coupled with the distinction between "regular jobs" and "casual jobs", as already developed in some detail by Hicks in *The Theory of Wages*.[3]

By a "regular job" is meant an employment relationship that is expected by both parties to have some stability and to extend over such duration as circumstances will permit, with neither party forcing termination whimsically. The stability may be guaranteed through an explicit contract. Due to the difficulty of covering enough relevant contingencies in formal terms, the typical contract will be largely implicit and rely on accepted norms of behaviour, to which both parties are expected to conform.

Table 1. Life hours of work in the United Kingdom
(thousands)

Year	Men	Women	All workers
1891	153	51	102
1911	146	46	96
1921	130	39	84
1931	126	41	83
1951	118	40	79
1961	113	40	76
1971	100	40	69
1981	88	40	64

Source: P.J. Armstrong, *Technical Change and Reductions in Life Hours of Work*. The Technical Change Centre, London, 1984.

"Casual jobs" carry no expectation of stability. They are fully defined by the performance of a specific task over a specific time span (typically short) against a given wage. Neither party commits itself, not even implicitly, to continue the relationship.

There are many cogent reasons why regular jobs are a superior form of employment relationship, *from the viewpoint of firms and workers alike*. Relevant considerations include the following:

(i)   Most jobs are performed better with the benefit of experience, including some experience specific to the workplace itself. When the job involves team work, the experience is an attribute of the team and needs to be rebuilt whenever a member of the team is replaced.

(ii)   Most firms are complex organizations, where individual workers stand in relationship with many other members of the firm (supervisors, personnel department, maintenance or inventory services, etc.). These relationships are facilitated by repeated contact.

(iii)   The employer-employee relationship is in itself complex, involving a measure of trust and mutual understanding which can only be developed gradually.

(iv)   A longer-run employment contract provides opportunities not present in short-lived contracts. Thus rewarding realized performance *ex post*, averaging between good and bad years or between periods of pressure and slack, is possible with regular, but not casual jobs.

Table 2. Annual hours worked per person: 1890-1979

	1890	1913	1929	1950	1970	1979
Austria	2,760	2,580	2,281	1,976	1,848	1,660
Belgium	2,789	2,605	2,272	2,283	1,986	1,747
Canada	2,789	2,605	2,399	1,967	1,805	1,730
France	2,770	2,588	2,297	1,989	1,888	1,727
FRG	2,765	2,584	2,284	2,316	1,907	1,719
Italy	2,714	2,536	2,228	1,997	1,768	—
Japan	2,770	2,588	2,364	2,272	2,252	2,129
Sweden	2,770	2,588	2,283	1,951	1,660	1,451
UK	2,807	2,624	2,286	1,958	1,735	1,617
US	2,789	2,605	2,342	1,867	1,707	1,607
Median	2,770	2,588	2,285	1,982	1,825	1,690

Source: A. Maddison, *Phases of Capitalist Development*, Oxford University Press, 1982.

From the viewpoint of workers, the workplace is one among many areas of life where regular relationships, developed over time on a continuing basis, are essential to the pursuit of human goals. (The foremost examples are of course the family and friendship.) Medical care, education, community relationships, trades services, leisure activities, and so on, provide additional examples. An important indirect benefit from a regular job lies in the prospects which it affords for founding a family, buying a house, establishing consumption patterns, etc. In modern economies, fringe benefits and social security benefits are more extensive for holders of regular jobs, thereby increasing their attractiveness. These benefits form a growing part of overall compensation.

It is thus safe to assume that *most individuals attach a positive value to having a regular job*. Within the context of such jobs, they supply hours (and effort) in accordance with the traditional assumption that the marginal disutility of work (relative to leisure) increases with working time, resulting in an upward sloping supply curve for hours. This eminently sensible view is not incorporated in standard textbook treatments of labour supply, because it is technically unwieldy.[4] It is however incorporated indirectly in the models of "learning by doing" and "embodied human capital", which aim at capturing the advantages of regular jobs mentioned under (i) and (ii) above, or in the models of employment over time under uncertainty, where a simple assumption of risk aversion brings in the aspects mentioned under (iii) and (iv) above.[5]

For a proper appraisal of work-sharing measures, the significance of recognizing the positive value to workers of regular jobs is twofold. First comes the immediate implication that the distribution of an aggregate number of hours over individual jobs matters to an extent imperfectly captured by the supply of hours. A distribution over more jobs carries the advantage of shorter hours and more leisure for all concerned; *in addition*, it carries the advantage of endowing more individuals with positively valued regular jobs.[6]

Second, it is important to recognize that the value attached to a regular job varies considerably, both across individuals and for given individuals over time. That different individuals may value differently the stability of employment is an immediate corollary of the diversity of tastes. There is no need to elaborate, but one specific point should be mentioned. The idiosyncracies of attitudes towards labour also concern the supply of hours. At given wage rates, different individuals would prefer different working times. Yet it is a commonplace observation that most regular jobs specify standard working times, imposed on whole sets of employees, with little room for individual variations.

Moreover, these standard working times vary little from firm to firm. There are understandable reasons for that uniformity. (Discussing them would be peripheral to my purpose). Hopefully, standard working times may reflect the preferences of a "median worker", being too long for half the labour force and too short for the other half. When faced with the choice of either working the standard time or not at all, each worker takes an all-or-none decision. Other things being equal, the net value of the job will be higher the closer standard working time comes to an individual's preferences. In particular, those who would prefer definitely shorter hours will benefit less from holding the job. It would seem plausible that older workers fall into that category and hence place a lower net value on regular jobs.

There are two additional reasons why the value to any individual of having a regular job is bound to decline as the age of retirement draws near. On the one hand, the period over which a stable relationship is anticipated becomes shorter, and hence less significant. On the other hand, the link with other durable patterns of behaviour (family, house, ...) becomes less important, as these are well established already.

The significance of individual variations in the value of regular jobs is of course that they offer prospects for gains through redistribution — a point that is central to some work-sharing measures and is taken up in Section II.1 below.

The four considerations, given above, pointing to the superiority of regular employment relationships for both firms and workers, all point to significant benefits to the firm. They also suggest two important characteristics of regular jobs.

First, *the provision of a regular job requires an initial investment on the part of the firm* — the "toll" discussed at length by Okun[7] which turns labour into a "semi-fixed factor".[8] Obviously, the benefits of experience acquired on the job, of integration in a work team and in the firm's organization, of mutual trust, or of averaging rewards over time and across states will accrue only progressively after a period of initiation. There will often be a period of training, during which a worker's productivity may be insufficient to cover his or her wage. Furthermore, because workers are heterogenous, firms will attempt to identify the more promising candidates through screening. Expenses associated with training and screening are in the nature of a fixed cost attached to each new hiring. Also, to the extent that the firm is offering some degree of income and employment stability,[9] it is undertaking a commitment which may prove costly under adverse circumstances. The present value of whatever costs or risk premium may be associated with that commitment is another component of the fixed cost of a new hiring.

144

An important implication of this initial investment, or toll, is the typical preference of firms for hiring employees on a full-time rather than a part-time basis. By "typical", I mean here that special advantages linked to part-time work must be present in order for that form of employment to be offered. (The foremost example comes from peak loads within that week, as in retailing, where part-time work is indeed widespread.) Otherwise, the initial investment is basically the same whether a person works full-time or part-time. (This is obvious for screening and training costs. It is also true for on-the-job learning. If it takes 500 hours to learn a job well, two half-time workers will need 1000 hours together; and so on.) Consequently, full-time work is altogether cheaper, and part-time work is "typically" confined to casual jobs, pending special inducements.

Second, *regular jobs are not created at will; they must correspond to some real employment prospect in the firm.* At the start, this requires the availability of a working post, the existence of demand for the output, and relative prices at which the additional job is profitable. In addition, the firm must anticipate that the additional employee will remain wanted with sufficient probability for a sufficient time. Adverse anticipations or considerable uncertainty about technological developments, demand, or relative prices would destroy the prospect of potential employment. The disconcerting fact is that so many conditions must be fulfilled *simultaneously* in order for a regular job to be forthcoming, whereas failure of any *one* condition is enough to destroy the prospect.

An important implication of the combination of real factors needed for the existence of a regular job is that the supply of such jobs is bound to be highly inelastic to their short-run cost. Specifically, temporary wage cuts or employment subsidies will not be very effective in increasing the supply of regular jobs. First, the other elements must be there (working posts and demand for output). Second, the relevant cost consideration is the long-run cost over the prospective period of employment, of which the short-run cost is only a part. Thus, temporary employment subsidies will at best move forward in time hirings that were contemplated anyway.[10] and stimulate casual employment. Desirable as these effects may be, they remain limited in scope.

These remarks also help to put the issue of severance pay in sharper perspective. It is often stressed that rights to severance pay deter firms from hiring additional workers who could profitably be employed in the short run. Clearly, if the prospect for continued employment is there, severance pay (though relevant) is not a major issue. But if the prospect for continued employment is lacking, then no regular job is at hand, irrespective of the severance pay issue. One should thus not expect a reduction of severance pay to have a major influence on the supply of regular jobs. At the same time, severance pay for casual jobs, where it exists, will deter that form of employment. There is also scope for deception about the extent to which a job is casual or regular. It is thus understandable that proposals to reduce severance rights are regarded with suspicion by unions. It might be more judicious to promote labour contracts of fixed duration instead.[11]

I.2. Short-run fluctuations

The short-run equilibrium between supply and demand for regular jobs is subject to numerous hazards — as we know only too well from recent experience. There are several independent factors affecting either the supply or the demand for regular jobs. When a number of them operate simultaneously to reduce the supply and inflate the demand, a serious imbalance may result. A long time may be needed to correct that imbalance, during which time self-perpetuating forces are apt to be at work. There are clear signs of such an unhappy combination of circumstances in the present situation.

To begin with the supply of jobs (demand for labour), four main factors should be listed as exerting macroeconomic influences. (These factors may of course affect specific labour markets differently; the point of interest here is that, when these factors affect many specific labour markets or a given country, or set of countries, in the same direction, then macroeconomic implications become noticeable.)

(i) The demand for output may be slack, due to an excess of savings over investment, to a fall in the demand for exports, to a contractionary fiscal policy, to a combination of these, etc.

(ii) Labour-saving technological progress may reduce the demand for labour at given levels of output.

(iii) Relative factor prices may induce substitution of capital for labour, or substitution of production elsewhere for production in the home country.

(iv) The capital stock physically available, or susceptible of profitable use, may become insufficient to offer an adequate number of jobs.

Looking at a given country at a given time, the first three factors may set in exogenously. (This is obvious for technological progress. The slack of final demand may originate abroad, and the shift in relative factor prices may reflect, for instance, the progress of industrialization in developing countries.) These factors may also originate in the country itself, as when domestic labour costs undergo an autonomous movement, which may in turn direct research and development towards labour-saving technological progress. In either case, the response of fiscal policy is basically an endogenous factor — but that does not guarantee the proper response! A self-perpetuating force sets in when public deficits originating in the reduced levels of employment and activity are deemed unbearable and fought through reduced public expenditure.

Most significantly, as the demand for domestic output slackens, investment is discouraged, plants are scrapped, and the capital stock is brought down to the level warranted by current output. While the low level of investment further reduces aggregate demand, the fourth factor comes into play: there are no longer enough working posts to generate adequate employment. Reflating the supply of jobs now requires investment in new capacity. The growth of employment is bound to be slow, even in the face of a demand upheaval; and demand management is discouraged by the fear that insufficient capacities lead to inflationary pressures.

Turning to the demand for jobs (the supply of labour), the main factors operating in the short run are the demographic and migratory movements and the changes in participation rates. In some European countries, female participation rates have gone up steadily over the past decades, resulting in significant increases in labour supply through the recession.

Although there is frequent reference in the literature to the so-called "discouraged worker effect", it may be the case that unemployment discourages some workers (especially married women) from *quitting* jobs which they would otherwise have given up temporarily. At the same time, unemployment may induce others to register as job seekers, even though they might otherwise have postponed entry in the labour force. In this way, unemployment becomes subject to self-perpetuation.

Regular jobs during recessions

The two characteristics of regular jobs discussed above (that they require an initial investment by the firm and that their supply is based on long-run rather than short-run cost considerations) take on additional significance when the prospect of sizeable short-run fluctuations is recognized.

First, because regular jobs entail an initial investment, prospective fluctuations shift the terms of trade against them and in favour of casual jobs. In particular, at times of high *uncertainty* about demand, technology, and real wages in the future, one may expect a temporary increase in the reliance on casual employment. Unfortunate as this development may be, given the well-founded preference of employees for regular jobs, it is to some extent unavoidable and is still compatible with efficiency. In particular, postponing the investment in a new hiring until it can be directed more effectively may be desirable. This would call for accepting a development of casual jobs during a recession, and waiting for the signs of recovery before incurring the tolls of job creation in those activities which do not benefit from the recovery.

There is some casual evidence that the private sector is relying more intensively on casual employment (including sub-contracting and contracting *ad interim*) in times of recession and uncertainty, like nowadays. In the public sector, special employment programmes make sense in such times, especially those providing casual jobs for the young. The attractiveness of these programmes comes from the relative ease and speed with which they can be set up, from their low net costs, and hopefully from the social value of the associated output.

Second, because the supply of regular jobs is inelastic to wage costs in the short run, relying on wage flexibility to clear the markets for regular jobs is not a realistic prospect. Indeed, market-clearing wages could drop to very low levels in response to a conjunction of adverse shocks. Most likely, wages could drop to a level sufficiently close to the opportunity cost of workers (including unemployment benefits) that the "market clears" because many workers become unattracted by employment (although still registered as "involuntarily" unemployed, to collect the benefits).

There are two compelling reasons why *that kind* of flexibility is undesirable. The first, of a microeconomic nature, is that it would generate an extent of income uncertainty which would place an excessive burden on workers holding regular jobs. That argument is taken up in the next section and extended to a discussion of wage discrimination between workers under contract and new recruits. The second reason of a macroeconomic nature, is that a major drop in labour incomes would depress aggregate demand further, leading to an "equilibrium" with very low levels of output and employment. The fact that the resulting unemployment can be labeled "voluntary" provides little solace. Given our imprecise estimates of the wage elasticity of labour demand and of the income multiplier, not to mention our near ignorance of the implications of wage moderation for government budgets, it is safer to look at incomes policy as a long-run instrument and not to rely on it as a short-run stabilizer of employment.

I.3. Labour contracts and market failures

Implicit (labour) contracts theory

How then does one reconcile the idea that most people want to have a regular job and stable income with the prospect of recurrent fluctuations in the demand for labour? This very question is taken up in recent theoretical work on labour contracts, known as "implicit (labour) contracts" theory.[12] The merit of that theory consists in looking at the shocks affecting labour markets *ex ante*, from the time when an employment relationship is initiated *with some prospect for duration.* A current limitation of the theory is that it looks only at employment patterns within pre-existing contracts and does not address itself to disequilibrium on the market for contracts. I shall consider the two issues successively, then sum up the argument.

The main premises of implicit contracts theory are:

(i) in the face of fluctuations in output and labour demand, regular jobs offer scope for pursuing employment and compensation policies which are Pareto optimal (economically efficient) *ex ante* from the viewpoint of the firm and its employees;

(ii) workers, being unable to diversify their labour supply, are more risk-adverse than firms, whose shareholders can hold diversified portfolios;

(iii) incentives, moral hazard, information asymmetries, the illegality of involuntary servitude, and so on, place limitations on implementable contracts.

This is not the place to review or summarize a sizeable and growing literature, to which accessible introductions are available elsewhere.[13] The main point of relevance to us here is that *efficient labour contracts will embody an element of risk-sharing*, whereby labour incomes are to a sizeable extent protected from the vagaries of supply and demand shocks. If wages were allowed to jump up and down in response to these shocks, the resulting income uncertainty would cost workers more than it would benefit the less risk-averse firms. Hence the prospect for Pareto superior arrangements, where the *labour contracts include a form of income insurance through downward wage rigidity.*

The insurance premium should be paid partly through lower wages during the early period of employment (explaining to some extent the practice of seniority bonuses), partly through reduced upward wage flexibility (to the extent compatible with incentives). A Pareto-optimal arrangement would combine an efficient degree of risk-sharing (whereby, in particular, labour incomes become immune from firm-specific risks and bear a less-than-proportional share of economy-wide risks)[14] with privately efficient levels of employment (whereas the marginal value product of labour is equal to its opportunity cost for workers at all times).

The combination of downward wage rigidity and efficient levels of employment implies that wages actually paid out do not correspond to the marginal value product of labour at all times, but only do so *in expectation*. In particular, during a recession wages in many firms will exceed the marginal value product of labour. These firms will be said to practise "labour hoarding". It is an immediate implication of the theory that such firms will not hire new workers, *even at wages lower than those which they currently pay*; new hirings will start only at wages lower than the marginal value product of labour, with all employees under contract working full hours. For these firms (which could well be a majority during a deep recession), the elasticity of employment with respect to wage decreases is zero.[15]

As for workers under contract, their employment will be cut when, but only when, their marginal value product falls below opportunity cost. With the downward rigid wage, the resulting unemployment *appears to be involuntary* — and is definitely perceived as such by the individual worker; or else, laid-off workers should enjoy full income insurance, which is seldom observed in practice (probably because firms cannot afford to supply that much insurance).

Efficient arrangements again call for work-sharing among employees under contract, who should preferably be laid-off on a part-time basis at times of slack employment, to the extent compatible with incentives and the organization of work. There are two reasons for this. First, when laid-off workers do not enjoy full income insurance, the extent of income uncertainty is reduced by laying-off two workers half-time instead of either one full-time. Second, under increasing marginal disutility of hours worked, it is Pareto-efficient to allocate work and leisure uniformly among workers. In practice, that approach seems applicable only to blue collar workers; temporary layoffs, whether on a part-time or full-time basis, are practically unknown among white collars.[16] Even part-time layoffs for blue collars are often discouraged by the rules governing unemployment compensation, which is not always forthcoming on a flexible, part-time basis.

Evidence of implementation

There is very little hard evidence on the extent to which the recommendations of implicit contract theory are implemented in

Table 3. Entrants and leavers in steel industry: EC-9

	Europe 9 1981	Europe 9 1982	FRG 1981-82	FRG %	France 1981-82	France %	Italy 1981-82	Italy %	UK 1981-82	UK %
Number of employees (end of year)	548,767	513,565	175,946		95,200		91,456		74,475	
Retirements	23,181	19,495	12,091	21	6,713	26	3,925	21	14,203	28
Early retirements	19,760	16,897	10,212	18	6,246	24	2,400	13	13,455	26
Dismissals and redundancies	19,591	11,215	6,383	11	644	2	673	3	21,555	42
Voluntary resignations	14,372	9,477	8,868	15	2,194	8	7,403	39	2,906	6
Other leavers	20,104	20,178	20,185	35	10,411	40	4,564	24	-1,045	-2
Total leavers	97,008	77,262	57,739	100	26,208	100	18,965	100	51,074	100
Total entrants	47,484	41,441	36,279		16,625		10,932		13,458	
Leavers minus entrants	49,524	35,821	21,460	12	9,583	10	8,033	9	37,616	50
Entrants minus other leavers	27,380	21,263	16,094		6,214		6,368		14,503	

Source: Eurostat, *Emploi et Chômage*, Bulletin Statistique, No. 4, 1983.

practice,[17] beyond the easy observation of widespread downward rigidity of wages, either real (as in most European countries) or nominal (as in the US). The extent to which firms use labour at marginal products below nominal wages in bad times (and conversely in good times) is not easy to ascertain, beyond the general belief (corroborated by econometric studies) that firms practise "labour-hoarding" during recessions. Neither do we know precisely how reductions of labour inputs are distributed over workers under contract — a subject on which some evidence should now be available in Europe.[18] Collecting and analyzing that evidence would seem worthwhile, if only for the light it could throw on the related issue of including the unemployed in work-sharing schemes.

A partial indication of the distribution of reductions is available at the European level for employees of the steel industry. Some recent figures are reproduced in Table 3. It is unfortunate that no details are given on the category "other leavers", whose content seems to differ between countries. (Presumably, it includes temporary layoffs in France and the Federal Republic of Germany, but not in Italy and the UK). Still, there are interesting insights. The very low level of dismissals and redundancies in France and Italy, compared with the FRG and UK, is striking. The net reduction in employment for the UK — 50% in two years — stands out. It is also interesting to note the significance of early retirements.

As for temporary layoffs and part-time unemployment, there is evidence that they move counter-cyclically. Some recent figures are reproduced in Table 4. They suggest that the phenomenon is both significant and limited in scope.

The implicit market failure

The existing literature about labour contracts does not explain why we observe prolonged spells of mass unemployment, with large numbers of workers without regular jobs (without contracts). The existing theory deals with properties of efficient contracts in economies where the markets for contracts clear; it does not deal with disequilibrium on these markets. To understand the issue of work-sharing, we must go beyond the findings of implicit contract theory and consider situations of disequilibrium on the market for regular jobs. Of course, the existing theory has useful implications for these situations as well, some of which are spelled out below. But a major extension is needed, which calls for a model with successive generations.[19]

Consider again *ex ante* the prospect of sizeable fluctuations in the supply of regular jobs (in the marginal value product of regular labour), taking into account the fact that a new generation of

Table 4. Temporary layoffs
(thousands of employees)

	FRG SESPROS[1]	France SESPROS	France INSEE[2]	Belgium IRES[3]
1973			119	33.3
1974			133.4	41.9
1975	773		427.2	82.5
1976	277	180	309	58.5
1977	231	319	136.9*	69.1
1978	191	230	162.7	69.8
1979	88	139	90.3	69.6
			57.4*	
1980	137	185	101.5*	80.3
1981	347	398	191.3	93.6
			116.2*	
1982	606	220	75.3	82.5
1983	675	233	109.1	81.7

Sources: 1. SESPROS: Eurostat, *Protection Sociale*, No. 2, 1984. These numbers are annual averages and include temporary layoffs due to weather conditions.
2. INSEE: *Enquête Emploi* (annual volumes). These numbers apply to a single week in March or April, and do *not* include temporary layoffs due to weather conditions. * denotes a single week in October.
3. IRES: A. Sonnet and PO. Defeyt, "Le marché du travail en Belgique", Bulletin No. 94, 1984.

workers will enter the labour market in the future, under conditions that may be either "good" or "bad". If conditions are "good", there will be full employment of both initially employed workers and newcomers. If conditions are "bad", there will not be enough regular jobs for everybody at full hours. How could the prospect of excess demand for regular jobs under "bad" conditions be eliminated?

The answer which is implicit in the labour contracts literature is the following. *Assume that the members of the new generation are present, or represented, when the initial labour contracts are drawn.* It will then be possible for firms to hire the newcomers *forward*, specifying the compensation and terms of employment simultaneously for the "good" and "bad" conditions. The newcomers would thus be under contract from the start, on par with earlier generations, the only difference being that actual employment of the newcomers starts later. In so far as clearing the market for contracts is concerned, all workers (the old and the new) would be treated symmetrically, and a global equilibrium could be characterized. Under that global equilibrium, everybody would work full hours under "good" conditions, *and everybody would take part in some form of work-sharing under "bad" conditions* — hopefully, to such an extent that the marginal value product of labour would be equal to the opportunity cost of *hours.* In such a world, no excess demand for regular jobs would occur in bad states; instead, a proper degree of labour-hoarding and work-sharing would be built into the private contracts, leaving no scope for public intervention. In particular, old and young would participate symmetrically in the labour-hoarding and work-sharing arrangements.[20]

Of course, the *assumption* that potential future workers take part in a market clearing process ahead of time is a preposterous idea, to say the least. Yet that is the very stretch of imagination required to rescue the "magic of the market" in our context, which is loaded with "market failures".[21]

Wage discrimination

An intriguing question, not explicitly answered by the labour contracts theory literature, is that of wage discrimination between employees under contract and new recruits. I have alluded in concluding Section I.2 to two reasons, one microeconomic and one macroeconomic, why it may not be desirable to let *wages of workers under contract* fall to market-clearing levels during recessions. But these reasons do not by themselves preclude a form of wage discrimination, whereby new contracts would stipulate wages different from those of extant contracts. Specifically, new recruits could be paid wages that clear the labour market for new contracts, while previously employed workers would keep their earlier wages. Evidence that such is not the case comes from the observation of mass unemployment and from casual empiricism to the effect that wage discrimination *by hiring dates* is not a widespread phenomenon.

Of course, some degree of discrimination by dates of hiring is consistent with the available evidence. It is also known that the quality of new recruits at given job characteristics improves during recessions and deteriorates during booms.[22] But there is no doubt that downward wage rigidity applies to new contracts as well, with limited wage discrimination *vis-à-vis* previously employed workers.

It could well be that such discrimination is regarded as impractical by firms and as undesirable by firms and workers alike. Wage settlements, including differentials by occupation and seniority, are complex enough already. Adding an extra dimension to the existing differentials would increase that complexity, to an extent possibly regarded as impractical. Moreover, it certainly goes against the grain of accepted ethical norms to accentuate pay differences for equal work.

It is, however, a direct, and to my mind compelling, consequence of implicit contract theory that some degree of wage rigidity *for new contracts* should emerge. For otherwise new firms (or expanding established firms) could hire newcomers at very low wages and outbid established firms *on the product markets*, thereby reducing further their output and employment. It is thus in the joint interest of established firms and their (unionized) employees to prevent, if they can, the wages specified in new contracts from dropping to market-clearing levels (at which all unemployment becomes voluntary). Furthermore, a majority of newcomers is apt to endorse that attempt, whenever the market-clearing wages fall very low (say, close to the level of unemployment compensation). Indeed, all workers with a reservation wage higher than or equal to the market-clearing level stand to gain from the wage rigidity, as do those with a reservation wage slightly inferior to the clearing level.[23]

The absence of market mechanisms leading to wage discrimination between workers under contract and new recruits has led to a number of proposals for *marginal employment subsidies*.[24] As I have noted above, such subsidies should be substantial and durable in order to affect significantly the long-run cost of a regular job, and hence employment. In addition, the argument presented in this section suggests that existing firms and their employees may object to such subsidies as generating unfair competition on the product markets.

Implications for job seekers

We can now summarize the implications of labour contract theory *for the workers seeking employment during a recession* (the new entrants as well as those who have lost their jobs). These job seekers are facing two kinds of firms, those engaged in labour-hoarding (which cut back employment), and those (including new firms) which hire new workers. The former, which may well be a majority during a severe recession, operate at a marginal value product of labour inferior to wage costs and equal to the opportunity cost of their employees. Routine demographic replacements, which will normally absorb all new entrants in stationary conditions, are not taking place. Newcomers are excluded both from the labour-hoarding and from whatever work-sharing is organized among employees under contract. These firms will not respond to wage cuts by new hirings until the gap between wage costs and the marginal value product of labour has been bridged. Thus competition between workers under contract and newcomers is shut off.

Expanding firms and new firms hire labour to the point where its marginal value product covers wage costs, but not beyond. They practise little or no wage discrimination between workers under contract and newcomers.

We thus have three groups of workers:

- those under contract in firms which are not hiring, where they are employed at a marginal value product below their wages;
- those employed in new and hiring firms, with a marginal value product equal to their wage; and
- the unemployed.

There are two sources of inefficiency in this situation. *First*, employment should increase in the expanding firms, to the point where the marginal value product of labour is equal to the opportunity cost of the unemployed. It is not clear how this can be achieved without some form of wage-cost discrimination between workers under contract and newcomers.

Second, the distribution of jobs and hours worked between the employed and unemployed is inefficient. Indeed, I adduced in Section I.1 some quite compelling arguments to the effect that *some* newcomers at least will place a higher value on finding a regular job than *some* workers under contract attach to keeping theirs. (In particular, young workers may be more eager to start a career than workers close to retirement are to bring their own to term.) Hence, some redistribution of regular jobs between workers under contract and newcomers would be desirable — but will not be naturally forthcoming. In addition, as the supply of *hours* is definitly upward sloping within the context of regular jobs, it would be desirable to increase the number of employees and redistribute aggregate hours among them — a standard argument. Thus, whether we look at positively valued jobs or at negatively valued hours of work, we conclude that the allocation of work between newcomers and workers under contract is inefficient.

Of course, to say that the allocation of jobs and hours is inefficient does not imply that the inefficiency can be eliminated *costlessly*. (For instance, I have noted above that firms cutting employment resort less to work-sharing than the theory might suggest, if only because temporary lay-offs are unknown for white-collar employees.) Assessing the costs would be required to define an optimal amount of work-sharing. The simpler point made here is that market failures prevent the natural emergence of optimal arrangements through private contracts and thus provide scope for intervention.

Finally, it is easy to understand why little or no work-sharing takes place among newcomers in the form of part-time jobs. With firms facing fixed costs of screening and training, and with half the newcomers prepared to work more than full-time (as must be the case if standard working time corresponds to median worker preferences), there is ample scope for mutually agreeable contracts on a full-time basis. The special motivation of risk-sharing embodied in a long-term contract would be needed to organize work-sharing in the form of part-time employment. That motivation does not apply to work-sharing in the form of part-time work for newcomers. Again, special measures will be needed to overcome the market failure and bring about a more efficient allocation of regular jobs.

The upshot of these arguments is precisely what we observe today in Europe! Namely,

• a prolonged spell of deeply depressed demand for labour,

• employment declining in many firms (especially in the manufacturing sector, exposed to international competition),

• downward rigid wages there,

• a modest degree of work-sharing among workers under contract;

• very high unemployment rates among the young entrants to the labour market (and older workers who have lost their previous jobs), and

• a fair degree of wage rigidity on new contracts.

The resulting allocation of work among all workers is definitely inefficient because little or no work-sharing takes place between workers under contract and newcomers or among newcomers finding employment. More efficient work-sharing thus requires special measures.

I.4. Scope for intervention

Market failures provide a motivation for public intervention aimed at correcting inefficiencies. In the case under discussion, that motivation is enhanced by the existence of social externalities. Unemployment is not only a burden on individuals, who are frustrated in their desire to work and to enjoy a stable employment relationship. It also entails additional real burdens for society — for instance when prolonged inactivity leads to delinquency or health deterioration. Of course, the most immediate externality comes from the existence of unemployment compensation schemes.

In the light of the arguments reviewed above, it is obvious that public unemployment compensation schemes are important and should be maintained, in spite of some obvious drawbacks.[25] This compensation accrues to the unemployed at no private cost; but it is paid out of public funds which need to be collected somehow,[26] and thus entail a social cost. This creates an externality. Any measure resulting in less unemployment also results in less public expenditure on unemployment compensation. More positively, the money spent on unemployment compensation could more profitably be spent on reducing unemployment. *One way is to subsidise work-sharing, thereby providing financial incentives to overcome the market failures.*

There are two additional reasons, specific to the issue under discussion, why public measures aimed at promoting work-sharing could *possibly* be effective.

First, in most European countries, social security has become a complex legal system, with many provisions introducing additional distortions in the already imperfect functioning of labour markets. An obvious example arises when ceilings or other regressive formulae for social security contributions (employment taxes) impose a penalty on part-time jobs as compared with full-time jobs. Eliminating those distortions which discourage work-sharing, possibly creating distortions which favour it, offers scope for public intervention.

Second, the organization of working time is a complex social phenomenon, involving coordination of all kinds of activities, with numerous externalities; it falls largely outside the sphere of market allocation. To take an obvious example, think back to the transition from the six-days week to the five-day week. Although five days became the norm for blue-collar workers shortly after World War II, it took nearly 20 years before that schedule became universal, with schools adopting it late. It is probably fair to say that consumption patterns fully adjusted to a five-day week for all are still spreading. With further reductions in working time below 40 hours per week now emerging here and there, a number of alternative patterns of work are possible. The coordination aspects and externalities provide scope for public initiative in sorting out the costs and benefits *for society* of these alternative patterns, then for public leadership in promoting the most desirable pattern and anchoring individual expectations in that respect.

These points are taken up again in Part II.

II. Applications — how and how not

Before turning to consider specific measures aimed at promoting work-sharing and recent experience with them in Europe, it is suggestive to speculate briefly on how a substantial decline in the demand for regular labour would be handled in a decidedly cooperative environment — like a kibbutz, a network of cooperatives (as in Mondragon), or an integrated set of family businesses.

Consider a hypothetical kibbutz where the major use of labour (entirely supplied by the members) goes into manufacturing of some gadget sold outside. Normally, young members are taken into the factory work-force and trained to replace retiring older members. Assume now that a non-negligible decline occurs in the need for labour input, one that was not anticipated with certainty, although its possibility may have been contemplated. Let the decline be expected to last for some time, with progressive resorption over a period of months or years at a highly uncertain speed. How would the kibbutz community react to such an event?

Most likely, a whole set of measures would be combined, such as:

• diverting some labour to other, casual uses, previously endowed with lower priority, like improving the grounds, repainting the buildings, etc.;

• excusing from work in the factory the older, less able, or less motivated workers, as well perhaps as some with high productivity alternatives (like young mothers, or members with valuable personal projects);

• reducing effective working times across-the-board, through shorter hours, longer vacations, or occasional days off;

• calling some of the young workers into the work-force on a part-time basis, with the rest of their time devoted to continued education, or to the other casual work mentioned above.

The list could be extended. The point I wish to make is that various forms of work-sharing would be introduced *naturally*; it is highly unlikely that a large number of young members would remain totally inactive for prolonged periods. There is room for speculation as to who would carry out the casual activities. Would these be mostly entrusted to the young, or would some of the members previously employed in the factory turn to such tasks? More specifically, would one observe simultaneously the introduction of some young members into the factory work-force and the diversion of some factory workers to casual tasks — either part-time or full-time? There is no compelling answer to that question. The only safe consideration is the following. If it were anticipated that future needs for labour would be qualitatively so different from current needs that training acquired now would be of little value in the future, then young workers would be mostly oriented towards casual activities and would not be trained now for factory work. This digression provides a useful background against which to evaluate the alternative forms of work-sharing which have been considered recently by European policy-makers. I will group them under three headings:

- *trading jobs*: replacing a worker under contract by a newcomer;
- *sharing jobs*: filling a single working post by more than one person; and
- *trading hours for jobs*: reducing working time for workers under contract to create new jobs.

II.1. Trading jobs

Trading jobs between workers under contract and unemployed persons is the simplest, and in a way most natural, form of work-sharing. In particular, it does not interfere at all with the organization of work. Because the value to individuals of regular jobs varies from one person to the next, there is scope for mutually advantageous trading.[27]

By definition, the holder of a regular job places a non-negative value on that job — otherwise, s(he) would quit. But that value could be small — in which case a small "bribe" would induce the holder to give up the job. If the "bribe" per year falls short of the level of unemployment compensation, the state can "buy" the job for an unemployed person, at no net cost (the compensation paid to the quitter is no longer paid to the new employee). This generates a positive externality, namely the value of the job to the new employee.

Also, the value of a job is often blown up artificially by the social legislation. For instance, some statutory pensions are proportional to average salary over the last five years prior to retirement age; consequently, quitting during these five years entails a cost far in excess of the salary itself.[28] The state could then step in to correct the externality, say by neutralizing the effect of early quitting on the pension.

These two ideas are combined in early retirement schemes, as introduced in several European countries over the past decade (in 1976 in the Netherlands and Belgium, in 1977 in the UK, in 1981 in France, complementing earlier measures, in 1984 in the FRG). As explained in Section I.1, workers close to retirement are natural candidates for giving up jobs, under moderate financial incentives (but subject to suitable adjustments in pension rules). All the schemes under consideration permit early retirement, with no loss of pension rights after the normal age of retirement and with an income allowance over the intermediate years. The level of that transitory income and its sources vary from scheme to scheme.

Typically, the basic component corresponds to unemployment compensation, with an additional allowance sometimes provided by the firm or the state. In several schemes, the retired worker must be replaced by an unemployed person (in Belgium, a young one), or else the firm must make a case that it operates with excess labour, so that early retirements are a substitute for dismissals. Although most schemes provide incentives for voluntary retirements and none makes it compulsory across the board, there are undoubtedly many cases where the worker's hand is forced by defining unappealing alternatives (being laid off, or transferred, etc.) There are also undoubtedly cases where the employer's hand is forced towards entering a programme with mandatory replacements.

I have not seen a systematic account and analysis of early retirement programmes at the European level. But the fragmentary country data which I have come across indicate clearly that these programmes can involve substantial numbers of people.

In the UK, the *Job Release Scheme*, introduced in 1976, offers a weekly allowance to older workers retiring early, provided their employer agrees to replace them by unemployed persons. The allowance is paid until the age of normal retirement and varies (from £48 to £61 per week) with family and health status. The age of eligibility for men has varied over time from 64 to 62; it is 59 for women and 60 for disabled men. Participation in the programme is entirely voluntary. Davies and Metcalf[29] refer to 272,100 *entrants* into the programme over the period 1976-1984, with 75,000 people participating in 1985. They also quote a 92% replacement ratio (new hirings per entrant) and claim that "the Job Release Scheme has the lowest net cost per person off the (unemployment) register" of all the Special Employment Programmes implemented in the UK. (In 1985, the net cost was £1,650 per person-year, obtained from a gross cost of £3,250 after netting out the savings in unemployment allowances.) They also claim that the scope of the programme could be more than doubled by extending eligibility to all men aged 60-64.

In France, several early retirement programmes have been implemented. One, with mandatory replacements, was initiated in 1981 (*Contrats de solidarité*); the others, without mandatory replacements, were initiated earlier. According to Marchand[30] as of the end of 1983 there were nearly 700,000 beneficiaries of early retirement programmes in France, namely:

Contrats de solidarité	180,000
Previous programmes:	
early retirement due to dismissals	284,000
voluntary early retirements	230,000
Total	694,000

The replacement ratio is known only for the *Contrats de solidarité*, where it is reportedly close to 95%. The ratio is of course null in cases of dismissals, and held to be relatively low under the previous schemes which did not include mandatory replacement provisions. The gross cost of these programmes, as estimated from national accounts, seems to be of the same order of magnitude as in the UK (around £3,200 per beneficiary per year). As of April 1983, the *Contrats de solidarité* programme was discontinued; instead, voluntary retirement was offered to all workers aged 60 or more having 37.5 years of labour force seniority. Apparently, no mandatory replacements are involved.

In Belgium, a number of early retirement schemes have been implemented since 1977; the age of eligibility has been mostly 60 for men and 55 for women. Except in the case of dismissals, replacements by an unemployed person aged less than 30 is mandatory. Observed replacement ratios reach 63% overall and 83% if dismissals are set aside. As of October 1984, the total number of beneficiaries was 138,000.[31]

These data are very fragmentary and leave unanswered many questions worthy of further investigation. Still, it seems safe to draw two conclusions from the British, French, and Belgian experiences. The first conclusion is that a *mandatory replacement provision seems to make a crucial difference in terms of job creation*. In contrast to the very high replacement rates quoted above for the UK, France, and Belgium, figures as low as 10 or 20% are reported for non-mandatory programmes, for instance in the Netherlands.[32]

(These figures may be partly illusory, to the extent that one might expect replacements to be staggered over time, with the high mandatory rates concealing some hirings unrelated to the scheme and the low voluntary rates failing to take account of subsequent hirings.)

The second conclusion is that the potential reduction in the effective labour supply of *workers under contract* through early retirement is definitely substantial, as witnessed by the French and Belgian figures. With legal pension schemes largely financed through redistribution rather than through accumulation, the official retirement age is (like standard working time) a "public good", hopefully corresponding to a median worker's preferences.[33] In that case, about half the labour force should have a potential interest in early retirement, at a transitory income close to retirement income, with the proportion of volunteers increasing smoothly with the income replacement ratio. Surveys conducted in France and the Netherlands confirm these common-sense observations.[34]

In the same way that the attractiveness of early retirement varies across individuals, it also varies across firms. One important aspect is the extent of seniority bonuses, which provide an inducement to replace senior workers by less costly beginners. Another aspect is the extent to which firms try to update the skill composition of their work-force; early retirements provide advance opportunities for doing so with constant employment.

Further empirical research is obviously needed to assess the practical limitations, quantitative scope, and budgetary implications of work-sharing through early retirements.

II.2. Sharing jobs

This form of work-sharing occurs whenever a single working post is filled by more than one person. Two separate issues will be considered under this heading, namely early retirement on a part-time basis with replacement on the same basis, and part-time work in general.

Part-time early retirement

In 1982, the UK introduced a Job Splitting Scheme, under which (among other provisions) a worker could retire early on a half-time basis and be replaced on the same basis by an unemployed person. After 12 months of operation, the Job Splitting Scheme had covered 578 jobs!

In 1983, the French *Contrats de solidarité*, which had been used by 180,000 people over a two-year span, were replaced by a scheme offering incentives to half-time early retirement with replacement. That scheme, parallel to the British Job Splitting Scheme, was equally unsuccessful.[35]

These experiences are definitely sobering, for progressive retirement would seem to convey a number of advantages in comparison with abrupt retirement. When reporting on the results of sample polls about the preferences of workers regarding earnings and working time, the Conference Board in Europe[36] noted that diversity of preferences is the rule. There was a single exception where a large majority emerged: in a 1979 IFO survey of German workers, *70 percent of respondents were in favour of progressive retirement!*

The apparent failure of progressive retirement schemes in France and the UK should be considered in the light of broader trends concerning part-time work.

Part-time work

Some data about part-time work in Europe are collected in the Appendix. The more striking features revealed by these data are summarized below.

(i)   Part-time workers are almost exclusively women; the percentage of men working regularly on a part-time basis is extremely small. Although that percentage has grown slightly in recent years, the growth is accounted for by older workers or younger workers in special programmes. *There is little or no indication of systematic job-sharing among men.*

(ii)   The percentage of women working regularly on a part-time basis varies substantially across countries, ranging from 40-45% in such countries as the UK and Denmark, down to 20% or less in France and Belgium. *Variations across countries are much more pronounced than variations over time.*

(iii)   High percentages of part-time work tend to be associated with above average labour force participation rates for women; when participation rates are translated into full-time equivalents, their variability across countries is sharply reduced. This observation suggests that the promotion of part-time work would increase participation rates, so that the increased employment would not be matched by a commensurate fall in unemployment.

(iv)   In a country like the UK, where part-time work of women is widespread, the percentage of part-time workers varies substantially with age and family composition. This is consistent with the hypothesis that the extent of part-time work largely reflects the preferences of workers, accommodated by firms, rather than the other way around. A more conclusive test of that hypothesis would be welcome, but is not easy to construct. In surveys in other countries where part-time work is less widespread (like the FRG and France), 40-45% of women respondents implied a desire for part-time work, close to the level observed in the UK and Denmark.

In France, the percentage of part-time workers is low, but it has increased uniformly across industries since 1980. In the UK, on the other hand, the percentage of part-time work is stationary. These observations are again consistent with the hypothesis that high rates of part-time work reflect worker preferences, with less (but growing) accommodation of these preferences (by firms, unions, or both) in the countries where part-time work is less developed.

(v)   In all countries, part-time work is more widespread in services than in industry. In all sectors, it is concentrated in jobs

164

entailing less responsibility and requiring lower qualifications. Hourly earnings of part-time workers are lower than those of full-time workers.

(vi) Hours worked by part-time workers are largely concentrated at or near the half-time mark. Yet, there is a potential supply of part-time work near the 30 hours, three-quarter mark. That supply does not seem to be matched by a corresponding demand.

(vii) An attempt was made in 1984 in the Benelux countries to hire public servants on an 80%, four days-a-week, basis. No systematic report on that experiment is available yet. Casual evidence suggests that it was not very successful due to insufficient reorganization of work. That experiment clearly deserves further study.

The conclusions emerging from this brief survey are fairly clear. Job-sharing through part-time work has not developed in Europe as a means of alleviating cyclical unemployment. It has not spread among men. The countries where part-time employment of women is growing are the countries where that form of employment is still abnormally infrequent, and where one would expect it to spread irrespective of the recession.

Although I have not seen hard data, I suspect that part-time work has not been practised either as a means of work-sharing for workers under contracts in firms with declining employment.

The reasons seem to lie in a natural preference for full-time contracts, shared by firms and male workers, and in a lack of flexibility in providing part-time jobs on a more-than-half-time basis.

If job-sharing were to be used systematically as a way of absorbing fluctuations in the supply of regular jobs, a natural approach would consist in promoting new hirings on a 75% or 80% basis, combined with reorganization of work aimed at extending sumultaneously the rate of utilization of capital. The latter measures would be particularly appropriate at times when spare capacity is scarce. Some speculative remarks on that theme are offered in Section III.2.

II.3. Trading hours for jobs

In the long run, reductions in hours worked have been an important component of welfare gains, accounting for something like 25% of overall gains by a crude estimate.[37] At the same time, these reductions have played an important role in reconciling full employment with productivity gains. (See Tables 1 and 2 above. Of course, the respective extents to which shorter hours have been triggered or permitted by technological progress are not separately identified.)

These are long-run trends. The question of interest here is short-run fluctuations. During recessions, hopefully viewed as temporary, could one stimulate employment (create jobs) by *anticipating* trend reductions in hours? Offhand, this is a tempting suggestion. In practice, it seems difficult to implement. It was tried in France in the 1930s, with little practical impact on effective working time and a questionable immediate impact on employment. Over the past decade, the theme of a 35 hours week has been the subject of much controversy, enlivened for instance by the strike of German metal workers in 1979 or by official pronouncements (of the Belgian Government in 1978, of the French Government in 1981, etc.). As of today, there is no indication that stimulating employment through shorter hours is feasible on a significant scale in the short run, and longer-run effects remain subject to much uncertainty. At best, the nature of the difficulties associated with this approach become progressively better understood.

I begin by reviewing the theoretical arguments for and against this approach, then summarize the more recent experience.

Theoretical arguments

The theoretical ground for advocating shorter hours during a prolonged recession is of course the prospect for correcting the inefficient distribution of work between employees under contract and job seekers. (It was explained in Section I.3 why the market fails to generate an efficient allocation.) If a given number of hours is to be shared more efficiently between the two groups, it seems natural to impose shorter hours on workers under contract, with identical hours for newcomers. (At least, this is more natural than laying off workers under contract to hire newcomers.) Hopefully (wishfully?), new hirings might occur in the same proportion that hours are reduced.

There is an important qualification, however. The logic of implicit contracts theory is that firms should use labour up to the point where its marginal value product is equal to the opportunity cost of workers, which is typically well below the full wage cost to firms in a recession. That logic applies to workers under contract — not to newcomers, who are hired only when their marginal value product covers their full wage cost. Consequently, if hours of workers under contract are reduced, firms operating at a marginal value product of labour below full wage costs will not hire replacements, unless the reduction in hours is sufficient to

166

bring the marginal value product of labour up to the full wage cost. Put more simply, *firms engaged in labour-hoarding will not respond to shorter hours by new hirings,* for the same reason that they do not offset natural attrition of their work force by new hirings. (Also, such firms will show relatively little reluctance to reduce hours, since they have excess labour anyhow.)

Shorter hours will induce additional hirings only in those firms which are already hiring, to offset quits or expand employment. Such firms are a minority during a prolonged recession and they are concentrated in specific sectors.[38] These firms will also show great reluctance to reduce hours. In order to increase employment, it might be preferable to create incentives for these firms to hire newcomers on a part-time basis — say 75% or 80% — with the prospect of switching to full-time work in these expanding firms as the pressure of unemployment abates.

Of course, if the newcomers had been part of a market clearing process *ex ante,* they would be part of the labour-hoarding today, and shorter hours would be an attractive alternative to layoffs. The problem is again one of asymmetry between sharing work among workers under contract versus sharing work between workers under contract and the unemployed. To overcome that asymmetry (i.e., to bridge the gap between the marginal value product of labour and full wage costs), one may consider the more radical measure of shorter hours with mandatory new hirings. That is, one may consider imposing on each firm an increase in employment by a fixed percentage, while reducing hours for all.

Clearly, measures of that kind entail a high degree of arbitrariness and are difficult to implement. To say that new entrants into the labour force would have a job today if they had been able to contract yesterday, is not to say that the employment in *every firm* would thereby be increased in *the same proportion.* (That arbitrariness would be alleviated, but not eliminated, if the hiring obligations were tradeable among firms.) Also, wages today would be different, and so on. Only if the measures under discussion had been fully anticipated could one claim that it would be non-discriminatory; but existence of a rational expectations equilibrium under proportional quantity constraints is open to question. It is also clear that once such a measure were announced as a contingent plan, it would discourage normal hirings to an extent which could be quite harmful.

Two additional pit-falls of a mandatory general reduction in hours should be mentioned.[39] The first concerns effective hours of plant utilization. In firms operating one or two shifts for a conventional number of hours, reducing weekly hours is apt to result simply in reduced plant utilization and output, with no effect on employment. (A typical example is offered by automobile plants working two shifts, with little or no possibility of keeping plant hours constant when weekly schedules of workers are reduced by a few hours.) It is only when the number of shifts is simultaneously increased that employment will rise naturally. (The limiting example is offered by plants operated on a continuous basis, where shorter hours per worker entail the need of additional employment.)

The second pit-fall concerns effective wage costs. If shorter hours result in higher hourly wage costs, whatever positive effects on employment may be associated with work-time reduction must be weighed against the negative effects associated with the wage increases. These may have two sources. On the one hand, effective wage costs may rise due to the fixed costs of hiring, training, and screening now spread over fewer hours, and due to the capital costs, similarly spread over fewer hours if plant utilization is linked to the working schedules of employees. On the other hand, workers on shorter hours may attempt to protect their disposable income by claiming higher hourly wages and a less than proportional reduction in take-home pay.

The risk that shorter hours result in higher effective wage costs will be tempered by the extent to which employment-conscious unions substitute hiring claims for wage claims. The difficult question, ultimately, is to assess the long-term incidence of hours worked on effective wage costs. The instantaneous increase arising from shorter hours at unchanged take-home pay may be partly compensated by slower wage increases thereafter, whereas the instantaneous wage moderation accompanying demands for more employment may be partly compensated by catching up later. In either case, speculation about future wage patterns is needed to draw firm conclusions.

Finally, there is a presumption that many firms are able to offset a gradual reduction in weekly hours by productivity increases without new hirings.

Recent European experience

The salient features of recent European experience with hours worked per week seem to be the following.

• Over the past 10 years, average hours worked have declined, whether measured per week or per year. (See Tables 5 and 6.) The main explanation for this decline lies in the near disappearance of overtime work. On the one hand, there was less need for overtime work due to the depressed demand for output. On the other hand, unions and governments discouraged overtime work in order to stimulate new hirings.[40]

Table 5. Annual hours worked: 1974-82

	Full-time blue-collar workers			All employees		
	1974	1982	1982/ 1974	1974	1982	1982/ 1974
Belgium	1,620	1,470	.910	1,700	1,500	.884
Denmark	1,830	1,760	.961		n.a.	
France	1,780	1,610	.905	1,820	1,700	.936
FRG	1,820	1,690	.931	1,740	1,640	.941
Italy	1,700	1,600	.949	1,690	1,650	.979
Netherlands	1,720	1,650	.959	1,790	1,670	.931
UK	1,910	1,800	.944	1,770	1,620	.917
Sweden	1,740	1,590	.913	1,630	1,530	.938
Canada	1,920	1,880	.979	1,830	1,720	.938
US	1,950	1,900	.975	1,710	1,610	.940
Japan	2,090	2,120	1.015	2,100	2,080	.992

Source: Commissariat Général du Plan, *Aménagement et Réduction du Temps de Travail*, La Documentation Française, Paris, 1985, p. 75. (From OECD data.)

Table 6. Average weekly hours worked: blue-collar workers in manufacturing
(adjusted for absences)

	1972	1975	1978	1979	1980	1981	1982
Belgium	41.7	37.1	37.6	38.1	35.7	35.9	34.9
France	45.0	42.4	41.3	41.1	40.9	40.6	39.4
FRG	43.2	40.9	42.0	42.1	41.6	41.3	40.0
Ireland	—	42.2	43.4	43.4	42.3	42.5	41.7
Italy	41.9	41.5	39.4	39.7	38.4	38.6	37.5
Luxemburg	43.9	40.9	40.2	40.8	40.2	40.6	39.0
Netherlands	43.9	40.8	41.1	41.1	40.8	40.7	40.6
UK	43.0	41.8	42.2	42.0	40.7	41.4	41.4

Source: Eurostat, "Gains horaires, durée du travail", No. 2, 1983.

• In those cases where a reduction in hours with mandatory new hirings has been put forward, it has met with adamant opposition from employers. A proposal by the Belgian Government in 1979 to subsidize a reduction of the standard working week from 40 to 38 hours, with new hirings corresponding to 3% of extant employment, was rejected by the employers and some unions.[41] When offered to individual firms on a voluntary basis, the proposal met with negligible success. In France, the *contrats de solidarité* in 1982 offered inducements to new hirings offsetting either reductions in working time or early retirement. Out of some 12,500 contracts signed by September 1982, only 4.5% were concerned with shorter hours, while 10 times as many new hirings resulted from early retirements.[42]

• Where a reduction in standard hours was introduced without mandatory new hirings, it seems to have been conducive to very few new hirings in the short run (with one exception, mentioned below). At least, *those who have looked for evidence of the new hirings do not seem to have found it.* Such was the case, in particular, for surveys conducted in Belgium in 1980 and more recently in France.[43] The only clear cases of new hirings came from firms operating on a continuous basis with several shifts. Shorter hours per shift necessarily implied some new hirings, but they were less than proportional.[44]

These findings are sobering, and confirm the theoretical warnings that reductions in hours will not create many jobs in the short run. At the same time, advocates of shorter hours seem to proceed from a *presumption* that shorter hours per week somehow imply more jobs in the long run — other things being equal. The reasoning apparently calls on arithmetic. The analogy with wages is instructive. The short-run elasticity of employment with respect to real wages is generally believed small, whereas the long-run elasticity at constant output should be close to unity on grounds of constant factor shares. Similarly, the short-run elasticity of employment with respect to hours per week is apparently small, for the reasons just indicated, whereas the long-run elasticity should be close to unity on grounds of arithmetic. Both arguments of course assume that productivity, technology, and output are related to wages or hours, and departures from these assumptions may well prove significant in the long run. Moreover the arithmetic *presumption* rests on the unproven *assumption* that hours and workers are perfect substitutes.

This is an area where uncertainties are substantial. Several attempts have been made to throw some light on the issue by simulating macroeconomic models.[45] Simulations typically compare employment forecasts, with and without reductions in weekly hours, under alternative assumptions about wage developments. Sometimes explicit hypotheses about the elasticity of output with respect to hours are also introduced.

My own attitude towards these simulations is one of polite scepticism. Too little is known about the elasticity of employment with respect to weekly hours *in a context of general recession* for these simulations to be reliable. Estimates of production functions where hours and numbers of employees appear as separate arguments, based on time series data covering the past thirty years, are not apt to measure that elasticity accurately, and I have not seen estimates based on recent microeconomic data. Accordingly, I regard the fragmentary information from the surveys mentioned above, concerning government subsidies for reduced hours, as more instructive for short-run purposes and I refrain from drawing long-run conclusions.

III. Policy prospects and conclusions

Hopefully, Part I of this essay may have convinced the reader that:

• some form of work-sharing could be used for efficient absorbtion of sizeable fluctuations in the demand for labour;

• market institutions fail to organize work-sharing between workers under contract and the job-seekers, or among job-seekers themselves; and

• there is scope for public intervention in correcting that market failure through promotion of work-sharing during deep recessions.

It is thus not surprising that interest in work-sharing as a means to alleviate unemployment should be lively in Europe today and that a set of specific measures meant to promote work-sharing should have been introduced by European governments. The brief review of our experience with these measures in Part II reveals three basic findings.

• Early retirement schemes with some form of income mainte-nance have pulled large numbers of senior workers out of the labour force and have led to roughly commensurate numbers of new hirings, but only when the schemes specified mandatory replacements.

• Part-time work has not spread as a means of sharing work among job-seekers, or between job-seekers and workers under contract. (The total failure of part-time early retirement schemes being particularly striking.)

• Those who have looked for evidence of job creations induced by reductions in weekly hours have not found any appreciable short-run effects. This leaves open the question of potential longer-run effects, which is surrounded by the related uncertainties of capital utilization, wage costs, and productivity adjustments.

These empirical findings are generally consistent with theoretical considerations, to the extent that:

• the (positive) value of holding a regular job varies substantially across individuals and over an individual's working life, suggesting in particular that a substantial proportion of the members of the older generations could be induced at little cost to hand over their jobs to new recruits;

• the fixed costs of hiring and training deter firms from using part-time labour outside of special circumstances (like peak loads within the week), whereas enough workers eager to work full time are forthcoming;

• firms engaged in labour-hoarding, which may well be in a majority during deep recessions, will not respond to shorter hours (or lower wages,) by new hirings; firms which are hiring new employees will resist reductions in hours.

It is always comforting for an economist to reconcile facts with theoretical predictions. It is definitely useful to understand better why some measures prove relatively effective and others do not. Looking at the issues of work-sharing from the viewpoint of contracts for regular jobs seems helpful on that score.

At the same time, it is discomforting to be left with a situation where clearly identified market failures offer scope for Pareto improvements through intervention, but where the effectiveness of intervention is limited in the short run. Such a situation seems to prevail on the work-sharing front.

III.1. Short-run implications

There are four immediate implications of this essay for policy purposes.[46]

Early retirement with mandatory replacement stands out as the most promising approach to work-sharing in the short run. In several countries, that approach has hardly been used. It offers a genuine prospect for some alleviation of unemployment, especially youth unemployment, if replacements are reserved for the young. More detailed work aimed at quantifying that prospect, both as to numbers and costs should be encouraged.

Shorter weekly hours stand out as the least promising and most uncertain approach to work-sharing in the short run. This approach should not be used indiscriminately. It will produce positive employment effects in those sectors (including metal working?) where plants are operated on a continuous basis, but it will produce negative output effects without gains in employment in those sectors where hours of plant utilization are given by the working week. Moreover, longer-run effects will be negative if shorter hours imply higher effective hourly wage costs.

If one accepts the view that firms engaged in labour-hoarding will not respond to either lower wages or shorter hours by new hirings, *one should concentrate the promotion of work-sharing on expanding and new firms.* In these firms, part-time work by the new employees may well be the more natural pattern of work-sharing.

The potential for part-time work to alleviate unemployment, which could be substantial, has not been exploited at all in recent European experience. This is particularly disappointing since part-time early retirement would seem so much more natural and appealing than abrupt early retirement. Given the substantial measure of success met by early retirement programmes and the overwhelming interest expressed by workers for gradual retirement, it is doubly disappointing to observe the total failure of the timid attempts in that direction. *Although efforts to promote part-time work are bound to be slow in producing their effects,* because they call for substantial reorganization of work, *such efforts are worth undertaking in a long-run perspective.*

III.2. Long-run implications

From the longer-run viewpoint, three interrelated questions must be faced, to which only speculative answers can be given today.

• How long will it take to restore a measure of full employment in Europe (say, with unemployment rates for the young of 5% or so)?

• Will the historical trend towards a shorter working week maintain itself in the future?

• How seriously should we entertain the prospect of other deep recessions, comparable to those of the 1930s and the 1980s, in the future?

If one fears that full employment will not be restored in Europe for several years to come (and this is my personal reading of the EC forecasts), and that deep recessions may occur again (for the reasons explained in Section I.2), then one should look seriously at part-time work as a means of sharing jobs during such recessions. If in addition one fails to see why the historical trend towards shorter hours should come to a halt, then one should take seriously the issue of maintaining the periods of use of capital and of provision of services. Indeed, as the working week becomes shorter, it is increasingly important to uncouple individual working hours from the period of business activity (over which capital is used and services are provided). For otherwise overhead costs will creep up and the benefits of additional leisure will be partly offset by the deterioration in availability of services. This remark is linked to the previous one because *uncoupling individual working hours from the period of business activity is bound to open up new prospects for part-time work*, at a gain in overall efficiency as well as in labour-markets flexibility.

A number of schemes to that effect have been proposed, ranging from the generalization of half-day shifts six days a week, to rotating vacation periods of up to three months per year.[47] The most appealing scheme to my mind would be a generalization of the four day working week with six days of activity. A working post then corresponds to one full-time and one half-time job, or two 75% jobs, or three half-time jobs, or one and a half full-time jobs with three full-timers filling two working posts. Aside from the obvious advantages of reducing commuting time for workers by 20% and increasing the use of capital by up to 35% (six days of nine hours versus five days of eight hours), this scheme would generate flexibility in the provision of part-time work, especially on a 75% basis. Hopefully, it would also generate flexibility in the provision of part-time early retirement and facilitate job-sharing through part-time work among the new employees of expanding and new firms. A new perspective would thus be opened for resorting to part-time work as a means of work-sharing to absorb fluctuations in the markets for regular jobs. A theme of the present paper is that such a perspective is needed, but not easy to find.

Of course, a four-day week with six days of activity is a highly speculative as well as controversial proposal. It is speculative because we lack solid information, beyond the isolated experience of a few firms which have chosen to operate on that basis for reasons of their own.[48] It is controversial because six days of activity means Saturday work (typically two weeks out of three) and a reversal of the trend towards longer weekends with less and less organized activity then. Reversing that trend has an obvious welfare cost, which must be weighed against the associated efficiency gains. On the other hand, it may be indispensable to protect the period of activity and the use of capital if the working week is to be reduced further; and it may be natural to reduce working time further as technological progress accelerates.

174

I have no particular authority to discuss this speculative proposal. But I refer back to two points made earlier, which are of relevance here. The first is that, in a world where firms and (male) workers have a common preference for full-time regular jobs, temporary reliance on 75% jobs when there is excess supply of labour will require inducements of some kind or other. It is a challenging task to think through a coherent approach to this issue. The open questions are numerous and the answers are not obvious. At a time when only three out of four new entrants into the labour force are employed, if one had a four day week with six days of activity, should one penalize full-time work or subsidize part-time work, or both? If there is a penalty, should it be levied on the employer or the employees, or is that issue immaterial? Should hours above the average effectively worked, including the unemployed, carry social security benefits, like rights to pensions and unemployment compensation? A whole set of intriguing questions arise which require a logic combining *ex ante* risk-sharing considerations and incentives considerations.

The second point made earlier (Section I.4) is that a major reorganization of work involves numerous externalities and therefore calls for guidelines and cooperation from the public sector. In particular, a four-day week with six days of activity requires a new coordination beween production activities, services, leisure activities, schools, etc. Such coordination can only evolve over time and is facilitated if the pattern is known ahead of time. It also involves the public sector directly, through the provision of public services. It would certainly make sense at this time for the post office, administrative services open to the public, and the like to consider six days of activity with more reliance on part-time workers.

This may well be the *only* fruitful direction in which thinking about the working week should be oriented. As I said, the suggestion is speculative *at best*. Moreover, it is not clear that governments are able to implement such far-reaching policies. But there are obvious merits to channelling the current debate about work-sharing in those directions which experience and theory alike suggest are the more realistic.

Appendix: part-time work in Europe

(The six sections of this appendix correspond to the six paragraphs on pages 160 and 161.) Tables 7–20 are on pages on 180 to 187.)

1.   An overview of the extent of part-time work in Europe and of trends over the last decade, is presented in Table 7. This gives the proportion of male and female employees working part-time in nine European countries over the period 1973-1983. The percentages for men are uniformally low and hardly rising. The percentages for women are 10 times as high on average and rising in some, but not all, countries. Table 9 shows that the share of women in the total number of part-time employees is accordingly high in all countries.

A further indication is provided by Table 8, which gives the percentage of male and female part-time workers in four age groups in the 10 EC countries in 1983.   The contrast between the situation for men and women is now much sharper. Rates of part-time work for men are lowest in the "prime age" group (25-49), highest after retirement age, and next highest among the young (14-24).   For women, the rates are rising continuously with age; in the prime age group, the 1983 figures stand uniformly above the average rates of Table 7.

2.   Tables 7 and 8 reveal that the percentage of active women working part-time varies substantially across countries, ranging from 40-45% in the UK and Denmark down to 20% in France and Belgium. One would like to understand the nature and the causes of these inter-country differences.

3.   A first observation is that high rates of part-time work tend to be accompanied by high rates of labour force participation. Table 10 lists side by side the gross labour force participation rates (GPR) for women in nine European countries and the proportion of employed women working part-time (PPT). The data are reproduced in Figure 1, together with the regression line GPR = 16 + .43 PPT. In order to compute an adjusted labour force participation rate (APR), I have treated part-time employees as if they worked half-time and have assumed identical unemployment rates among full-time and part-time workers. The results of the computations are given in column (3). Figure 2 reproduces the data on APR and PPT, together with the regression line APR = 18 + .2 PPT (where the coefficient .2 is not significant). Thus, adjusted participation rates are not significantly affected by the extent of part-time work. The relationship of gross to average participation rates is depicted in Figure 3, where the regression line GPR = -4 + 1.35 APR gives a very good fit. (Thus gross participation rates are adequate for comparison purposes, but somewhat misleading for assessing levels.)

4.   In all countries, labour force participation rates of women vary with age and marital status (Table 11); these variations are quite systematic. (In the age group 14-24, married women display the highest participation rates; in the age group 25-49, single women display the highest rate and married women the lowest; after 50, single women display the highest rate while the rates for married women, widows, and divorcees are equal.)

176

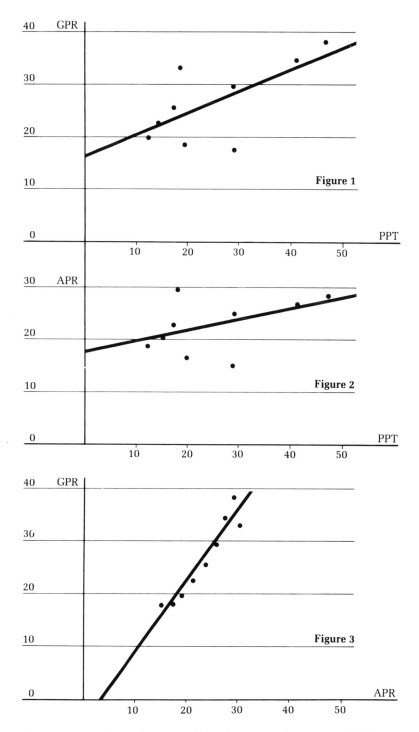

Figures 1-3. Labour-force particiaption rates for women: EC9

177

In the UK, the high percentage of part-time women workers conceals substantial differences related to marital status. Table 12 reveals a percentage of 50% for married women, as against 20% for unmarried women. The difference is most pronounced at young ages and declines steadily to near equality. Equally striking differences emerge in Table 13, where the variables of classification are marital status and the age of the youngest child. Married women with young children are most inclined to work part-time; unmarried women with no young children are least inclined to do so. It seems difficult to impute all these differences to the behaviour of individual employees and much more natural to see them as reflecting workers' preferences.

Survey data about preferred working time, collected in countries where part-time work is less prevalent, point towards the same conclusion. Thus, in a survey conducted in the Federal Republic of Germany in 1978 (the results of which are summarized in Table 14) some 40% of women respondents expressed a preference for working less than 35 hours a week. (The corresponding percentage for men is 14%). 40% is very close to the actual part-time percentage in the UK. Analyzing the results of a survey conducted in France in the same year, Baroin concludes that the percentage of active women working part-time could easily double, if the demand for that kind of job were accommodated.[49] (Because 60% of the increase would come from women switching from full-time to part-time work, no change in output is at stake.) If doubled, the percentage of employed women working part-time in France would come close to the actual British level.

One naturally wonders whether the growth in the rate of part-time work of women in countries like Belgium, France, and the Federal Republic is due to a generalization of that pattern of work, or whether it simply reflects the more rapid growth of sectors where that pattern is more prevalent (like retail trade). French data, available annually for 38 sectors, answer that question unequivocally: the proportion of part-time workers for 1983 is the same, whether the proportions in individual sectors are weighted by employment for the sector in 1983, in 1980, or in 1975 (namely, .200, .198, and .197); the same results hold for services (namely, .209, .208, and .209) and nearly so for industry (.113, .112, and .107). (See Table 15.) There is thus clear evidence of an economy-wide generalization of part-time work, probably reflecting growing accommodation of workers' preferences.

5.   The higher rates of part-time work in services than in industry apply to all European countries and to men as well as women. This is shown in Table 16 where the single diverging observation concerns men in Greece.

The facts that part-time workers hold jobs of lesser responsibility (Table 17), requiring less education (Table 18), and yielding lower pay (Table 19), seem fairly robust. In particular, they are verified across sectors or occupations.

6.   Data on hours worked by women employees with regular part-time jobs (Table 20) reveal a high concentration (45 to 50%) near the 20 hours mark and a very low concentration in the 30-34 hours range. The country data (not reproduced, but available from the same source) are homogeneous in that respect. This may be contrasted with the expressed preference of Table 14. Interpreting the preference for 35 hours or more

as a preference for full-time work, one would be left with more than 50% of the part-time workers in the 30-34 hours range (20.6 out of 38.7 percent of the sample). It would seem that women eager to work 30 to 34 hours end up either working half-time or working full-time — probably due to lack of opportunities.

Table 7. Proportion of employees working part-time, by sex: 1973-83
(% of total employment, same sex, regular and casual jobs)

	Men						Women					
	1973	1975	1977	1979	1981	1983	1973	1975	1977	1979	1981	1983
Belgium	1.0	1.0	1.2	1.0	1.3	2.0	10.2	13.0	16.7	16.5	16.3	19.7
Denmark	—	4.7	5.4	5.2	5.6	6.6	—	45.2	46.3	46.3	46.5	44.7
France	2.6	3.0	3.1	2.5	2.3	2.5	14.7	16.7	17.8	17.0	17.4	20.0
FRG	1.8	1.9	1.8	1.5	1.6	1.7	24.4	26.7	28.3	27.6	28.9	30.0
Ireland	—	2.6	2.7	2.1	—	2.7	—	16.9	18.9	13.0	—	15.6
Italy	3.7	3.4	3.3	3.0	2.9	2.4	14.0	12.7	11.9	10.6	10.1	9.4
Luxemburg	1.3	1.3	1.3	1.0	—	1.2	19.4	17.6	14.4	18.1	—	18.0
Netherlands[1]	2.4	2.4	2.5	2.8	9.7	6.9	26.3	28.8	28.3	31.6	49.0	50.3
UK	2.3	2.3	2.3	1.9	3.1	3.3	39.2	41.0	40.8	39.0	40.0	42.1
EC-9	—	2.6	2.6	2.2	2.8	2.8	—	26.0	26.4	25.6	26.7	27.6

Note: 1. In the Netherlands, a change in definitions occured between 1979 and 1981.
Source: Eurostat,"Labour Force Sample Survey", *Emploi et Chômage*, No. 2, 1985.

Table 8. Proportion of employees working part-time, by sex and age: 1983

	Men				Women			
	14-24	25-49	50-64	65 up	14-25	25-49	50-64	65 up
Belgium	3.8	1.4	1.9	13.8	14.7	20.4	23.2	37.5
Denmark	20.2	2.7	4.8	20.5	30.2	44.5	54.4	46.5
France	4.5	1.4	3.0	37.6	14.4	19.6	25.2	39.2
FRG	1.5	0.9	1.6	39.4	6.0	36.7	36.5	55.7
Greece	6.7	2.4	3.3	16.7	10.1	10.9	13.0	51.4
Ireland	5.8	1.6	2.6	—	6.9	19.4	27.3	—
Italy	3.7	1.1	3.1	25.3	7.8	29.8	13.1	29.9
Luxemburg	—	—	—	—	6.7	22.2	20.0	—
Netherlands	11.0	5.3	7.5	46.4	22.0	59.9	66.1	55.6
UK	6.0	1.0	2.6	57.9	15.9	47.1	51.1	74.5
EC-10	4.6	1.4	2.8	35.8	12.1	29.8	34.8	—

Source: Eurostat, *Emploi et Chômage*, No. 2, 1985.

Table 9. Proportion of women among part-time employees: 1972-83

	1972	1975	1977	1979	1981	1983
Belgium	82.4	85.1	87.0	89.3	85.8	84.0
Denmark	—	86.8	85.4	86.9	86.9	84.7
France	77.9	78.0	78.8	82.0	83.3	84.6
FRG	89.0	89.6	90.5	91.6	91.9	91.9
Ireland	—	71.4	73.7	71.2	—	70.7
Italy	58.3	58.7	61.3	61.4	61.4	64.8
Luxemburg	83.3	85.7	83.3	87.5	—	80.0
Netherlands[1]	80.2	81.4	81.1	82.5	69.4	78.3
UK	90.9	91.5	91.9	92.8	89.6	89.6
EC-9	—	84.7	85.3	86.8	84.8	85.7

Note: 1. In the Netherlands, a change in the definitions occured between 1979 and 1981.
Source: Eurostat, "Labour Force Sample Survey", *Emploi et Chômage*, No. 2, 1985.

Table 10. Adjusted labour-force participation rates for women: 1977

	Gross participation rate (1)	Proportion of part-time employees (2)	Adjusted participation rate (3)	Un-employment rate (4)
Belgium	25.7	16.7	23.3	10.9
Denmark	38.2	46.3	28.6	8.9
France	33.0	17.8	29.9	6.1
FRG	29.5	28.3	25.2	3.8
Ireland	18.6	18.9	16.7	7.4
Italy	19.9	11.9	18.7	7.0
Luxemburg	22.4	14.4	20.8	1.5
Netherlands	17.6	28.3	15.0	3.3
UK	34.7	40.8	27.3	4.4
EC-9	28.5	26.4	24.5	5.3
Mean absolute deviation (unweighted)	6.63	10.04	4.55	—

Definition: $(3) = (1) \left[1 - .5\,(2) \left\{ 1 + \frac{(4)}{100} \right\} \right]$
Source: Eurostat, "Labour Force Sample Survey", *Emploi et Chômage*, No. 2, 1985.

Table 11. Labour-force participation rates for women, by marital status and age: 1983

	Single					Married					Other				
	14-24	25-49	50-64	65 up	Total	14-24	25-49	50-64	65 up	Total	14-24	25-49	50-64	65 up	Total
Belgium	27.6	81.3	45.7	—	33.8	76.1	56.5	17.8	(1.1)	40.1	(68.6)	67.9	17.3	(0.7)	16.3
Denmark	54.6	88.0	53.6	—	59.1	86.8	85.6	51.5	5.9	65.0	—	89.0	46.1	(1.7)	32.8
France	38.4	87.0	58.4	5.1	48.3	67.1	63.8	36.8	2.0	49.7	76.8	85.0	41.8	1.5	26.5
FRG	44.8	85.1	58.2	4.6	49.6	58.6	53.3	31.2	3.4	42.1	69.5	77.8	33.4	2.1	21.8
Greece	34.8	74.4	32.3	—	41.7	29.2	41.0	31.4	12.6	34.5	—	63.7	23.5	3.8	14.9
Ireland	50.3	85.5	52.0	(8.5)	53.5	46.8	28.9	17.1	—	24.7	—	50.3	24.7	(3.6)	13.2
Italy	38.8	75.0	36.8	3.6	42.7	43.9	43.7	19.1	2.7	32.4	(42.4)	72.6	19.5	1.4	13.2
Luxemburg	47.3	87.0	51.2	—	51.7	58.8	36.4	13.3	—	28.3	—	72.8	(19.2)	—	18.7
Netherlands	40.5	84.3	47.5	—	47.1	62.5	39.9	16.5	(1.0)	31.4	(46.2)	49.4	15.8	(0.8)	15.2
UK	53.0	83.2	47.2	3.5	52.6	54.3	60.9	45.2	3.8	49.0	35.9	65.7	38.6	2.8	20.0
EC-10	43.1	82.5	48.8	4.1	47.8	56.6	53.9	31.4	3.3	42.2	59.0	74.5	32.2	2.0	20.4

Note: Figures in parentheses are based on small cells, i.e., the part of the overall sample falling in this category is small.
Source: Eurostat, *Emploi et Chômage*, No. 2, 1985.

Table 12. Proportion of female employees working part-time in the UK, by marital status and age: 1977

Age	Married	Unmarried
14-19	17.2	4.1
20-24	19.3	4.3
25-34	51.5	14.9
35-44	57.5	20.7
45-54	48.0	21.5
55-59	49.4	33.3
60-64	64.7	50.0
65 up	80.2	70.5
Total	50.2	21.1

Source: J.P. Jallade (ed.), *L'Europe à temps partiel*, Economica, Paris, 1982, p. 132.

Table 13. Proportion of women aged 16-59 working part-time in the UK, by marital status and age of youngest child: 1977

Age of youngest child	Married	Unmarried
0-4	78	49
5-9	70	52
10-15	56	35
16 up	52	34
No dependent child	31	6

Source: J.P. Jallade (ed.), *L'Europe à temps partiel*, Economica, Paris, 1982, p. 149.

Table 14. Preferences about working hours expressed by FRG sample survey of respondents: 1978

Preferred length of working week, hours	Men	Women
less than 20	0.9	1.3
20-24	1.2	9.3
25-29	1.7	7.5
30-34	10.1	20.6
35-39	47.3	37.7
40 up	38.8	23.6
	100.0	100.0

Source: J.P. Jallade (ed.), *L'Europe à temps partiel*, Economica, Paris, 1982, p. 76.

Table 15. Role of sectoral distribution in growth of part-time work in France: 1975-83

Average proportion of active women working part-time		Economy-wide (38 sectors)	Industry (23 sectors)	Services (14 sectors)
Unweighted	1975	.107	.077	.144
	1980	.120	.093	.152
	1983	.140	.104	.184
Weighted by current employment	1975	.154	.078	.163
	1980	.162	.086	.173
	1983	.200	.113	.209
Weighted by 1975 employment	1980	.161	.081	.174
	1983	.197	.107	.209
Weighted by 1980 employment	1983	.198	.112	.208
Standard deviation of sectoral proportions	1975	.067	.057	.039
	1980	.079	.082	.043
	1983	.076	.064	.042

Source: Calculations based on INSEE, *Enquêtes sur l'Emploi*.

Table 16. Percentage of part-time employed persons among employed persons, by sex and sector: 1983

	Men			Women		
	Industry	Services	Total[1]	Industry	Services	Total[1]
Belgium	1.0	2.7	2.0	9.0	22.3	19.7
Denmark	3.5	9.0	6.6	33.3	47.5	44.7
France	1.2	3.1	2.5	11.3	20.9	20.0
FRG	0.7	2.0	1.7	6.2	31.9	30.0
Greece	4.4	2.1	3.7	8.4	12.1	12.1
Ireland	1.8	3.0	2.7	7.5	14.6	15.6
Italy	1.4	1.8	2.4	6.0	8.0	9.4
Luxemburg	—	(1.2)	(1.2)	(12.1)	17.5	18.0
Netherlands	3.0	9.5	6.9	38.9	51.3	50.3
UK	1.3	5.1	3.3	26.1	46.0	42.1
EC-10	1.3	3.4	2.8	18.0	30.3	27.6

Note: 1. Includes agriculture.
Source: Eurostat, *Emploi et Chômage*, No. 2, 1985.

Table 17. Distribution of blue-collar women by job qualification, FRG: 1978

| | Job qualification[1] | | | |
	I	II	III	Total
Industry				
Full-time workers	6.5	41.8	51.5	100
Part-time workers	5.6	38.5	55.8	100
Total	6.3	41.2	52.3	100
Services[2]				
Full-time workers	11.9	20.7	67.3	100
Part-time workers	5.3	12.5	82.0	100
Total	8.1	15.9	75.7	100

Notes: 1. I = Highly specialized jobs with genuine responsibility; II = skilled jobs;
III = unskilled jobs.
2. Trade, banks, and insurance.
Source: J.P. Jallade (ed.), *L'Europe à temps partiel*, Economica, Paris, 1982, p. 120.

Table 18. Distribution of female employees by education, UK: 1978

Educational group: highest degree received	Percentage of women in given educational group working		Percentage of given educational group among all women working	
	full-time	part-time	full-time	part-time
University	81.7	18.3	4.5	1.5
Non-university higher education	70.0	30.0	10.7	6.9
High school:				
complete	82.8	17.2	4.1	1.3
incomplete	69.2	30.8	15.3	10.2
2 years	62.7	37.3	12.6	11.3
No degree	53.5	46.5	52.8	68.8
Total	60.0	40.0	100.0	100.0

Source: J.P. Jallade (ed.), *L'Europe à temps partiel*, Economica, Paris, 1982, p. 142.

Table 19. Earnings of female employees in the UK: 1977

	Average weekly hours		Average hourly earnings (£)		
	full-time	part-time	full-time	part-time	ratio[1]
Food and beverages	38.1	21.7	1.21	1.08	.89
Electrical appliances	38.5	22.4	1.23	1.17	.96
Textiles	38.3	22.8	1.08	1.02.	.94
Garments, shoes	37.9	24.8	1.02	0.98	.96
Transport, communication	37.2	21.1	1.45	1.16	.80
Retail trade	37.9	20.9	1.03	0.91	.88
Banks, insurance	35.4	20.0	1.38	1.13	.82
Professional services	35.3	19.5	1.66	1.21	.73
Other services	37.9	20.8	1.17	0.98	.84
Public servants	37.0	19.8	1.47	1.19	.81
Total	36.8	20.4	1.37	1.09	.80
Whole economy	36.9	20.6	1.34	1.09	.81

Note 1. Part-time/full-time.
Source: J.P. Jallade (ed.), *L'Europe à temps partiel*, Economica, Paris, 1982, p. 139.

Table 20. Distribution of hours worked by women employees with regular part-time jobs, EC-9: 1981

	Industry	Services
0	6.7	7.1
1-14	12.5	23.1
15-19	36.7	35.0
20-24	11.9	11.6
25-29	23.2	16.6
30-34	3.7	2.6
35 up	5.3	4.0
	100.0	100.0

Source: Eurostat, Labour Force Sample Survey, *Emploi et Chômage*, No. 2, 1985.

Notes and sources

1. OECD, *Employment Outlook*, Paris, 1983, and *Employment Growth and Structural Change*, OECD, Paris, 1985.

2. See R.C. Fair, *The Short-Run Demand for Workers and Hours*, North-Holland Publishing Company, Amsterdam, 1969, for an early account.

3. J.R. Hicks, *The Theory of Wages*, Macmillan, London, 1932, pp. 63-74.

4. More precisely, a worker's utility function should be specified in terms of two distinct arguments, namely hours of casual work h_c and hours worked under a regular job h_r. Although utility may be assumed diminishing in both arguments, there is a jump (discontinuity) at $h_r = 0$:

$$U = \begin{cases} u(\cdot, h_c), \ h_r = 0 \\ k + u(\cdot, h_c, h_r), \ h_r > 0. \end{cases}$$

(More generally, two distinct functions could be used; or else, the benefits flowing from a regular job should be spelled out explicitly.)

5. The standard reference on "firm-specific human capital" is G.S. Becker, *Human Capital*, Columbia Univerisity Press, New York, 1964; see also R.A. Hart, *The Economics of Non-Wage Labour Costs*, George Allen and Unwin, London, 1984.

6. There are, of course, offsetting disadvantages, including those implied on page 13.

7. A.M. Okun, op. cit., Chapters 2 and 3.

8. W.Y. Oi, "Labor as a Quasi-Fixed Factor", *Journal of Political Economy*, 70 (6), 1962, pp. 538-555; see also R.A. Hart, op. cit., or C.C. Holt, F. Modigliani, J.F. Muth, and H. Simon, *Planning Production, Inventories and Work Force*, Prentice-Hall, Englewood Cliffs, 1960, for an early application at the firm level.

9. See Section I.3. below.

10. See L. Phlips, "Selective Manpower Policies in Germany, with Special Reference to Wage-Cost Subsidies" in *European Labour Market Policies*, National Commission for Manpower Policy, Washington DC, 1978, pp. 223-258.

11. These remarks apply to new contracts. Reducing severance rights of employed workers is apt to promote dismissals, not employment.

12. See, C. Azariadis, "Implict Contracts and Underemployment Equilibria", *Journal of Political Economy*, 83 (6), 1975, pp. 1183-1202; M. Baily, "Wages and Employment under Uncertain Demand", *Review of Economic Studies*, 41 (1), 1974, pp. 35-50

and D.F. Gordon, "A Neo-Classical Theory of Keynesian Unemployment", *Economic Inquiry*, 12 (4), 1974, pp. 431-459 for the seminal contributions; J.H. Drèze "Human Capital and Risk-Bearing", *The Geneva Papers on Risk and Insurance*, 12, 1979, pp. 5-22 for a non-technical presentation of the main ideas; and the more recent accounts in the *Quarterly Journal of Economics*, Supplement 1983, or in the surveys by C. Azariadis, "Implicit Contracts and Related Topics: A Survey" in *The Economics of the Labour Market*, Z. Hornstein *et al.* (eds), HMSO, London, 1979; T. Ito, "Implicit Contract Theory: A Critical Survey", University of Minnesota, 1982; and S. Rosen, "Implicit Contracts: A Survey", *Journal of Economic Literature*, 23 (3), 1985, pp. 1144-1175.

13. Violation of this condition is a major drawback of the otherwise attractive profit-sharing scheme advocated by M.L. Weitzman, *The Share Economy: Conquering Stagflation*, Harvard University Press, Cambridge, 1984. Firm-specific risks should not matter to holders of diversified portfolios. That argument does not apply to privately owned firms, however.

14. This statement applies to new hirings. The retention rate of workers under contract will be enhanced by wage cuts in firms facing bankruptcy; again, these firms can be numerous in a deep recession. See for instance J.H. Drèze, and H. Sneessens, "What, If Anything, Have We Learned from the Rise of Unemployment in Belgium, 1974-1983", Louvain, CORE Discussion Paper 8521, 1985.

15. That seniority bonuses are more significant for white collars than for blue collars is consistent with this observation.

16. See, however, J. Abowd and O. Ashenfelter, "Anticipated Unemployment and Compensating Wage Differentials", in S. Rosen (ed.), *Studies in Labour Markets*, University of Chicago Press, Chicago, 1981, pp. 141-170.

17. See, however, the sample information about Belgian and French firms mentioned in Section II.3, *Theoretical arguments*.

18. Pages 152-155 in Section I.3 reflect work in (slow) progress on "labour contracts with overlapping generations". After completing this paper, I read a paper by A. Lindbeck and D.J Snower, "Explanations of Unemployment" (*Oxford Review of Economic Policy*, Vol. 1, No. 2, 1985, pp. 34-59), which gives a summary account of "Insider-Outsider" theories of unemployment as developed in several unpublished papers by the same authors. That work seems to be directly relevant to pages of the present paper.

19. Some known private labour contracts stipulate that the more senior workers are laid off last, whereas other such contracts stipulate that they are laid off first; see M. Feldstein, "Temporary Layoffs in the Theory of Unemployment", *Journal of Political Economy*, 84 (5), 1976, pp. 937-957.

20. Another problem arising with this forward contracting is the difficulty for the firm of collecting an insurance premium before the contingency.

21. See A.M. Okun, op. cit., pp. 67-68, and references given there, pp. 79-80.

22. Let s(w) and d(w) denote respectively the supply and the demand for new contracts at the wage level w. Assume that, when demand exceeds supply, the probability of finding a job is well approximated by s(w)/d(w). The expected utility of a worker is then

$$Eu = \frac{s(w)}{d(w)} u^e(w) + [1 - \frac{s(w)}{d(w)}]u^u = \frac{s(w)}{d(w)} [u^e(w) - u^u] + u^u,$$

where $u^e(w)$ and u^u denote the utility level of employed and of unemployed respectively. Then, denoting derivatives by subscripts and elasticities by y (i.e., $y_{s.w.} = \frac{w}{s(w)} \frac{ds(w)}{dw} = \frac{w}{s} s_w$):

$$\frac{\partial EU}{\partial w} = \frac{s_w d - s d_w}{d^2} [u^e(w) - u^u] + \frac{s}{d} u_w^e$$

$$= \frac{s}{d} \{(\frac{s_w}{s} - \frac{d_w}{d}) [u^e(w) - u^u] + u_w^e\}$$

$$= \frac{s}{d}\{(\eta_{s.w.} - \eta_{d.w.}) \frac{u^e(w) - u^u}{w} + u_w^e\}$$

$$> 0 \text{ if and only if } \frac{u^e(w) - u^u}{u_w^e} < \frac{w}{\eta_{d.w.} - \eta_{s.w.}}.$$

This condition will hold whenever $\dfrac{u^e(w) - u^u}{u_w^e}$ is small enough.

23. See R. Dornbusch et al., "Macroeconomic Prospects and Policies for the European Community", in O. Blanchard et al., (eds.), *Restoring Europe's Prosperity*, The MIT Press, for the Centre for European Policy Studies, London and Cambridge (Mass.), 1986, or A. Steinherr and B. Van Haeperen, "Approche pragmatique pour une politique de plein emploi: les subventions à la création d'emplois", *Recherches Economiques de Louvain*, 51 (2), 1985, pp. 111-151.

24. The most fashionable of these drawbacks, namely the negative impact on job search, is of little consequence during a deep recession, when employment is only very weakly linked to labour supply. The possible impact of wages is a more serious matter.

25. In the case of new entrants into the labour force, or workers dismissed from bankrupt or closed-down firms, there is no scope for charging part of the cost to the employer, for instance through experience-rated contributions.

26. Could such trading be organized through markets? In exceptional cases, something resembling a private market for individual jobs

exists; but closer scrutiny reveals that the "jobs" in question are in the nature of independent practice or casual jobs, and lack the dimension of a lasting employment relationship. For regular jobs, the presence of a third party, the employer, complicates the trading: the employer must accept (recruit) the "buyer" of a job; and if jobs in a firm had positive market values, this might provide incentives for the firm to reduce wages and capture the "rent". I am not aware of serious work on this topic. It should also be realized that our complex social legislation does not facilitate market trading of individual jobs. Would a seller be eligible for unemployment compensation? Would a buyer inherit the seniority rights of the seller? Basically, social security rights are not transferable.

27. See R.A. Hart, *Shorter Working Time*, OECD, Paris, 1984, p. 27.

28. See G. Davies and D. Metcalf, *Generating Jobs*, Simon and Coates, London, 1985.

29. O. Marchand, "L'Emploi en 1982-83: Simple répit dans la divergence entre demande et offre", *Economie et Statistique*, 166, 1984, pp. 25-38.

30. See A. Sonnet and P. Defeyt, "Le marché du travail en Belgique", *Bulletin de l'IRES*, 94, 1984, pp. 1-99.

31. Commissariat Général du Plan, op. cit.

32. The relevant preferences concern the trade-off between the age of retirement and the level of pension, for instance.

33. According to a survey conducted in France in 1980, 50% of the workers would have retired at age 60 instead of 65 if offered the same retirement income. In the Netherlands, when older teachers were given the option of reduced working time in pre-retirement years, 90% of those eligible took advantage of the scheme.

34. In a sample of 34 firms surveyed in 1984 by a Commission of the French Planning Office, 27 firms had adopted some form of work-sharing or of working-time reduction, but only one case of progressive (part-time) retirement was mentioned. See Commissariat Général du Plan, op. cit.

35. Conference Board in Europe, 1981, op. cit.

36. OECD, *Employment Growth and Structural Change*, Paris, 1985, p. 201, quoting P. Douglas, *The Theory of Wages*, Macmillan, New York, 1934.

37. Collecting microdata on employment changes in individual firms and analysing these should be both feasible and instructive.

38. They are discussed at greater length in J. H. Drèze, "Réduction progressive des heures et partage du travail" in Quatrième Congrès des Economistes de Langue Française, 5-7, 1980, pp. 61-87, where an attempt is also made at quantifying their implications.

40. S. Rosen, op. cit., Section V, outlines a simple model of "returns to hours" in a contracts framework, where firms use overtime in good states and layoffs with constant hours in bad states.

41. The proposal also called for "wage moderation".

42. R.A. Hart, *The Economics of Non-Wage Labour Costs*, op. cit., p. 80.

43. Quatrième Congrès des Economistes Belges de Langue Française, *Réduction Progressive des Heures et Partage du Travail*, Commission 3, Charleroi, CIFOP, 1980 and Commissariat Général du Plan, 1985, op. cit.

44. Firms operating on a continuous basis typically operate five, and sometimes even six, shifts of variable size.

45. See, for instance, J. Charpin and J. Mairesse, "Réduction de la durée du travail et chômage", *Revue Economique*, 1, 1978, pp. 189-205, W. Driehuis and M. Bruyn-Hundt, "Enige Effecten Van Arbeidstijd Verkorting", *Economisch Statistische Berichten*, 3197, 1979, pp. 289-300, or J. Plasmans and A. Vanroelen, "Arbeidsduurverkorting: Een mogelijke oplossing voor (jeugd) werkloosheid?", mimeo, UFSIA, (SESO), Antwerp, pp. 1-40.

46. Since every form of work-sharing has both opponents and advocates, none of these implications is "original". My only hope is to have convinced the reader that my own stand is consistent with both theory and recent experience.

    Cf. for example, T. Palasthy, "Six heures de travail par jour", *Les Dossiers Wallons*, 6, 1978, pp. 3-40 and J. Van den Broeck, E. Hendericks, and L. Coenaerts, *Roterende Vakantie*, RUCA, Antwerp, 1984.

47. I know of one industrial firm which adopted the scheme a few years ago to expand capacity by 35% without new investment or multiple shifts, and one savings bank which has adopted the scheme to impose team-work on its staff.

48. D. Baroin, "Le travail à temps partiel en France", p. 36, in J.P. Jallade (ed.), *L'Europe à temps partiel*, Economica, Paris, 1982. The percentage of active women working part-time in that year was 17.5%. Baroin asserts that this number could increase by 70% (to 29.5%) due to full-time workers switching to part-time work, and by 50% (to 38.5%) due to inactive women working part-time. This would result in 38.5 out of 109 active women working part-time, i.e., 35% or twice the initial rate of 17.5%. (The 109 consists of an original group of 100, plus the additional 9% of inactive women attracted into the labour force.)

Comments

by Christopher A. Pissarides

I shall discuss two issues raised by Drèze's paper, one micro-economic and one macroeconomic. The microeconomic issue concerns the efficiency of the free market and whether policy should encourage work-sharing as a device for improving efficiency. The macroeconomic issue concerns short-run fluctuations in economic activity; the question here is whether work-sharing can reduce employment fluctuations. Drèze comes out in favour of work-sharing on both grounds. I am convinced by the microeconomic arguments, but I have some doubts on the macroeconomic side.

Microeconomic efficiency

I find it useful to consider the microeconomic issues raised by Drèze within a steady-state equilibrium model. We can think of firms and workers as coming together in the way Drèze suggests, to form "regular" jobs in which wages and conditions of work do not fluctuate very much. We can go further and suppose that workers come and go for a variety of reasons and that firms experience varying fortunes, some expanding and some contracting. In steady-state equilibrium, aggregate demand and aggregate supply are equal to each other and constant, and prices and wages are such that each firm has maximum profits and each worker maximum utility. Are there any inefficiencies in this kind of economy and can work-sharing help in any way? Drèze argues that there are two kinds of inefficiencies, both of which arise from the nature of the employer-employee relationship in regular jobs. Firms bear some fixed costs to setting up a regular job and finding a suitable worker. They cannot insure against these costs, so the only way they can regroup them is through the future profits they expect to make from the job. The implications of these fixed costs are two:

(i) Expanding firms and firms with replacement vacancies are less likely to recruit quickly, because they want to make sure that the present and future profitability of the job are high enough to justify paying the fixed costs. Hence in recession firms are likely to cut back on recruiting much more than would be implied by conventional marginal productivity considerations.

(ii) Firms prefer to reduce the need to hire many workers by requiring more weekly hours from those they do hire. Thus a situation arises where those in employment may be faced with the choice of working longer hours than they really want or not working at all.

Drèze believes that both these factors give rise to inefficiencies that work-sharing can correct. Employed workers — especially older ones who have met most of their financial commitments — are forced to work longer hours than they want because it is still better than unemployment. Young workers, who are eager to have regular jobs, are unable to get them as fast as a competitive market would give them, because of the caution of expanding firms and the longer hours of the older generation.

Early retirement

The main proposal Drèze considers — early retirement with mandatory replacement — gives sufficient financial incentives to older workers to induce them to leave and forces firms to recruit a new, and presumably younger, worker to the job. Of course, the departing worker becomes unemployed, but he is not counted as such. He is counted as a retired person. However, there is no escaping the fact that what this proposal amounts to is that the government should spend a certain amount of public money to force firms to replace one employee by another, something which will itself cost the firm money. Two questions arise. Why does the replacement improve efficiency, and if it does, why does the private market fail to implement it?

I am in complete agreement with Drèze on the reasons for the efficiency gain, though I want to argue that most of the gain is almost certainly not the improved efficiency but the improved distribution of the national cake: the young are likely to want the jobs much more than the old.

There is some improvement in efficiency because the old are likely to be less productive (and less enthusiastic in devoting effort to the job) than the young. The young have much more incentive to work hard than the old, most of whom merely have to satisfy the minimum requirements of their contract to qualify for their pension. Also, the unemployment of the young is likely to introduce many more externalities of the kind Drèze raises — unemployment benefits and how to finance them, loss of human capital, crime, etc. — than the early retirement of the old. Thus some efficiency gains exist.

But far more important is the fact that the young are likely to want the jobs much more. Faced with the question, "Would you like a regular job which was taxed to raise the money needed to pay for the extra pension of those retiring earlier than anticipated?", a young person would almost certainly answer "yes".

Firms, of course, would also have to be compensated for the increased rate at which they pay the fixed cost of recruitment, but this does not seem to be too prohibitive. However, it is omitted from Drèze's suggestions. If the reason for the efficiency gain in the first place is the firm's fixed cost, it is only fair that the firm should not be forced by law to pay more of it.

If early retirement is such a good thing, why hasn't the free market adopted it? There seem to be compelling reasons for the failure of the market in this connection. Young workers obviously cannot go up to the old and bribe them to give up their jobs. An old worker may consider the job as his or hers for as long as he or she is holding it, but no worker can sell the right to the job to a worker of his or her choice.

Could the firm take on a worker at reduced wages and use the money saved to pay an early pension to one of its older workers? Although this would seem to be a mutually beneficial trade in the short run, it is not a viable policy in the long run. The day will come when today's young workers will be the early-retiring workers. The firm will choose the wages of the young on the basis of the present value of their expected marginal product and of their present and future wages. When present and future conditions are taken into account, the firm is likely to choose a contract that gives relative overemployment to older workers, because of the reasons explained by Drèze: older workers will be expected to work longer hours and they will not be replaced fast enough. It is not to the firm's interest to renege on that contract when new workers come knocking on the door.

Reducing hours

Early retirement is not the only work-sharing idea that can reduce these inefficiencies. Reducing each worker's hours of work directly, but keeping the length of the working week the same, is another. Although this proposal is more difficult to implement in a world where, for better or worse, we have come to regard a job as the holder's property, it should also prove good in the circumstances. If anything, when the problem is excessive hours, it should prove better than early retirement.

Macroeconomic stability

Moving now on to macroeconomic issues, it is worth emphasizing that Drèze considers work-sharing to be as much a solution to Europe's cyclical problems as to its secular ones. Early retirement is proposed as a way to reduce unemployment, and work-sharing in general is put forward as a policy that would reduce employment fluctuations in the face of aggregate shifts in the demand for output.

Whatever the merits of work-sharing as an anti-recession policy, it is important to remember that the adoption of new work-sharing rules brings with it institutional changes in the economy. Institutions do not change easily in today's economies, especially in Europe. If we were to advocate fundamental institutional change in response to the current recession, we had better make sure that the new institutions would not prove too rigid in more normal times.

I was disappointed not to find a discussion of work-sharing in booms. The recommended policies, which may reduce unemployment and absorb some of the negative output shocks in recession, may prove too inflationary when the output shocks are positive. When the discussion is of institutional change which is not easy to reverse (like early retirement), the desirability of the policy can only be judged by looking at the economy's responses to shocks in both slump and boom.

I have another, more basic, objection to Drèze's recommendations for dealing with the recession: he ignores inflation. He is, of course, aware of it. But I wonder how far one can discuss Europe's present recession within a real model which does not explain inflation. I am firmly of the view that the implicit contract model is unhelpful as a model of macroeconomic fluctuations and that it has misled many people when some of its proponents have tried to apply it to macroeconomic equilibrium and change.

As with every other macro policy, we must look at work-sharing within the context of the inflation-unemployment trade-off, or, if it is preferred, within the external-internal balance trade-off. I will confine my remarks here to the inflation-unemployment trade-off. In a steady state, the rate of inflation is equal to the difference between monetary and real growth, and work-sharing has no effect on it. Unemployment is at the natural rate and it may be affected by work-sharing — through the substitution of retired workers by unemployed ones, for example. But work-sharing will not affect the total number of hours worked. Suppose now we take a view of recessions as a situation where actual unemployment is above the natural rate because inflation needs to fall. Whether we believe work-sharing is beneficial or not then depends on the view we take of the reason inflation falls when unemployment is above the natural rate.

To see that problems may arise with work-sharing even under fairly conventional macro models, consider the case where nominal wages are set by collective bargains. Unemployment exerts a moderating influence on the negotiated wage rate because of the implications it has for the employability of the union members. The higher the chance of employment, the bigger the union's wage demand. Work-sharing reduces unemployment but does not affect employment. Thus with work-sharing the chances that a typical union member will find another job improve. The union raises its wage demand and inflation sets in. If the high unemployment was a temporary set-back designed to reduce inflation, work-sharing would defeat its purpose.

Of course other, equally plausible models may have different implications. For example, suppose we take the view that Europe's current recession is the result of adverse supply shocks which reduced productivity and — at given levels of demand — raised prices. Then if real hourly wages are rigid, work-sharing is a way of reducing unemployment without serious inflationary consequences. At the given level of demand, supply of output would either stay the same or (if the young are more productive than the old) rise with work-sharing, so prices might even fall.

In the first model, inflation is driven by union wage demands which are moderated by unemployment; in the second, inflation is determined by supply and demand while union wages are indexed. In one case work-sharing does not help; in the other it does. My point is that to remove any scepticism about work-sharing as a counter-cyclical policy we need a model of the cycle. Drèze's paper does not have one.

Comments

by Lars Calmfors

The starting point for Drèze's paper is that the existing distribution of employment is inefficient and can be improved through work-sharing. Several forms of work-sharing are discussed, such as substitution of young workers for old through early retirement schemes, sharing jobs through part-time work, and trading hours for jobs, which involves either a shorter work week or a shorter working-day.

The basic argument is the existence of a market failure because new entrants to the labour market (outsiders) are excluded from the benefits of income — and some employment — stabilization which, according to implicit contract theory, firms offer to the already employed (insiders). Both insiders and outsiders could gain from a redistribution of work. In the case of trading hours for jobs, the former benefit from increased leisure and the latter from obtaining a regular job. In the case of substitution of young workers for old, the young are likely to attach greater utiility to having a job than the old. In addition, positive externalities, such as less wastage of human capital, are likely to arise.

One problem I have with the analysis is that it only focuses on the welfare effects for workers. Although *workers as a collective* are likely to gain from the redistribution of a given amount of hours from insiders to outsiders, it does *not* follow that there need be welfare gains for *society* as a whole. Indeed firms are likely to lose, as evidenced by the opposition of employer federations to reductions of working-time. This, in my view, is the main reason why work-sharing has not been established by the market itself. Moreover, profit-maximizing firms will react to reductions of working-time in various ways, so the amount of work demanded will not remain constant. Hence we cannot be sure that reduced working-time will actually result in work-sharing. Therefore the welfare consequences for workers also become uncertain. Any discussion of work-sharing must therefore focus on the responses that a reduction of work-time is likely to trigger. My main criticism of the paper is that these aspects are treated only casually.

On the basis of existing literature one can enumerate at least six different channels through which working-time reductions have negative effects on employment (i.e., the number of persons employed). I shall discuss them one by one.

1. Effects on wage costs

A first effect arises because some of the firm's costs for workers —
e.g. for screening, training, firing, and many fringe benefits — are
fixed per employee and thus unrelated to the number of hours
worked. A reduction of working-time therefore increases the
firm's wage cost per hour even if wage rates stay constant, and
thus reduces the total number of hours demanded. This effect is
likely to be limited in size but it is not negligible.

Say that fixed costs per employee amount to 20% of total costs; a
reduction from an eight to a six hour working-day then raises
wage costs per hour by 6%. With a unitary elasticity of labour
demand, total hours will fall by as much. This is a significant
offset to the 25% employment increase that would otherwise occur
at an unchanged demand for hours (provided that hours and
workers are perfect substitutes in the production of labour
services).

2. Effects on wage rates

A second effect arises if *hourly wage rates* do not stay constant. It
is not immediately obvious which theory to use in analysing wage
responses. If one believes that the equilibrium rate of
unemployment (the NAIRU) is unaffected by working-time, the
long-run wage response is to restore the original level of
employment. But this is, of course, a very naive hypothesis. A
more sophisticated alternative is to use a model of union wage-
setting, according to which unions trade off the benefits of real
income gains against employment losses.[1]

This framework will basically show that the issue is a complex
one. On the one hand, a reduction of working-time tends to reduce
real wage income. Therefore the marginal utility of wages
increases, and the utility loss of becoming unemployed decreases.
Both these factors tend to raise wages. But on the other hand, the
increase in leisure works in the direction of raising the utility of
being employed, which tends to increase the utility loss of
becoming unemployed. Hence this works in the opposite direction.

Under reasonable assumptions the hourly wage will indeed rise,
but not by the full amount necessary to keep real income of
employees constant.[2] Let us suppose that a 1% reduction of
working-time causes a 0.7% increase of the hourly wage. Again,
assume also that workers and hours are perfect substitutes in the
production of labour services, that labour demand is unit-elastic
with respect to the real wage cost, and that fixed costs per
employee amount to 20% of total costs. Then a 25% reduction of

working-time (from eight to six hours a day) results in a 14% increase of hourly wage costs and an equally large fall in total hours demanded.

3. Effects on labour productivity

A third effect arises if labour productivity is affected by a reduction of working-time. This will be the case if hours and workers are *imperfect* substitutes for each other. Labour productivity tends to rise to the extent that workers can increase their intensity of work. It tends to fall to the extent that a larger share of working-time will be devoted to "unproductive" uses (starting and stopping work, etc.). The former effect tends to reinforce and the latter to reduce positive effects on employment (although the productivity effect cannot by itself cause a fall in employment as long as the marginal productivity of hours with respect to output is decreasing). The empirical evidence on the net direction of the labour productivity effects is mixed.[3] My conclusion is that this effect is not likely to be very important, although the risk that labour productivity effects will be negative must be larger today than in the past, when reductions in working-time were made from a higher level.

4. Effects on overtime

A fourth effect can arise because a reduction of working-time may not be binding. Such a reduction is likely to affect only *standard* working-time, but this will differ from actual time to the extent that there is overtime work. Suppose that overtime premia are unaffected by a reduction of standard working-time. Then the relative cost of employment compared to hours increases, because the cost of an employee working a given number of hours increases. This creates an incentive to substitute (overtime) hours for employment. In addition, the cost increase gives rise to a negative scale effect.[4]

It is hard to judge the magnitude of these effects. But one should not minimize them with reference to the relatively small importance of overtime at present. A major reduction of working-time will make overtime profitable for a large number of firms now working without it. The potential importance of this factor is recognized if we do the calculations with 40% overtime premia and 20% of total costs being fixed per employee. A reduction of standard working-time from eight to six hours a day then raises the cost per employee by around 8% (for an unchanged actual working-time).

5. Effects on capital utilization

A fifth effect arises if the operating-time of the capital stock falls *pari passu* with the reduction of working-time. In principle, operating-time and employment can be regarded as separate factors of production, which the firm tries to combine in an optimal way. But the majority of firms find themselves operating at corner solutions with one-shift systems, in which working-time and operating-time coincide. Therefore this effect *may* be very significant. It causes a reduction of the utilization rate of the capital stock that will have negative effects on employment.

Consider as a benchmark a firm for which output is proportional to working-time. This will be the case with a linearly homogeneous production function in terms of capital and labour services, if working-time and operating-time are perfect substitutes for employment and capital respectively *and* if the number of shifts is constant.[5] Then the only effect of a reduction of working-time will be a proportional fall in output; employment will be unaffected. Even worse, any increase in the wage rate per unit of time will cause employment to *fall*. Of course, all firms do not operate one-shift systems, and some that now do might change to a multi-shift system. Still, the example demonstrates the possible importance of this factor.

6. Effects on labour supply

The sixth effect arises because labour is not homogeneous. At any point in time, specific skills will be in short supply. For these categories of employees a reduction of working-time thus acts in very much the same fashion as a reduction of the effective capital stock. The way to avoid this is to increase overtime, but this raises labour costs. In addition, resulting excess demand pressures for these types of workers can trigger wage increases that may spread generally.

Conclusions

For pedagogical reasons I have varied some of the assumptions in my examples, so one cannot simply add up the effects I have enumerated. Nevertheless it is clear that the idea that a reduction of working-time will redistribute a given amount of work is completely misleading. Indeed a reduction of working-time is as likely to *reduce* employment as to increase it.

It is true, of course, that the effects will vary somewhat between different forms of working-time reductions, as pointed out by Drèze, who comes out in favour of early retirement schemes. A major difference between a shorter working-life and, say, a shorter working-week is that the former does not imply any reduction of the operating-time of the capital stock. But the other effects will still be there, so I find it hard to share Drèze's enthusiasm about the employment prospects of such schemes.

However, it is not obvious that one should view a reduction of working-time as an isolated event. Drèze has an interesting and speculative discussion about the possibilities of separating working-time from operating-time through more shiftwork: he specifically discusses a four-day working-week and a six-day operating-week. This has the advantage of both maintaining the effective capital stock and ensuring a reasonable supply of services. But the welfare effects of such combined measures are quite different from those of an isolated reduction of working-time. Working irregular hours obviously has negative welfare implications for the workers involved, since shift premia are necessary to induce the supply of such hours. Moreover, it is not clear how such an increase in operating-time would be realized. Firms would not necessarily find it in their interest to increase shiftwork; to the extent that they did, it might represent a substitution of capital for labour services.[6]

I also find Drèze a bit unclear about how a reduction of working-time should come about. Is it through collective agreements, through legislation, or through the creation of incentives subsidizing employment and penalizing long hours? It is crucial to distinguish between various methods. My discussion has been in terms of a reduction of working-time that is imposed exogenously on firms. It is, of course, possible to devise incentive systems that induce a substitution of employment for working-hours. The Swedish system of high marginal tax rates and separate taxation for spouses is one such arrangement which has proved very "efficient" in this respect.[7] My arguments then basically become arguments why such policies are likely to produce significant output losses (as they seem to have done in the Swedish case[8]). These would have to be weighed against the positive welfare effects of the redistribution of employment. But this requires a much more detailed analysis than in the Drèze paper.

In a more complete analysis we would also have to compare such incentive systems with other policies. Natural candidates are measures aimed directly at the distortions in the wage-setting process, e.g. tax incentives for profit-sharing schemes, à la Weitzman,[9] in order to increase both aggregate and relative wage flexibility. An alternative method is to "roll back" employment protection laws with the aim of reducing expected fixed costs per worker.[10]

Thus my position is that employment considerations do not provide a rationale for reducing working-time. There are better reasons: for instance, that it is nice to work shorter hours and that it provides more equal opportunities between the sexes. These are strong arguments for rising living standards to be enjoyed as significant — but gradual — further reductions of working-time. To me the upshot of the paper is that we should think very carefully about *how* these reductions of working-time should be made in order to gain the maximum positive welfare effects. Here one can easily point to conflicting aims. A shorter working-day may be preferable for families with children and two full-time wage earners. Some long-distance commuters may instead prefer a shorter working-week. Others may prefer longer holidays or a shorter working-life. Unfortunately, as Drèze points out, it cannot be left to the market alone to sort these choices out. The character of working-time as a collective good with strong externalities means that collective decisions need to be taken as well.

Notes and sources

1. This has been done, for example, by L. Calmfors, "Work Sharing, Employment and Wages", *European Economic Review*, Vol. 27, 1985; and A. Booth and F. Sciantarelli, "The Employment Effects of a Shorter Working Week", Discussion Paper No. 263, Department of Economics, University of Essex, 1985; and C. Wyplosz, "A Note on the Reduction of the Work Week", mimeo, INSEAD, Paris, 1985.

2. See L. Calmfors, op. cit., note 1.

3. For a survey of the empirical estimates, see R.A. Hart and P.G. McGregor, "The Returns to Labor Services in West German Manufacturing Industry", International Institute of Management, Wissenschaftszentrum, Berlin, 1984.

4. These effects have been analysed, for example, by R.A. Hart, in "Work Sharing and Factor Prices", *European Economic Review*, Vol. 24, 1984; and L. Calmfors and M. Hoel, in "Work Sharing and Overtime", mimeo, Institute for International Economic Studies, University of Stockholm, 1986.

5. This case has been discussed by M. Hoel, in "Nedsettelse av arbeidstid — et virkemiddel mot arbeidsledighet", Department of Economics, University of Oslo, 1983.

6. This has been analysed by L. Calmfors and M. Hoel, "Work Sharing, Employment and Shiftwork", mimeo, Institute for International Economic Studies, University of Stockholm, 1986, where the authors show that a reduction of working-time is likely to increase the relative factor cost of employment versus shifts. The marginal factor cost will fall less for employment than for shifts because of the existence of costs that are fixed per employee.

7. See G. Burtless, "Taxes, Transfers, and Swedish Labour Supply", in B. Bosworth and A. Rivlin (eds.), *The Swedish Economy*, Brookings Institution, Washington DC, 1987, and the comments by I. Hansson in the same volume.

8. Ibid.

9. M. Weitzman, "Some Macroeconomic Implications of Alternative Compensation Systems", *Economic Journal*, Vol. 93, 1983.

10. For a review of various costs imposed by such laws, see M. Emerson, "Regulation or deregulation of the labour market: the case of policy regimes for the recruitment and dismissal of employees in the industrialised countries", *Economic Papers*, Commission of the European Communities, Brussels, 1987.